PHILOSOPHERS·IN·CONTEXT

LEIBNIZ

Stuart Brown

Reader in Philosophy,
The Open University

D0104623

University of Minnesota Press   Minneapolis

Published by the University of Minnesota Press,
2037 University Avenue Southeast, Minneapolis MN 55414

Printed in Great Britain

Library of Congress Cataloging in Publication Data

Brown, Stuart, C.
  Leibniz.

  (Philosophers in context)
  Bibliography: p.
  Includes index.
  1. Leibniz, Gottfried Wilhelm, Freiherr von, 1646–1716.
I. Title. II. Series.
B2598.B74 1984 193 84–13205
ISBN 0–8166–1390–7
ISBN 0–8166–1391–5 (pbk.)

The University of Minnesota
is an equal-opportunity
educator and employer.

To the memory of my father, John D. Brown, who first aroused my interest in philosophical questions.

Contents

Preface

Leibniz is commonly reputed to be one of the strangest of the great philosophers in the Western tradition. His relative inaccessibility is partly due to the scope and profusion of his writings. It is also partly due to the obscurity of some of the figures of the preceding centuries to whom he acknowledged an intellectual debt. But in large measure the strangeness commonly found with Leibniz's writings is due to wrong expectations about what he was trying to do. These wrong expectations have been fostered by generations of expositors and teachers. They have a variety of roots, from long-standing assumptions about what philosophy ought to be like to the conveniences of the curriculum. The 'stock' Leibniz makes up, with Descartes and Spinoza, the classical trio of 'Rationalists' to counterbalance the opposing school of Empiricism. But it is hard to recognize this 'stock' Leibniz in his actual writings. In consequence those writings are seen as more difficult than they need be.

This book is offered as a fresh interpretation of Leibniz's philosophy, outlined in the Introductory Essay. It does not pretend to be comprehensive. It gives little attention, for instance, to Leibniz's books—the *New Essays on Human Understanding* and the *Theodicy*. It concentrates more on writings in the last two decades of the seventeenth century, particularly on the *Discourse on Metaphysics* and the *New System*. It is concerned to bring out the problems with which Leibniz was centrally preoccupied and to look at his various solutions to them as they developed through that period. Such a study cannot, in the present state of Leibniz scholarship, hope to be definitive. The book will have served much of its purpose for specialists if it convinces others of the philosophical value of such a diachronic study of Leibniz's writings.

Although the book departs from such consensus as there is about what sort of philosopher Leibniz was, I have not written it with Leibniz specialists primarily in mind. The main text is intended to be intelligible to a reader who knows a little about Descartes, perhaps, but little or nothing about Leibniz. Most of my comments on other commentators have been confined to the footnotes. I have quoted Leibniz more liberally than is customary in a scholarly work, partly with this wider readership in mind. But there is also a further purpose in such quotations, namely, to encourage more people to set about reading Leibniz for themselves, without relying on books like this to tell them what he thought. Leibniz has, more than most of the great philosophers of the past, become something of a prisoner of his commentators. With the increasing availability of good English translations students of Leibniz are better placed than formerly to use the secondary literature as no more than an aid to their own study. This book attempts to provide such an aid.

Acknowledgements

I am grateful to a number of colleagues for discussions which helped me in various stages of writing this book: particularly to R. Niall D. Martin who has been working with me on the Leibniz-Foucher correspondence. Others have also read a draft: Oswald Hanfling, Tony McWalter, Professor G.H.R. Parkinson, George MacDonald Ross and Tom Sorell. Their comments have been helpful in a number of ways. I am grateful to Professor Stephan Körner for encouraging the project in the first place and to Daniel Garber for his constructive criticisms as a publisher's reader. The task of producing the book has been much eased by the patience and accuracy of the Philosophy Secretaries at the Open University, Jackie Wootton and Angela Sheffield.

Abbreviations

A   *Leibniz: Sämtliche Schriften und Briefe*, ed. Deutsche Akademie der Wissenschaften, Darmstadt and Leipzig, 1923- (incomplete)

BW   *Leibniz: Basic Writings: Discourse on Metaphysics: Correspondence with Arnauld: Monadology*, La Salle, Ill., Open Court, 1902

C   *Opuscules et Fragments inédits de Leibniz*, ed. L. Couturat, Paris, 1903

F de C *Nouvelles Lettres et Opuscules inédits de Leibniz*, ed. Foucher de Careil, Paris, 1857

G   *Die Philosophischen Schriften von G W Leibniz*, ed. C.I. Gerhardt, 7 vols, Berlin, 1875-90

GM   *Mathematische Schriften von G W Leibniz*, ed. C.I. Gerhardt, 7 vols, Berlin, 1849-60.

NEHU   *G.W. Leibniz: New Essays on Human Understanding*, trans. and ed. P. Remnant and J. Bennett, Cambridge, Cambridge University Press, 1981. The authors of this edition have indicated the page numbers of the Akademie edition in the margins of their text and it is this number that is given in what follows.

PW   *Leibniz: Philosophical Writings*, ed. G.H.R. Parkinson, trans. Mary Morris and G.H.R. Parkinson, London (J.M. Dent and Sons), Totowa, N.J., Rowman and Littlefield, 1973

PPL   *Gottfried Wilhelm Leibniz: Philosophical Papers and Letters*, trans. and ed. L.E. Loemker, 2nd Ed., Dordrecht, Holland, D. Reidel, 1969

S   *Leibniz: Selections*, ed. P.P. Wiener, New York, Charles Scriber's Sons, 1951

1 Introductory Essay: Bearings on Leibniz's Philosophy

Great philosophers have commonly emerged out of the chaos of social and intellectual revolution. Gottfried Wilhelm Leibniz is a case in point. He was born in Leipzig in 1646, in the twenty eighth year of a ghastly and bitter war which left Germany in a highly fragmented and ruined state. The Thirty Years' War concluded nothing, except that the institutions of the Holy Roman Empire were fast becoming an anachronism. These institutions were a symbol of European, but particularly German unity. With a united Germany at its heart there was some defence of European civilization from the East. Against the 'barbarians', as the Turks were known, the peoples of Europe had once been able to make common cause in the name of Christendom. But the seventeenth century saw the gradual disintegration of 'Christendom' as political reality. France, under Louis XIV, emerged first as the only power able to uphold it and then, by her exclusive pursuit of her own national interests, as one of its greatest threats.

Leibniz grew up in a Germany divided into hundreds of states all owing allegiance to the Emperor. His brilliance at jurisprudence was recognized by the offer of a professorship at the University of Altdorf (in Nuremberg) but he was drawn into the political service of the Elector of Mainz. He was enlisted by Baron Johann Christian Boineburg, a statesman who encouraged Leibniz in what was then his ambition—to restore the intellectual, spiritual and political unity of Europe.[1] As a young man living in the shattered heart of Europe it naturally seemed to Leibniz that this cause was identical with that of the Holy Roman Empire. His dedication to this cause brought him, in later life, the title of Baron of the Empire. But by that time Leibniz had come to recognize that the reunification even of Germany under the Emperor was unthinkable. The modern nation state was there to stay and the hope of peace in Europe lay in a balance of power rather than in allegiances which transcended state boundaries.

Leibniz spent his whole adult life in the service of princes, most of it in the service of the Dukes of Brunswick, later Hanover. He sought, on several occasions, to secure a post which would allow him more time to pursue his philosophical studies. But either his religion or his nationality or sometimes both turned out to be an obstacle. So he remained at Hanover until his death in 1716. In the last thirty years and more of his life he fell increasingly out of favour with his employers. The Duke who employed him in the first place encouraged his efforts to promote Church unity and left him free to pursue his own interests. But his successors were men of affairs who had little use for a philosopher—even an internationally famous one—in their service. In the attempt to retain their favour he was lured into proposing schemes which were either disastrous (like his plan to improve the mines in the Harz) or were to prove an impossible burden, as did his history of the House of Brunswick. His failure to complete this history put Leibniz out of favour with the last of his employers (who became George I of Great Britain a few years before Leibniz's death) and indeed no one from the Hanover court attended his funeral.

The disintegration of Christendom as any kind of political reality was hastened by the fragmentation of spiritual and intellectual authority. Leibniz, although himself a Lutheran, believed that the Protestant communions could yet be reconciled to a reformed Catholic Church. In seeking to discover a basis for this reconciliation he had influential allies on the Catholic side. But here too he was frustrated, not only by religious sectarianism, but by the schisms in philosophy itself. It would be oversimple to represent this as a division between Scholastic and Modern philosophy, for neither party spoke with one voice. Leibniz himself was confronted with this division as a student at Leipzig and, with some difficulty, decided in favour of the Moderns. But he soon became aware that, as he put it, there were many names 'among whom the mantle of philosophy is torn apart' (PPL 93, G i 15). There would be no political unity without religious unity and no religious unity without intellectual unity. And yet, or so it seemed to Leibniz, European philosophy itself was imbued by the same factious spirit that prevented agreement between politicians or religious leaders. The 'empire of reason' itself was in disarray. The task of rebuilding it was immense but it was to become Leibniz's mission in life to take it on.[2]

Leibniz's more tangible successes were largely confined to Germany. There he helped to build academic institutions and something like his philosophy, as systemized by his disciple Christian Wolff (1679-1754), became established in the German universities. In this way Leibniz became the father of Modern German philosophy and an important influence on Immanuel Kant (1724-1804). He had his disciples in France also,[3] at least for a while, but both in France and in Britain Leibniz's philosophical influence was largely eclipsed by that of John Locke (1632-1704). Leibniz wrote, but refused to publish, a critical appreciation of Locke's *Essay*. When Leibniz's *Nouveaux Essais sur l'Entendement Humain* was eventually published in 1765, it came to Kant's attention. The contrasting positions of Locke and Leibniz impressed themselves sufficiently on Kant that he was led to represent his *Critique of Pure Reason* as an attempt to mediate between the two.[4]

Leibniz's reputation has suffered from the very sectarianism he spent his life opposing. He is now acknowledged by historians of mathematics as an independent inventor of the infinitesimal calculus. But his name was long-abused in Britain by supporters of Newton who accused Leibniz of plagiarism. In philosophy his position as contrasted with that of Locke was long distorted even to the point of supposing him to belong, together with Descartes and Spinoza, to a 'school' of philosophy called 'Rationalists' diametrically opposed to that of Locke and the (British) Empiricists. These two injustices were even to be compounded by a third, which represented Leibniz as a secret plagiarist from the philosophy of Spinoza.[5]

1.1 Leibniz's Alleged 'Rationalism'

The practice of talking as if there were a 'school' of Rationalists is seriously misleading. What is true is that in the seventeenth century there was a widespread demand that any claim to real knowledge should conform to the standards of geometry. But the existence of such a demand reflects the uncertainty of the age. Geometry remained as an indisputable achievement of the human intellect when philosophy was in disarray and its practitioners could find little common ground. The demand itself was an ancient one and so was the response of sceptics who thought it could not be met and who concluded that no real knowledge of the world is possible. There were others, known as 'dogmatists' (a word which had not yet acquired its abusive undertones), who sought to respond more positively to this demand. Among these were Descartes and Spinoza, though their responses were very different. For a while Leibniz too was concerned to respond to this demand in a more satisfactory way than Descartes. And, for a while, Leibniz did indeed take a keen interest in Spinoza's work.

From the early 1680s, however, Leibniz's philosophical method changed.[6] It is significant that he sought to justify this change by proposing that his method was the one actually adopted by geometers. It seems that, had he not done so, he would have had little reason to expect that his claims would be taken seriously. Thus he was led to contrast his approach with that of Descartes in the following way:

> ... it is astonishing to me to see that that famous philosopher of our times Descartes, who has recommended so much the art of doubting, has so little practised it in good faith on the occasions when it would have been most useful, contenting himself with ideas which Euclid and other Geometers have very wisely refused to begin with; this is also the way to cover up all sorts of illusory ideas and prejudices. However, I agree that we can and should often be content with a few assumptions, at least while waiting until they can be made into theorems some day; otherwise we should sometimes be holding ourselves back too much. It is always necessary to advance our knowledge, and if it were only to establish many things on a few hypotheses, that would still be very useful. Then at least we should know that there remain only these few hypotheses to be proved in order to arrive at a full demonstration, and in the meantime we should at least have the hypothetical ones which will lead us out of the confusion of disputes. That is the method of Geometers... (S 35f., G vii 165)

In Leibniz's later philosophy the hope of arriving at a 'full demonstration' was never fulfilled and his central preoccupation remained with escaping from 'the confusion of disputes'. But his earlier view, as embodied in his paper 'On the General Characteristic', was that the issues should be treated in the form of a calculus. Disputes would be ended because one school would triumph. Leibniz's ambition at this stage seems to have been to succeed where Descartes had failed. Commenting on Descartes, he remarked:

> ... had he seen a method of setting up a reasonable philosophy with the same unanswerable clarity as arithmetic, he would hardly have used any way other than this to establish a sect of philosophers, a thing which he so earnestly wanted. For by applying this method of philosophizing, a school would from its very beginning, and by the very nature of things, assert its supremacy in the realm of reason in a geometrical manner and could never perish nor be shaken until the sciences themselves die through the rise of a new barbarism among mankind. (PPL 223, G vii 187)

A project which implemented such a method would undoubtedly qualify as 'Rationalist' as that word is commonly used.[7] But the patronage Leibniz sought for his work on a logical calculus was not forthcoming. He was able quietly to forget the extravagant claims he made for his logical language. He was soon to favour an altogether different strategy for escaping the confusion of disputes, a strategy based on the recognition that not everything can be demonstrated and on the expectation that universal assent to certain assumptions might nonetheless be found even though no proof could be given of them. Granted these assumptions, answers could be worked out for a number of controversial problems.

This strategy still calls for rigorous deductive argument. Where it differs from a 'Rationalist' strategy as generally understood is that Leibniz claimed no kind of self-evidence for the assumptions he employed. Indeed he came to think of any philosophy which so based itself as essentially sectarian, as having an appeal only to like-minded people. Only a Cartesian would find clear and distinct what Descartes claimed to find clear and distinct. Only a philosophy which based itself on what people did actually accept could be free from the risk of confounding the confusion of disputes still more. That risk is one which Leibniz was anxious to avoid.

1.2 Leibniz's Writings

The mistaken belief that Leibniz was a Rationalist philosopher is accompanied by the expectation that he ought to have written a book which did for his philosophy what the *Principles of Philosophy* did for that of Descartes or the *Ethics* for that of Spinoza. Leibniz wrote no such book. Accordingly those who have understood him to be a philosopher of the same 'school' as Descartes and Spinoza have undertaken to supply the deficiency.[8]

But, as I shall try to bring out, the expectation is itself based on a misunderstanding. Even when he believed his health to be in decline and set to putting together some legacy for posterity, Leibniz produced only a short paper (his 'New System of the Nature and Communication of Substances') outlining a way of solving two problems in the Cartesian tradition. He himself had no wish to write the kind of work Descartes (and Spinoza) had written, as he made clear by implication in his 'Memoir for Enlightened Persons of Good Intention':[9]

> An intellectual will have some opinions which he thinks great and fine. Thereupon he wants to turn himself in to the head of a sect.... He will make himself a learned magician's book, to which his disciples will so accustom themselves as to be unable to reason without it ... Good understanding and communication destroys this wilfulness. Then one recognises that he should not limit himself to [the doctrines of] his master, and that a single man counts for little compared with the union of several.

Whether or not these beliefs were justified, they provide an explanation of Leibniz's failure to write a book concerned exclusively with articulating his own philosophical point of view. He was induced in later life to provide shortened versions of what would have been 'learned magician's books', had they been expanded for publication. Works such as the *Monadology* (1710) have accordingly been seized upon as meeting something of the demand for which Leibniz generally refused to cater. His only published book—generally known simply as the *Theodicy* (1710)—gives considerable prominence to the thoughts of others, particularly to the sceptic Pierre Bayle (1647-1706). Leibniz had enjoyed a lengthy and amicable correspondence with Bayle in spite of there being a fundamental disagreement between them on whether faith could be reconciled with reason. Leibniz represented the *Theodicy* as the fruit of that debate. It is a wide-ranging work but much of it is peripheral to Leibniz's main metaphysical concerns.

Earlier Leibniz had written his *New Essays* in the form of a dialogue. He evidently hoped to secure Locke's approval and indeed it is remarkable that, having gone to some lengths to write the book, he refused to have it published. Locke died just as the book was nearing completion and Leibniz gave this as his reason for not releasing it to the public. This cannot have been the whole story, since he was not deterred by Bayle's death from publishing the *Theodicy*. Yet the fact was that Leibniz and Bayle had corresponded in a spirit of mutual deference and good will and there could be no suspicion that Leibniz was taking advantage of Bayle's death to have the last word. The *New Essays*, by contrast, might have been construed in just such an unfavourable light.

Readers of the *New Essays* can hardly fail to be struck by Leibniz's efforts both to represent the author of the *Essay Concerning Human Understanding* fairly and to find common ground with him. Leibniz was clearly anxious that the book should be acceptable not only to Locke but to his disciples. But Locke seems to have been suspicious of Leibniz and indeed had made it plain that Leibniz did not in his opinion deserve the reputation he enjoyed of being one of the great minds of Europe. Locke refused to be drawn into correspondence with Leibniz on the basis of a short and very favourable review Leibniz had written of his *Essay*. Locke's approval of the *New Essays* would have significantly increased Leibniz's acceptability in England—something Leibniz was at this stage anxious to secure. But to have pressed forward with its publication without that approval might, in the circumstances, have damaged Leibniz's reputation in England beyond repair.

Leibniz's refusal to write a 'learned magician's book' is a considerable inconvenience to those who want to understand his philosophy. For the history of philosophy is usually pursued by attending primarily to such books conceived as classics of the subject. There are indeed short works to which Leibniz himself referred his readers and correspondents as definitive statements of his views on certain subjects. But he did this to save himself from repetition. Leibniz was above all a collaborative philosopher who is best represented by his contributions through short papers and letters to the debates of his time. He enjoyed taking part in public correspondence in periodicals like the *Journal des Savants* and *Nouvelles de la République des Lettres*. His confidence in the possibility of moderate men reaching rational solutions of the disagreements between them is reflected in the way he conducted his part in these debates.

1.3 Leibniz's Conception of Metaphysics

In basing his later metaphysics on what was generally agreed Leibniz was departing from the demonstrative metaphysics of Rationalism. But that does not mean that he conceived of metaphysics as a merely 'dialectical' exercise whose aim was to arrive at an agreed verdict rather than a true one. On the contrary he seems to have believed that the capacity of a metaphysical theory to solve problems was a measure of its truth. Where debates had formerly been dogged by confused notions (e.g. of substance or of cause) and where, accordingly, each party was landed in difficulties, a true theory would enable one to derive distinct notions by means of which difficulties could be removed.

Central to Leibniz's conception of metaphysics is that it could in this way be progressive without being definitive. A metaphysical theory could be modified in the light of difficulties which still remained for it. The testing of a theory involved a dialogue with open-minded and judicious persons who could be counted on to point to difficulties not apparent to its author. This is how Leibniz himself proceeded. While he continued to think that the claims of his *Discourse on Metaphysics* were true in essentials, his 'system' was modified at important points of detail as a result of his correspondence with Antoine Arnauld in the late 1680s. Leibniz was delighted to have been able to convince the discerning Arnauld on some points of consequence. But on other points he was persuaded of the need to modify what he had written. He toyed with the idea of publishing the *Discourse* and the Arnauld correspondence together. That would certainly not have constituted a 'learned magician's book' but it might have been a way of recommending Leibniz's metaphysics as worth the critical attention of the reading public.

Leibniz had in the meantime produced a shorter statement of his 'system' for the *Journal des Savants* which he had hoped to debate publicly with his Paris ally and friend, Simon Foucher, in subsequent issues. Foucher entered the lists with a rather fierce critique and Leibniz made a careful reply. But unfortunately Foucher did not live to continue the discussion further. The *New System* seemed consigned to oblivion. But then Pierre Bayle, in his best-selling *Historical and Critical Dictionary* (first published in 1697), gave Leibniz the kind of attention he liked. Bayle was a critic but there was nothing dismissive about his criticisms. Leibniz responded with alacrity and was unstinting in his praise for Bayle's abilities to carry out the sceptic's role of articulating problems:

> No ancient academician, not even Carneades, could have brought out the difficulties better. Although Mr Foucher was most able in such studies, he does not approach these, and I myself find nothing in the world more useful in solving these same old difficulties. It is this that pleases me so in the criticisms of able and moderate persons, for I feel that they give me new powers, like Antaeus hurled to earth in the fable ... (PPL 582, G iv 567)

Leibniz's image as an arch-Rationalist, as the author of a 'learned magician's' metaphysical system if not of such a book, has made his associations with sceptics like Foucher and Bayle seem rather puzzling. In fact he became impatient with Foucher's insistence on refusing to proceed in philosophy except on secure foundations. The sceptics were inclined to demand too much just as the 'dogmatists' (like Descartes) were inclined to promise too much. But, if the sceptics were too negative and showed an insufficient sense of the need to make progress, their criticisms could nonetheless be turned to advantage. For, as it seemed to Leibniz, 'dogmatic' philosophers tended to have an insufficient sense of the difficulties and hence their works only tended to multiply intellectual sects and add to the confusion of disputes. Progress towards a restoration of intellectual unity, as it seemed to him, lay in a more gradual approach to developing metaphysics, one which attached a particular value to solving difficulties and testing out theories on discerning critics.

Leibniz's philosophy developed against a background of problems from both Scholastic and Modern philosophy. In Part One I shall trace some aspects of his intellectual heritage and context, insofar as this serves to clarify the problems with which Leibniz continued to be particularly concerned. In Part Two I shall also trace Leibniz's changing conception of philosophy and the formation of his philosophical agenda. Part Three will be concerned with Leibniz's metaphysical synthesis of the *Discourse on Metaphysics* and its subsequent modifications. It will be concerned in particular with his theory of substance. Part Four will be concerned with Leibniz's metaphysics as a system of principles, in particular with the relation of metaphysics to the special sciences. It will consider Leibniz's attempt to reconcile the purposive framework of religion with the mechanistic character of modern science. More generally, it will be concerned with the limitations of a metaphysics such as that pursued by Leibniz.

Notes

1 It is beyond the scope of this book to explain the full significance of this central preoccupation for Leibniz's philosophy. The interested reader may be referred to Paul Hazard's *The European Mind 1680-1715*, trans. J. Lewis May, Harmondsworth, Penguin Books, 1964 and especially R.W. Meyer's *Leibnitz and the Seventeenth-Century Revolution*, trans. J.P Stern, Cambridge, Bowes and Bowes, 1952 for more extended treatments of this theme.

2 This is evidenced by a tendency throughout his later philosophy, in particular to what has sometimes been taken for 'eclecticism', as exemplified in passages like the following statement about his own metaphysical system:

Consideration of this system also shows that when we penetrate to the foundations of things, we observe more reason than most of the philosophical sects believed in. The lack of substantial reality in the sensible things of the sceptics; the reduction of everything to harmonies or numbers, ideas and perceptions by the Pythagoreans and Platonists; the one and the whole of Parmenides and Plotinus, yet without any Spinozism; the Stoic connectedness, which is yet compatible with the spontaneity held to by others; the vitalism of the Cabalists and hermetic philosophers who put a kind of feeling into everything; the forms and entelechies of Aristotle and the Scholastics; and even the mechanical explanation of all particular phenomena by Democritus and the moderns; etc.—all of these are founded united as if in a single perspective centre from which the object, which is obscured from any other approach, reveals its regularity and the correspondence of its parts. Our greatest failure has been the sectarian spirit which imposes limits upon itself by spurning others... (PPL 496, G iv 523f.)

3 For a good account of Leibniz's reception in France, see W.H. Barber's *Leibniz in France from Arnauld to Voltaire*, Oxford, Oxford University Press, 1955.

5 According to Kant, Leibniz '*intellectualised* phenomena' where Locke '*sensualised* all concepts of the understanding'. Kant's account of each is questionable but his insistence that concepts without intuitions are empty and that intuitions without concepts are blind is evidently directed respectively, at what he took to be Leibniz's and Locke's positions. For Kant's account of his own position in contrast with Leibniz's see *Critique of Pure Reason*, A271/B327.

5 This has been a strangely recurrent theme in writings on Leibniz, even in his lifetime. The charge was revived by L. Stein in his *Leibniz und Spinoza* (1890) and is echoed in Bertrand Russell's *A Critical Exposition of the Philosophy of Leibniz* (1900). For a more recent appraisal of Leibniz's relation to Spinoza, see G.H.R. Parkinson's 'Leibniz's Paris Writings in Relation to Spinoza' in *Leibniz à Paris (1672–1676)*, Vol. 2 Wiesbaden, Steiner, 1978.

6 The earliest piece of writing in which, so far as I have been able to discover, Leibniz adopted this different view is in a paper dated around 1680. See S 35f., G vii 165, part of which is quoted in the main text.

7 I take Rationalism to be a view not simply that a deductive metaphysics is possible but that a *fully demonstrated* metaphysics is possible. Leibniz's later metaphysical system is, as I shall attempt to show, *hypothetico*-deductive. Its principles are assumptions rather than self-evident truths.

8 Russell's *Critical Exposition* is a classic and Nicholas Rescher's *The Philosophy of Leibniz* a good recent example of this genre.

9 Published in O Klopp *Die Werke von Leibniz*, Vol. 10 Hanover, 1884 and translated by Patrick Riley in *The Political Writings of Leibniz*, Cambridge, Cambridge University Press, 1972, pp.109f.

PART ONE

The 'Confusion of Disputes':
Leibniz's Philosophical Heritage
and Context

2 Youthful Scholasticism (1646–63)

You say that my estimate of the Schoolmen's metaphysics would be more favourable if I had read them. Yet I esteemed them most favourably, for I had written you, if I remember well, that I believe many excellent metaphysical demonstrations are to be found in them which deserve to be purged of their barbarisms and confusion. I would not have said this if I had not wanted you to believe that I have read them. And I did in fact read them, more immoderately and eagerly than my teachers approved, when I began to study philosophy at the universities. They feared, indeed, that I should cling too tightly to these rocks. You would have found me, then, making some original and profound comments (for so they seemed to others as well) on the principle of individuation, the composition of the continuum, and the concourse of God. And I have never since regretted having sampled these studies. (PPL 190, G i 197f.)

Leibniz was, of course, not unusual amongst the great so-called 'Modern' philosophers in having been trained in the Scholastic philosophy. So were Bacon, Hobbes, Descartes and Locke. Unlike these, however, Leibniz did not react against his Scholastic training in a radical way. Unlike Descartes and Locke he was not a 'clean-sheet' philosopher. His youthful Scholasticism is not merely of biographical interest. The problems which concerned him then continued, for the most part, to be important problems which he did not dismiss as irrelevant for a Modern philosopher but saw as continuing to demand an answer. Leibniz was from the start a problem-solving philosopher and remained unstinting in his praise for philosophers like Pierre Bayle who were able to state problems clearly. ' ... I myself find nothing in the world more useful in solving these same old difficulties' (PPL 582, G iv 564). Many of these 'difficulties' were simply ignored by other Modern philosophers or dismissed as mysteries the human mind could not penetrate.

Leibniz, who yielded to none of the Moderns in his belief in the intelligibility of the world, was reluctant to make divine mysteries out of philosophical problems. Partly for this reason, he continued to value the 'substantial discussions' of 'the deeper Scholastics' (NEHU 431).

2.1 Context

Leibniz was born to pious academic parents in Leipzig just before the end of the Thirty Years' War. He did not suffer materially on account of the War but he seems to have grown up with a keen sense of the fragility of civilization. His father, who died when Leibniz was still a boy, seems to have been profoundly disturbed by the spirit of sectarian bitterness between Catholic and Protestant which the War had only increased. He seems to have had the ambition that his son would become a peace-maker. Whether or not he was imbued with this ambition by his father, Leibniz was to become a tireless champion of order, peace and reconciliation.

We may be more certain of his father's part in encouraging the young Leibniz to a life of study. Leibniz mastered Latin when he was very young and spent a great deal of time reading books in his father's library. His early familiarity with and enthusiasm for the literature of Scholastic philosophy and theology seems to date from this time.

Partly because of the War, intellectual life in the German States was, by comparison with that in France, Italy, Holland or England, in a moribund state. Cartesianism had already made an impact in Holland before Leibniz was born. It was ten years later before Johann Clauberg introduced Cartesianism into Germany. The debate between Scholastic and Modern philosophy was only beginning to get under way in Germany when Leibniz became a student. Although he was later to read Descartes with great care, his original knowledge of him seems to have been largely mediated by Clauberg. He claimed to have undergone some sort of conversion from Scholastic to Modern philosophy while he was a student. But the evidence is that this was much less wholehearted than he made it appear when later writing for a journal amongst whose readers Cartesianism had become fashionable. Leibniz's youthful enthusiasm for

Scholastic philosophy became subject to considerable qualification. But there is almost nothing in Leibniz's writings to com-
pare with the iconoclastic attacks on Scholasticism which became commonplace amongst Modern philosophers and indeed turned the word 'scholastic' into a term of abuse.

It is possible to detect something of this anti-Scholastic
iconoclasm amongst Leibniz's writings in the period 1666-72.
But the mature Leibniz was always reserved in his criticism of
Scholastic philosophy. Indeed, as we shall see, he sought a basis
for reconciling it with Modern philosophy. In his youth, as he
admitted in the part of his letter to Hermann Conring in 1678
which was quoted at the beginning of this chapter, he was
reluctant to give up his adherence to Scholasticism. Two of the
problems to which he referred in that letter are ones which
continued to preoccupy him, off and on, throughout his long
period of flourishing philosophical activity. In a short paper
written in the late 1680s he went so far as to say: 'There are two
labyrinths of the human mind: one concerns the composition of
the continuum, and the other the nature of freedom ...' (PW
107, F de C 180). The problem of freewill, as Leibniz conceived
it, is one dimension of the general problem of God's concurrence with what happens in the world. The third problem is one
which was the subject of a dissertation which Leibniz produced
in 1663. In the case of this problem, however, Leibniz came to
conclude that it was misconceived. Whereas he thought the first
two problems were ones which were genuine and needed to be
solved, he came to think that this problem rested on a false
assumption and therefore needed to be dissolved by rejecting
that assumption. Leibniz's concern with these problems is not
just a fact about his early intellectual biography but is
importantly formative of his mature philosophy. But it is not
important, for an understanding of Leibniz's later philosophy,
to know how he attempted to solve these problems as a young
man. Accordingly my emphasis here will be on what these
problems were. I shall also attempt to indicate how they
continued to be of importance in Leibniz's philosophy after he
became a Modern philosopher.

2.2 Three Samples of Scholastic Studies

In his much-discussed book, *The Structure of Scientific Revolutions*, Thomas Kuhn distinguishes between two phases of scientific activity: between 'normal science' and 'revolutionary science'. *Normal science* is possible only within a framework of agreed theoretical assumptions and consists of the pursuit of a limited range of problems. The prospects of agreement as to the merits of proposed solutions to these problems are good since disagreements are about details and not about fundamentals. *Revolutionary science* is precipitated by a breakdown in the prevailing consensus about fundamentals. Kuhn himself envisaged, and historians of philosophy have not been slow to note,[1] that something like this distinction can be drawn in other forms of enquiry. 'Scholasticism' may be seen as a label for the discipline of *normal philosophy* as commonly practised and taught in universities for some centuries prior to the emergence of so-called 'Modern' philosophy.[2] Its discourse was heavily indebted to Aristotle though students were no more inducted into it by reading Aristotle's texts than are students of scientific subjects today taught by means of the classics of their subjects. They learnt a technical vocabulary, to see certain problems as constituting the agenda of philosophy and to debate about a range of possible solutions to them.

Philosophy in the German universities when Leibniz was a student was already entering a revolutionary phase and indeed, apart from his early induction into Scholastic philosophy, Leibniz knew nothing else but a revolutionary phase of philosophy. In a letter to his former teacher, Jacob Thomasius, in 1669 Leibniz lists nineteen distinguished contemporaries and complains how these are only a few of the names 'among whom the mantle of philosophy is torn apart' (PPL 93, G i 15). It can be very misleading to represent Descartes as 'the father of Modern philosophy', however much such a label may make just tribute to his eventual importance. In the late seventeenth century Cartesianism was perhaps the dominant philosophical 'sect' but it is not true that, after Descartes, a new phase of normal philosophy was established.

Kuhn, in characterizing the difference between normal science and revolutionary science, describes the former as being practised within an accepted 'paradigm' or 'paradigms' and the latter as a phase of competing 'paradigms'. A paradigm is, as I take it, a distinguished historical example of the practice of a discipline by reference to which it is taught to generations of students. Leibniz naturally took to be paradigms of philosophy what he found in his father's library—works such as, in all probability, the *Metaphysical Disputations* of Francisco Suarez (1548-1617). Such now largely forgotten works first aroused Leibniz's enthusiasm for philosophy and determined his view of what its business was. When Leibniz became a Modern philosopher he adopted some of the new paradigms of what reasoning should be like, such as Euclid's *Elements*. But he never ceased to believe that specimens of good philosophy could be found in the writings of the Scholastics and that many of their problems were genuine, important and potentially soluble. The three which Leibniz himself mentions as of particular value for him are not the only ones.[3] But they may be taken as representative.

2.2.1 *The Principle of Individuation*

An assumption of much philosophy over the past 300 years has been that persons are unique. What has become known as *the* problem of personal identity is the problem of finding a general criterion or set of criteria for determining how to identify the same person on different occasions. The Scholastic search for a principle of individuation is evidently a forerunner of the modern problem of personal identity but is not to be confused with it. The Scholastics sought, not a criterion for deciding that someone remained the same individual but rather an *assurance* that he did. Whether persons were genuine individuals was a problem for Scholastic philosophers and remained a problem for Leibniz. In some remarks he wrote in May 1686 in connection with a letter from Arnauld, Leibniz states the problem like this:

> Suppose that a particular straight line A B C, represents a particular time and there is a particular individual substance, myself for example, which endures or exists during this time. Let us then consider, on the one hand, the me which exists during the time AB and, on the other hand, the me which exists during the time BC. Now, since people assume that it is the same individual substance which endures, or that it is the same me which

exists in the time AB at Paris which continues to exist in the time BC in
Germany, it is necessary that there be some reason why we can truly say
that I endure, or, in other words, that the me which was at Paris is now in
Germany. For were there no reason it would be quite right to say that it
was someone else. Of course my inner experience convinces me *a posteriori*
of this identity but there must also be some *a priori* reason. (G ii 43)

Leibniz goes on to offer his solution to this particular
problem, a solution which forms an important part of the
interconnected set of solutions to problems which he came to
refer to as his 'system'. His solution is not an answer to the
modern problem of personal identity but an answer to what that
problem presupposes, namely, that human beings are
substances each with a distinct identity. Leibniz wanted, and
eventually claimed to be able to give, an *a priori* guarantee that
this was so.

Leibniz's answer lay in his claim that there are no two
substances which are exactly alike. His solution lay in denying
what was, for the Scholastic philosophers, a commonplace,
namely, that there are many individuals which are exactly alike.
It is just this assumption which, he later claimed (see PPL 700, G
vii 395), led the Scholastics on their fruitless search for a
principle of individuation. Leibniz's dissolution of the
Scholastic problem is thus directly connected with his
affirmation of his important *principle of the identity of
indiscernibles*.

Leibniz himself acknowledged that it was 'paradoxical' to
deny that 'two substances may be exactly alike and differ only
numerically' (*Discourse* § 9) In saying that it was 'paradoxical',
however, he did not mean that it was necessarily false but only
that, since it was contrary to established opinion, it was
something which needed to be proved. It is a radical solution
though, as Leibniz was pleased enough to be able to point out, it
was foreshadowed by Aquinas' solution of the problem.

To understand this problem it is necessary to know a little of
the terms in which it was traditionally couched. The early Greek
philosophers had occupied themselves with questions about the
basic stuff of the universe, i.e. the stuff out of which everything
is composed. Plato and Aristotle directed attention away from
such questions to questions about the kinds of thing there are.
Science, they saw, should be concerned with general truths and

therefore with universals. The basic stuff came to be known as *primary matter* and the subject matter of science came to be directed to the forms which matter took. It was supposed that the same primary matter had the capacity to become a thing of a particular kind depending upon the form which was pressed upon it, rather like a piece of plasticine or putty is potentially any of a huge variety of things. General knowledge of the world, for Aristotle, was knowledge of *forms* or whatever it is in virtue of which a particular piece of matter is the kind of thing it is. Scientific knowledge is therefore knowledge of the *essences* of things.

These rudiments require much development and elaboration to even begin to look as if they might provide an apparatus with which philosophers might think about the world around them. The cluster of problems relating to the status of individuals is only one set of problems. However, even with the outline of the previous paragraph, it is possible to glimpse how there might be a problem of capturing what is unique about individual things or 'substances'. For two individuals might share the same essence or form as do any two individuals who are members of the same species. This, as it stands, is not an insuperable problem since it is possible to distinguish between those properties of an individual substance which are *essential* to its being a substance of a particular kind and those which are merely *accidental*. Thus one plant might have different markings from another. They would differ in their accidents but not in their essence. This answer, of course, invites questions about freaks or what we would nowadays call 'mutations'. That problem was made much of by philosophers who doubted the Aristotelian division of the world into different natural kinds, each with its own essence. But, letting that pass, there are still problems about individuality. For what if two individuals of the same species have exactly the same accidents? What was their 'principle of individuation'? An obvious answer would be to say that these individuals are distinguished by being comprised of different matter. To say this is to say that they are distinguished only numerically—'*solo numero*' was the Latin phrase and one commonly used by Leibniz—and that such individuals are not intrinsically or qualitatively different.

This may seem a more or less satisfactory answer to give if the individuals in question are plants. But what if they are human beings? Human beings have long been thought of as having a special kind of individuality which transcends the matter of which they are composed. Christians and Muslims go further and say that we retain our identities after we are dead and are rewarded or punished for the way we have lived. Aristotelian philosophy and these religions thus seemed incompatible on a vital point. Matters were brought to a head, to some extent, by the writings of one of the great mediaeval commentators on Aristotle, the Muslim philosopher Averroes (1126-78). Averroes allowed some kind of individuality to human beings while they were alive but, having no principle of individuation for souls, denied that this individuality was preserved after death. Human individuals after death became as drops in the ocean of a single universal spirit, namely, God. Averroes' solution seemed to many to be consistent both with sound philosophy and with piety. Indeed, what Leibniz took to be variations on it were common in the late seventeenth century. Spinoza put forward a picture of the world in which God was the only substance, and Malebranche put forward a theory in which He was the only cause. This may be one reason why Leibniz continued to take a keen interest in this problem. In 1702 he wrote a paper against the doctrine of a single universal spirit, implicating Spinoza and Malebranche in it. The paper begins with a summary of the doctrine in its original form and how it was received:

> Some discerning people have believed and still believe today, that there is only one single spirit, which is universal and animates the whole universe and all its parts, each according to its structure and the organs which it finds there, just as the same wind current causes different organ pipes to give off different sounds. Thus they also hold that when an animal has a sound organ, this spirit produces the effects of a particular soul in it but that when the organs are corrupted, this particular soul reduces to nothing or returns, so to speak, to the ocean of the universal spirit.
>
> Aristotle has seemed to some to have had an opinion approaching this, which was later revived by Averroes, a celebrated Arabian philosopher. He believed that there is an *intellectus agens*, or active understanding, in us and also an *intellectus patiens* or a passive understanding, and that the former, coming from without, is eternal and universal for all, while the passive understanding, being particular for each disappears at man's death. This was the doctrine of certain Peripatetics two or three centuries ago....

These men taught the doctrine in secret to their closest and ablest disciples; in public they were cautious enough to say that though the doctrine was indeed true according to philosophy—by which they meant pre-eminently that of Aristotle—it was false from the view-point of faith. This finally resulted in the disputes concerning the two-fold truth, a doctrine condemned in the last Lateran Council. (PPL 554,G vi 529)

The doctrine of the 'two-fold truth' was intended to avoid the problem of incompatibility between philosophy and theology. What might be true from the standpoint of theology (reward and punishment after death) might be false from the standpoint of philosophy. The two-fold truth was defended in the late seventeenth century by Pierre Bayle and this is one of the main points on which Leibniz opposes him in his *Theodicy*.

Averroism had caught on in some parts of the Christian world, particularly in Italy. But neither its denial of individual souls nor its dichotomy of faith and reason was adopted as the orthodox Catholic standpoint. The problem of reconciling Aristotelian philosophy to Christian theology remained. It was to be one of the great achievements of Thomas Aquinas (c.1225-74) to produce a synthesis of the two. Partly on account of Aquinas' achievement many of the Catholic seminaries remained bastions of Scholasticism long after it had been rejected elsewhere.

Aquinas sought not merely to oppose the Averroist doctrine of a two-fold truth by insisting that the truths of theology and philosophy must at least be compatible. He also sought to provide an alternative answer to some of the problems which made philosophers resort to the doctrine of a two-fold truth. Amongst these problems was that of the principle of individuation. What, roughly, Aquinas proposed was that the soul was the 'substantial form' of the body and that, although individual souls could exist apart from bodies, they retained this capacity to inform a body. The problem of individuating these substantial forms was, for him, the same problem as that of individuating angels. The answer is that no two of them are alike.

Leibniz's own eventual solution to this problem is, as he himself was to acknowledge,[4] really a generalization of what Aquinas claimed for certain kinds of substances to all substances. Thus, in Leibniz's mature philosophy, each individual substance is claimed to have its own 'full concept' and no two substances are exactly alike. As we shall see later, however, Leibniz's account of individual substances resulted also from his attempt to solve problems posed by Cartesian philosophy. No more than any other serious philosopher did he attempt to solve problems in isolation from one another.

2.2.2 *The Labyrinth of the Continuum*
The problem about the composition of the continuum is an abstract and general one which can be quite widely applied. Leibniz was particularly concerned with the problem as it applied to matter. Primary matter is not, in itself, divided into individual things or substances. It is a continuum. Primary matter as such can be divided up into smaller and smaller parts to infinity since primary matter, being itself what individual things are composed of, is not itself composed of individual things. This suggests that primary matter is merely ideal and not actual. For what is actual is a real being or is composed of real beings or substances. These considerations lead to a dilemma: either primary matter is a continuum or it is not: if it is, then it cannot be that out of which *real* beings are composed: if it is not, then it needs to be redefined.

The abstract problem is equally applicable to anything which is not divisible into individual parts. It goes at least as far back as the ancient Greek philosopher, Zeno. In representing it as an example of Scholastic studies, Leibniz probably had in mind a book which had impressed him entitled *Labyrinthus de Compositione Continui* (1631). This book was written by Libertus Fromond, a correspondent and critic of Descartes. Philosophers with a Scholastic training lost little time in pointing out that the problems about continua raised serious questions for matter as redefined by Descartes. For, on Descartes's account, the essence of matter consists in extension. Extension or spatial spread is itself a continuum.

Leibniz came to regard the problem of the continuum as a 'labyrinth' (following Fromond) from which it would be impossible for a Cartesian to escape without abandoning the central doctrine of the essence of matter. It was, for Leibniz, a problem which had to be solved in any satisfactory account of the composition of the material world. Thus, writing to Arnauld in 1687, he could say,

> Philosophers have also recognised that it is the form that gives determinate being to matter, and those who have not taken this into consideration will never escape from the labyrinth of *the composition of the continuum* once they enter it. (PPL 343, G ii 119)

Like his solution to the previous problem, Leibniz's answer to the problem about the composition of continua plays a crucial part in determining his 'correction' of the concept of substance. Whatever Leibniz may have thought the answer was when he was a student, he later toyed with different answers at various stages in his philosophical development. Here it is enough to note the Scholastic context of the problem and how it became a rallying-point for those opposed to the new account of matter put forward by Descartes.

2.2.3 *Divine Concurrence and Human Freewill*
Leibniz, as we have seen, came to represent the problem of the composition of the continuum as one of the two great labyrinths in which the human mind is caught. The other is that which relates to reconciling God's foreknowledge of what will happen in the world with human freewill. The problem may be put quite simply. If God is all-knowing and omnipotent, there is nothing which happens in the world except in accordance with God's will. But there are things which people do which are contrary to the divine will. The apparent inconsistency between these conventional beliefs about God and about human beings provided the starting point for much discussion amongst Scholastic theologians and philosophers.

Leibniz was well-versed in the literature which had grown up round this problem. He came back to it frequently and gave particular attention to it in his *Discourse on Metaphysics* and other writings of the late 1680s. He dissociated himself from the two radical solutions by which others had been tempted. There had been those (the Averroists and others) who so emphasized divine agency as to make God responsible for everything humans do and, at the other extreme, there were those (labelled 'Socinians') who so elevated human freewill as to deny God's providential foreknowledge.[5] Leibniz, like a number of Scholastics before him, sought a middle way through an account of the *concursus* ('concourse' or 'concurrence') of God's will with what happens in the world.

One of the Scholastics to whom Leibniz was particularly indebted for his thinking about this problem was the Portuguese Jesuit, Luis de Molina (1535-1600). Molina wrote a book with the (translated) title: *The Harmony of Freewill and the Gift of Grace, Divine Foreknowledge, Providence, Predestination and Punishment*. He maintained that all human action was by the grace of God but that this 'grace' might be either 'efficacious' or 'sufficient'. 'Sufficient' grace merely empowers someone to act in a particular way. 'Efficacious' grace extends to embrace his or her free consent in doing so. Thus divine grace does not, on Molina's account, pre-empt the possibility of human free choice. But, as it stands, it raises problems about God's foreknowledge. For it looks as if God's foreknowledge is restricted to knowledge of human opportunity and does not extend to all that they actually do. Not so, according to Molina, since God has a special knowledge, sometimes called the 'middle science' or better 'intermediate knowledge' (*scientia media*), of how any given human being will freely act in any given circumstance.

Molina's solution serves, of course, only to narrow down the problem by identifying where a solution to it might lie, namely, in an account of this intermediate knowledge. Without an illuminating explanation of *scientia media* the problem is only shifted. It was further refined by Suarez and others and it may have been in Suarez's writings that the young Leibniz first met the problem. However that may be, the mature Leibniz saw the key to the problem as lying in a clear account of *scientia media*. This, he believed, he was in a position to give. In a paper on freedom written around 1689, Leibniz wrote of God's foreknowledge in this way:

... He sees things which are possible in themselves by a consideration of his own nature, but he sees existent things by the consideration of his own freewill and his decrees, of which the first is to do everything in the best way and with supreme reason. What is termed 'mediate knowledge' is simply the knowledge of contingent possibles. (PW 111, F de C 184)

Leibniz's solution is to say that everything that there might be in the universe has a 'complete notion'. These complete notions are such that it is possible to deduce from them everything that is true of the individuals that would correspond to them. All our actions, including our free actions, are included in our complete notions. These in turn have existed in God's mind eternally together with the complete notions of all the other individuals there might have been—what Leibniz calls 'contingent possibles'. God selects, so to speak, the best team of individuals from the vast pool of 'contingent possibles', namely, the one which constitutes the best possible universe. God chooses certain individuals as part of his overall purpose who will use their freedom to act badly. God allows their evil yet is not responsible for it. But it is not that God did not know before hand everything that would happen. Such divine knowledge is knowledge of 'contingent possibles'.[6]

2.3 A Legacy of Problems

None of these problems could be resolved without a satisfactory theory of the nature of an individual substance. It became, for Leibniz, a requirement of a satisfactory theory that it provided the means of resolving them. Such a theory would need to explain both the uniqueness and the capacity for free action of that special category of substances called 'persons'. It would also need to distinguish individual substances proper—which are, in the Scholastic jargon, *unum per se*—from quasi-substances like a block of marble which have a merely accidental unity (are *unum per accidens*). It would need to explain how, if at all, there can be material substances and the relation of persons to the material world.

Some way of coping with such problems was found within the apparatus of 'substantial forms'. But this whole apparatus was, as we shall see in the next chapter, radically questioned by the leading Modern philosophers. Attention was turned to other problems. These old problems, however, continued to perplex Leibniz and others who thought that the reaction against Scholastic philosophy was excessive. To Leibniz it seemed that the attitude of the Moderns to these problems was at best shifty.

He was particularly critical of Descartes on this score. (See PW 107f., F de C 180).

Locke was also to incur Leibniz's disapproval, for ducking the question whether matter can think. 'I acknowledge that we must not deny what we do not understand, but I add that we are entitled to deny (within the natural order at least) whatever is absolutely unintelligible and inexplicable' (NEHU 65). No greater injustice could be done to Leibniz than to see his later revival of 'substantial forms' as a reactionary tendency. For it was a consequence of his pressing much further the insistence on intelligible explanations of the natural order. He was soon convinced that an appeal to 'substantial forms' had no place in the explanation of particular phenomena. But souls were, he thought, part of the natural order and therefore it was right to demand intelligible explanations of their nature and their place in the material world. The desire to find such explanations is an important part of Leibniz's motivation in metaphysics. And in this he believed that he had more in common with Descartes himself than with some of the Cartesians:

> The human soul somewhat shakes the confidence of some of our modern thinkers. Some of them acknowledge that it is the form of man, but add that it is the only substantial form in the known part of nature. M. Descartes speaks of it in this way; and he reproved M. Regius for challenging the soul's quality of being a substantial form and for denying that man is an *unum per se*, a being endowed with genuine unity. Some believe that this distinguished man did so out of prudence. I rather doubt that, since I think that he was right about it. (NEHU 317)

Whether or not Leibniz was right in attributing to Descartes a willingness to retain substantial forms at least as a mark of the uniqueness of human beings, this passage brings out the dilemma which Leibniz himself experienced when confronted by Modern philosophy. On the one hand, the mechanistic picture of the universe offered the hope of truly intelligible explanations of Nature. In this respect it represents a distinct advance on explanations in terms of substantial forms. On the other hand, the place of human beings in such a mechanistic universe is highly problematic. In that respect, a price had to be paid for the rejection of substantial forms. Nonetheless as we shall see in the next chapter, Leibniz initially decided that the price had to be paid.

Notes

1 See, for instance, Richard Rorty's *Philosophy and the Mirror of Nature*, Oxford, Blackwell, 1980, pp. 6-7 and *passim*.

2 It is worth observing, moreover, that Leibniz referred to Scholasticism throughout his life as 'the common philosophy'.

3 In the *New Essays*, Leibniz remarks: '...to be fair to the deeper Scholastics, such as Suarez..., it should be acknowledged that their works sometimes contain substantial discussions—for instance of the continuum, of the infinite, of contingency, of the reality of what is abstract, of the origin of forms, of the soul and its faculties, of God's communion with created beings, etc. and even, in moral philosophy, of the nature of the will and the principles of justice. In short, it must be admitted that there is still gold in that dross' (NEHU 431). All these topics are important in Leibniz's mature philosophy.

4 Having introduced his new concept of substance in the *Discourse on Metaphysics*, for instance, Leibniz goes on immediately to declare:

> There follow from this several notable paradoxes, as among others that it is not true that two substances should resemble each other entirely and differ *solo numero*, and that what St Thomas assures us on this point of angels or intelligences (*quod ibi omne individuum sit species infima* is true of all substances.... (§ 9)

5 This problem was clearly an important one in Leibniz's own time. L.E. Loemker, indeed, refers to it as 'the moral problem of the century ... in theological garb'. See Chapter 7 below, especially 7.3.

6 This is further discussed in Chapter 9 below.

3 Radical Modernism and Its Problems (1663–71)

I had penetrated deeply into the land of the Scholastics, when mathematics
and modern authors made me withdraw from it while I was still young.
Their beautiful ways of explaining nature mechanically charmed me, and
with good reason I despised the method of those who use only forms or
faculties of which nothing is understood....
(*New System* § 2)

In 1663 Leibniz completed his thoroughly scholastic
Disputation on the Principle of Individuation. Not long
afterwards he seems to have undergone something of a
conversion to Modern philosophy. In a letter to a friend written
fifty years or so later, he recalls having walked in a grove outside
Leipzig trying to make up his mind between Scholastic and
Modern philosophy and only deciding with some difficulty in
favour of 'mechanism' rather than 'substantial forms'. Later he
was to try to reconcile these two disparate and supposedly
incompatible standpoints. But at the time they confronted him
as stark alternatives. Leibniz reacted against the style of
philosophy he had previously emulated and now treated it with
what, for a Modern philosopher, was characteristic contempt.

The charge most commonly levelled at the Scholastics was
that they allowed themselves to be content with explanations
that were even more obscure and puzzling than what they were
intended to explain. They refined a complex vocabulary of
academic Latin, concocting new phrases which effectively did
no more than mark the spot where an explanation was needed.
This, I suggested in the previous chapter, was so with Molina's
reconciliation of divine foreknowledge and human freewill by
means of his doctrine of the *scientia media.* Leibniz himself had
not been wholly unsympathetic to Duns Scotus' answer to a
search for a principle of individuation—'*haecceitas*' ('thisness').

He was later to be caught up with the characteristically Modern insistence on clarity and distinctness.

That Nature is wholly intelligible and indeed in principle wholly intelligible *to us* is a corollary of Leibniz's principle of sufficient reason. So far as concerned the behaviour of bodies it was to be explained 'mechanically, that is through qualities of bodies, namely magnitude, shape and motion' (PW 173, C 12). The apparatus of 'occult qualities' invoked by the Scholastics failed to explain phenomena and only involved something more obscure. 'Substantial forms' were condemned on this ground.

3.1 Atomism (1666-68)

> At first, after freeing myself from bondage to Aristotle, I accepted the void and the atoms, for it is these that best satisfy the imagination.... (*New System* § 3)

For a short time Leibniz was taken by the atomism of Pierre Gassendi (1596-1655). It is natural that he should have been, given his inclination to believe (see Section 2.0 above) that the material world cannot be supposed to be infinitely divisible. But he later saw his atomistic phase as one in which he gratified the demands of the imagination and ignored those of reason. Thus, writing nearly half a century later, he wrote dismissively of his youthful atomism:

> All those who believe in the void allow themselves to be guided more by imagination than by reason. When I was a young man, I also fell into the snare of the void and of atoms; but reason brought me back. The imagination was a pleasing one. On this theory a limit is set to our researches; reflection is fixed and as it were pinned down; we suppose ourselves to have found the first elements—a *non plus ultra*.[1] We should like nature to go no further; we should like it to be finite, like our mind.... (PW 220, G vii 377)

Leibniz frequently makes very allusive references to Greek antiquity in order to give colour to his presentation of philosophical predicaments. The phrase *non plus ultra* in the above quotation is an allusion to the legendary sign at the entrance to the Pillars of Hercules—the ancient name for the Straits of Gibraltar—which might be rendered idiomatically into recent English as 'Thou shalt not pass'. The philosophical predicament with which Leibniz became obsessed was the thought that there might be limits to science, in particular a point beyond which it was impossible to go further in explanations of phenomena. It was only by supposing that there are such limits that it was possible for Leibniz to subscribe to belief in material atoms as the ultimate constituents of the physical universe. That there are no such limits became a watchcry of his philosophy from at least the late 1670s on. Fundamental progress required that we 'pass beyond the columns of Hercules' (S 58, C 182). The *Encyclopaedia* he planned was to be entitled 'PLUS ULTRA' (see, e.g. C 217). The possibility of passing 'beyond the columns of Hercules' was finally encapsulated in Leibniz's great 'principle of sufficient reason'. It is by reference to that principle, directly or indirectly, that Leibniz outlaws material atoms from his later metaphysics.

3.2 The Principle of Sufficient Reason

Leibniz writes of freeing himself 'from the bondage of Aristotle' but he was well aware that the obscurantism of the Scholastics was by no means entirely due to their acceptance of Aristotelian ideas. He knew that, in any case, the Scholastics often went well beyond Aristotle. Where Aristotle, for example, had distinguished four kinds of cause, many Scholastics were engaged in what became a preoccupation of Modern philosophers—the search for a unitary conception of causality. Leibniz himself largely despaired of the word 'cause' and indeed was to deny that substances strictly *interacted* with one another at all. He never departed from the belief, expressed in a publication of 1670, that the notion of an *influx*, which found some favour after the influential writings of Suarez, was unintelligible. He comments on the word *influx*:

On the invention of this last word Suarez prides himself not a little. The Scholastics before him had been exerting themselves to find a general concept of cause, but fitting words had not occurred to them. Suarez was not cleverer than they, but bolder, and introducing ingeniously the word *influx*, he defined *cause* as *what flows being into something else*, a most barbarous and obscure expression. Even the construction is inept, since influere is transformed from an intransitive to a transitive verb; and this *influx* is metaphorical and more obscure than what it defines. I should think it an easier task to define the term 'cause' than this term *influx*, used in such an unnatural sense. (PPL 126, G iv 148)

Leibniz's rejection of the Scholastic doctrine of *influx* led him to look with suspicion on Descartes's suggestion that mind and body interacted. Like a number of the Cartesians, most famously Nicolas Malebranche, he regarded Descartes' 'interaction' as no more intelligible than Suarez's 'influx' and sought an account of the 'mystery' of the union between soul and body on a different basis. Interaction was seen as a hangover from Scholastic ways of thinking which Descartes failed to account for in a way appropriate to Modern philosophy.

Leibniz and Malebranche were more or less exact contemporaries, though they did not meet till Leibniz's stay in Paris in the early 1670s. On a number of important points there was agreement between them. In a letter dated 1679 Leibniz declared that he 'heartily agreed' that (amongst other things) 'strictly speaking, bodies do not act on us' (PPL 210, G i 330). He did not object to Malebranche's reason for thinking this, namely, that it is impossible to conceive that a substance which is extended but lacks thought can act upon a substance which is unextended and 'has nothing but thought' (PPL 209, G i 327). But he insisted that he had 'always been convinced of this' for reasons of his own which rested on certain 'axioms' he claimed could be the means of proving a number of other important theses.

It is very likely that one of these 'axioms' is what he later referred to as his 'great principle', namely, the principle of sufficient reason. That principle, broadly stated, is that for every truth whatsoever there is a complete explanation of why it is true. That '*there is nothing without reason*' is stated by Leibniz as a 'fundamental principle' in a paper of 1671 (PPL 142, G iv 232). But the principle is presupposed in an earlier work in which Leibniz sought to illustrate the dictum of Francis Bacon that 'casually sampled philosophy leads away from God but that drunk more deeply, it leads back to him' (PPL 109, G iv 105).

Leibniz's argument begins with an affirmation of what he took to be the basic tenet of Modern philosophy, namely, 'that so far as can be done, everything should be derived from the nature of body and its primary qualities—magnitude, figure and motion' (PPL 110, G iv 106). But, he maintained, an explanation is needed for the origin of these primary qualities and this cannot be given from the nature of body alone. It is, for instance, in the nature of a body to be moveable, i.e. to be able to change space. But it does not follow from the fact that bodies can be moved that they will. On the contrary, 'when a body is left to itself' it will remain at rest. Hence 'no reason for motion can be found in bodies left to themselves' (PPL 111, G iv 108). It is to little purpose to explain the motion of one body by reference to that of an already moving body contiguous to it. For, as Leibniz puts it, '*the reason for a conclusion is not fully given as long as no reason is given for the premise*, especially since the same doubt remains in this case without end' (PPL 111, G iv 107, italics added). Motion, in short, is not inherent in bodies but requires to be continuously created in them.

It is clear that at this stage Leibniz was unfamiliar with Descartes' *Principles of Philosophy* and that his account assumes an Aristotelian conception of rest as the natural state of a body. Indeed his argument is like an Aristotelian argument why there must be a Prime Mover. But the point would have seemed to Descartes an obvious one. Descartes' mechanics required that God conserved a constant quantity of total motion in the universe and would have agreed with the necessity of assuming a Conserver or Continuous Creator of motion to explain the phenomena. Leibniz was later to be a critic of Descartes' conservation law and indeed of his own earlier physics. But he continued to use the principle of sufficient reason to establish the existence of God. He also continued to believe that matter, conceived of simply as what is extended, could not strictly be the cause of anything. *A fortiori* bodies do not strictly act on us.

What can strictly act (initiate change, including change of motion) must, Leibniz concluded, be something incorporeal, i.e. a mind. Modern philosophy, on a superficial view, might seem to support a materialistic and atheistic view of the universe. But if its own demands for intelligibility are pressed far enough, or so it seemed to Leibniz, it yielded quite the contrary view. Human minds are causally independent of the material universe and therefore not naturally destructable, being dependent only on God.

3.3 Mind and Matter

During the years 1668-71 Leibniz thought he was able to conclude that not only was Modern philosophy consistent with a religiously sanctioned view of man but that it was even possible to make it consistent with a partial retention of substantial forms. It all seemed to turn on providing a right account of the relation between mind and matter.

As we have seen, Leibniz was inclined to the view that only minds can act. It seemed to follow from this that minds were the only substances. For, he argued, a substance is something 'which subsists in itself' and therefore 'has a principle of action within itself' (PPL 115, A VI i 508). Bodies do not have a principle of action within themselves but derive their motion from something else. Bodies are, therefore, either not substances at all or are so only in virtue of a 'concurrent mind' (PPL 116, A VI i 508). Bodies thus require to be sustained by a mind in order to be substances. Leibniz thought his argument could explain how, in the Christian sacrament, the bread might be 'transubstantiated' into the body of Christ. All that is needed is for the mind of God to change and what sustained the matter as bread would sustain it as the body of Christ!

This argument only shows—as he himself later admitted—that Leibniz had at this stage no clear idea of how mind could act on matter. This account of material substance, though consistent (as notoriously Descartes' seemed not to be) with allowing the possibility of transubstantiation, represents the extraordinary as a special case of something ordinary. But then it does so at a price. Any action of a mind on a body becomes as deeply mysterious as the transformation of bread into flesh or water into wine. Leibniz was later to concede that action by a mind on a body is no more possible than the other way around and so this particular defence of transubstantiation represents only a passing phase in Leibniz's thought.

Leibniz agreed with the 'corpuscular philosophers', amongst whom he included Galileo, Bacon, Gassendi, Descartes and Hobbes, that 'in explaining corporeal phenomena, we must not unnecessarily resort to God or to any other incorporeal thing, form or quality ... but that so far as can be done, everything should be derived from the nature of body and its primary qualities—magnitude, figure, and motion' (PPL 110, G iv 106). The qualification 'so far as can be done' was backed up by a line from Horace to the effect that God should not intervene, except there be a knot worthy of his untying. But a dualistic theory of mind and matter was bound to make it mysterious and indeed miraculous that mind should act as matter or vice versa. Leibniz, in the early 1670s, seemed resigned to such an account. It is only in his later philosophy that we find him rejecting theories of mind and matter (e.g. those of Malebranche and Locke) on the ground that a philosophically intelligible account must be possible, by the principle of sufficient reason. On his later view the mind-body problem was not one to be solved by alleging a divine intervention. It was Leibniz's boast that his later account was the only intelligible one available (*New System* § 17).

Notes

1 The *Discourse* theory of the individual substance as having a unique 'notion or *haecceitas*' (§ 9) can be regarded as a characteristically Leibnizian attempt to rescue an unintelligible theory by giving a 'good sense' to *haecceitas*.

4 Platonic Scepticism

> Some distinguished men in our own times have also set their minds on metaphysics, but so far without success. It cannot be denied that Descartes has contributed some admirable things. Above all, he both restored the study of Plato by leading the mind away from the senses and thereupon added to it the doubts of the Academy. But he missed the mark because of a certain wavering or license in making assertions and failed to distinguish the certain from the uncertain. (PPL 432, G iv 468f.)

Leibniz had not studied Descartes' philosophy carefully before his mission to Paris in 1672. To judge from these remarks (published in 1694) it might appear that he never did. For Descartes, as a matter of diplomacy, tended to avoid references to earlier philosophy in his public writings. It is indeed certain that he had a high regard for Plato. But to represent him as some kind of Neo-Platonist is either to show ignorance of his writings or to be perverse.

In Leibniz's case we may confidently exclude the former possibility. By 1694 Leibniz had written a good deal about Descartes, including his *Critical Remarks on the General Part of Descartes' Principles of Philosophy*. He cannot have imagined that it was any part of Descartes' purpose to restore a study of Plato. In concluding that this was Descartes' main 'contribution' to metaphysics, Leibniz was referring to the effect of Descartes' work, insofar as it was beneficial, and not to his intentions. That Descartes' philosophy had this effect at all is ironic. For his disciples—the Cartesians—were notorious for their ultra-Modernism. The restoration of the study of Plato was fostered above all by a group of men who were united in opposition to the Cartesians. If the Cartesians had won the day, curricula would have been thoroughly modernized and the study of Plato, so far from being restored, would have effectively been abolished.

Leibniz's claim about Descartes' 'contribution' is thus partly autobiographical and it is so in two ways. In the first place it is a comment on the good that had come about (intended or otherwise) as a result of Descartes' work in metaphysics. In the second place, it is an expression of what Leibniz found of particular value in Descartes' own metaphysical writing. Insofar as it is the latter it is also a statement of what Leibniz took to be underlying affinities between him and his illustrious predecessor. However silent Descartes may have been about his own loyalties, he was, according to Leibniz, a follower of Plato and a philosopher in the tradition of Plato's Academy. Leibniz saw himself in much the same terms. It is not, however, that Leibniz was any sort of disciple of Descartes. On the contrary, what Leibniz believed, or affected to believe, was that Descartes belonged as a wayward disciple to the same school as that more faithfully followed by Leibniz himself.

4.1 Paris Connections

The occasion of Leibniz's visit to Paris in 1672 was a diplomatic mission. In the event, however, that mission formed a small part of his activities during his sojourn in Paris. He went to meetings of the Académie des Sciences and, both there and elsewhere, met many of the friends with whom he was to correspond in later years.

Leibniz applied himself to learning mathematics under the guidance of Christiaan Huygens (1629-95). He soon began to work on the problems which led eventually to his invention of the infinitesimal calculus, for which he is best remembered as a mathematician. While in Paris he constructed a calculating machine and became a fellow of the Royal Society in London. He aspired, but failed, to become one of the inner core of members of the Académie des Sciences. There is little doubt that, had it been at all easy for a foreigner who was a Protestant to live with honour in Paris, Leibniz would have dearly loved to do so. As it turned out, however, Leibniz was to take a position in the service of Duke John Frederick of Brunswick and for the last forty years of his life was based at Hanover.

As well as mastering mathematics and becoming, as he put it, a 'geometer', Leibniz spent some time while in Paris taking classes in Greek. These classes were conducted by Pierre-Daniel Huet (1630-1721), then assistant tutor to the Dauphin and later to become Bishop of Avranches. Huet was largely instrumental in Leibniz's rediscovery of Plato. Moreover he seems to have been a leading light in the anti-Cartesian circle with which Leibniz appears to have become closely identified.

4.2 Cartesians and Anti-Cartesians

While he was in Paris Leibniz made the acquaintance of two distinguished philosophers who are usually classed as 'Cartesians'—Antoine Arnauld (1612-94) and Nicholas Malebranche (1636-1715). But they might be classed more as sympathizers than as activists in the Cartesian cause. Those who were generally referred to as Cartesians were primarily a group of physicists, led by Regius in Holland and by Rohault and Regis in Paris. Leibniz does not seem to have met any of the Cartesians whom he indicted as having added nothing to the discoveries of their master. He had mistakenly included Spinoza in that indictment on the strength of a book which Spinoza had written expounding Descartes' philosophy.[1]

By the time that Leibniz came to Paris the teaching of Descartes' philosophy had more or less been banned on the ground that it was religiously subversive. The Cartesians were regarded as a sect, like the Jesuits, and not admitted to membership of the Académie des Sciences. Nonetheless Cartesianism was a high intellectual fashion in some of the salons and enjoyed some degree of protection because of its powerful patronage. The Oratory, for example, where Malebranche taught, trained young noblemen not only to equip themselves well with a sword but also to hold their own in the verbal duelling of the salon. But the attraction of Descartes' philosophy went deeper than mere fashionability. The manly Stoic ethic which it supported was more acceptable than Christian ethics as commonly presented. Cartesianism came to be seen as a threat to the established order in religion and an embarrassment to the new Académie.

Leibniz, when he was in Paris, appears to have been

cultivated by a group of anti-Cartesians who in varying degree were appalled by its ethical content and by its contempt for earlier philosophy. On the positive side this group seems to have had a particular enthusiasm for Plato and to have had strong sympathies for the sceptical tradition of Platonic Academy. Not all of the group were philosophers of any note. The man of the greatest social consequence among them was Huet, whose *Censura philosophiae Cartesianae* (1689) accused Descartes effectively of religious subversion.[2] Huet himself adopted a stance of Christian scepticism. So did the man who aspired to being the philosophical leader of the group, Simon Foucher (1644-97). Huet and Foucher were amongst the most formidable opponents of Descartes' philosophy and it has been argued that Foucher in particular played a crucial role in the downfall of Cartesianism.[3] However that may be, Leibniz became an ally with Foucher and Huet in attempt to curtail the spread of Cartesianism.

The relative seniority of Huet and his rapid rise in the ecclesiastical world made him a rather remote, though cordial, party to this alliance. Much closer were the relations between Foucher and Leibniz. Although they never met after Leibniz's stay in Paris, they corresponded for the next twenty years, usually in bursts, when one of them was embarked on some project in which he wanted the critical comment or assistance of the other. Foucher kept writing books which were either critiques of 'dogmatic' philosophers such as Descartes and Malebranche or histories of Academic scepticism, or both. At times, in their correspondence, he and Leibniz appeared to reach a degree of intellectual concord beyond what Leibniz ever shared with any other philosopher. Leibniz himself was even prepared to go so far as to put himself forward as a sceptic in the Academic tradition, as Foucher claimed to be. Writing to Foucher in May 1687, for instance, Leibniz expresses pleasure at reading a short discourse which Foucher had written on the opinion of St Augustine regarding the Academics. He could tell him without flattery that he found it entirely to his way of thinking: 'The laws [methodological rules] of the Academics which you extract from the remarks of St. Augustine are those of the true logic' (G i 390).

After Foucher's death in 1696 Leibniz sometimes said of him

that he sought to revive the 'sect' of the Academics much as Gassendi had sought to revive the sect of Epicurus. It is likely that members of Foucher's circle saw the rivalry between the Cartesians and the Gassendists as a case of history repeating itself. For the ethical doctrines associated with these philosophical parties—those of the Stoics and the Epicureans, respectively—constituted the two major forms of 'dogmatic' philosophy against which the sceptics of the Academy had launched their destructive criticisms. Some of the Academics were wholly negative but others, or at least so conjectured Augustine, had a secret positive doctrine. Foucher and Leibniz both embraced a sceptical standpoint over against the Cartesians. But neither denied that a positive philosophy was possible. Foucher, in practice, seemed to be content to play a purely critical role. Leibniz, by contrast, was too concerned with making progress in the sciences to be happy with merely correcting dogmatism. One of the laws of the Academics was to always search for new truth. Leibniz occasionally questioned how sincere Foucher was in professing to abide by this rule. Leibniz's scepticism bears heavily upon knowledge derived from the senses and in this respect he took himself to be a true disciple of Plato.

4.3 Scepticism and the Material World

One matter on which Foucher and Leibniz agreed, in opposition to Descartes, was that it was not possible to prove the existence of an external world. Descartes had tried to prove that there was a God whose goodness was incompatible with allowing us to be deceived as to the existence of a world outside us. Leibniz thought that, even if the arguments for the existence of God had been valid, they would not afford the kind of proof which Descartes desired. For, he claimed, we cannot know that it is inconsistent with the purposes of a good God that our lives should be one long dream. The very coherence of our experience gives us a high degree of assurance that our experiences are of something existing outside us. But it is a mistake to hope for proof. Such is the spirit of an early letter to Foucher:

This permanent consistency gives us great assurance, but after all, it will be only moral until somebody discovers *a priori* the origin of the world which we see and pursues the question of why things are as they appear back to its foundations in essence. For when this is done, he will have demonstrated that what appears to us is a reality and that it is impossible for us ever to be deceived in it. But I believe that this would very nearly approach the beatific vision and that it is difficult to aspire to this in our present state. Yet we do learn therefrom how confused the knowledge which we commonly have of the body and matter must be, since we believe we are certain that they exist, but eventually find that we could be mistaken. (PPL 154, G i 373)

Leibniz agreed with Foucher about two other major arguments he developed against Descartes' claim to knowledge of the material world. One is the argument against the distinction between primary and secondary qualities, which was taken up by Pierre Bayle and made known to the English speaking world by Berkeley. The other argument turns on the fact that matter, as defined by Descartes, is a continuum and is therefore exposed to the arguments turning on its infinite divisibility against matter, so defined, being substantial (see section 2.2.2 above). A central plank of Descartes' philosophy had been his claim to know that the essence of matter consisted in extension and could therefore be understood in terms of the primary qualities of size, figure and motion. In the *Discourse on Metaphysics*, Leibniz remarks that it can be demonstrated that 'the concepts of size, figure, and motion are not so distinct as has been imagined and that they include something imaginary and relative to our perceptions, as do also (though to a greater extent) colour, heat, and other similar qualities which one may doubt truly are found in the nature of things outside of ourselves' (§ 12). Such arguments were later to be developed by Berkeley, against Locke in particular. Leibniz, like Berkeley, was to deny an absolute space or absolute motion. Spatial properties were therefore, for him, relative to the perspective of a particular observer.

Leibniz acquired a copy of Berkeley's *Principles of Human Knowledge* when it was published in 1710. The short review which he wrote at the end begins as follows:[4]

Many things that are here seem right to me. But they are expressed rather paradoxically. For there is no need for us to say that matter is nothing. It is sufficient to say that it is a phenomenon like a rainbow. Nor need we say that it is substantial: rather that it is the result of substances. Nor need we say that space is more real than time: It is sufficient to say that space is nothing but the order of co-existing things and time the order of successive things.

Leibniz's later doctrine that matter is a 'well-founded phenomenon' turns on his solution to the problem of the composition of continua. Matter is not itself substantial, according to the later doctrine. It is not composed of substances but in some sense 'results from' them.

But, although Leibniz sought to provide room for belief in matter in his system, he did not claim to be able to prove it. Descartes, he concluded, had been mistaken in believing that in such matters it was possible to refute the sceptic. In his *Critical Remarks on the General Part of the Descartes' Principles of Philosophy* (1692), Leibniz sums up his attitude as follows:

> About sensible things we can know nothing more, nor ought we to desire to know more, than that they are consistent with each other as well as with rational principles that cannot be doubted, and hence that future events can to some extent be foreseen from past. To seek any other truth or reality than what this contains is vain and sceptics ought not to demand any other, nor dogmatists promise it. (PPL 384, G iv 356)

4.4 'Sceptics' and 'Dogmatists'

To understand Leibniz's attempt to find a middle way between 'scepticism' and 'dogmatism' we need to appreciate the extent to which seventeenth century debates about the possibility of science were seen by the participants as a resuscitation of debates which took place in ancient Greece. As R.H. Popkin has pointed out,[5] it is important to distinguish different kinds of scepticism. It is also important to realize—as is evident from the quotation at the beginning of this chapter—that Plato was associated more closely with scepticism than a modern reader would expect. Plato was seen as more of a sceptic, Aristotle more of a dogmatist, and their successors at Plato's Academy inclined to polarize the debate still further.

This is indeed how Descartes himself represents the matter in one of his rare attempts to place himself in relation to earlier philosophers.[6] He himself was engaged in trying to find a road to 'wisdom' which was 'incomparably more elevated and assured' than those conventionally trod. There have, he conceded, always been great men with similar preoccupations:

> That road is to seek out the first causes and the true principles from which reasons may be deduced for all that which we are capable of knowing; and it is those who have made this their special work who have been called philosophers. At the same time I do not know that up to the present day there have been any in whose case this plan has succeeded. The first and principal whose writings we possess, are Plato and Aristotle, between whom the only difference that exists is that the former, following the steps of his master Socrates, ingenuously confessed that he had never yet been able to discover anything for certain, and was content to set down the things that seemed to him to be probable, for this end adopting certain principles whereby he tried to account for other things. Aristotle on the other hand, had less candour, and although he had been Plato's disciple for twenty years, and possessed no other principles than his master's, he entirely changed the method of stating them, and proposed them as true and certain although there was no appearance of his having ever held them to be such. But these two men had great minds and much wisdom acquired by the four methods mentioned before, and this gave them great authority, so that those who succeeded them were more bent on following their opinions than in forming better ones of their own. The main dispute between their disciples was as to whether every thing should be doubted, or whether there were some things which were certain. And this carried them, both on the one side and on the other, into extravagant errors; for certain of those who argued for doubt, extended it even to the actions of life, so that they omitted to exercise ordinary prudence in its conduct; and those who supported the doctrine of certainty, supposing it to depend on the senses, trusted to them entirely.

Descartes, in this passage, distinguishes the scepticism he attributes to Plato (that certain knowledge is impossible but we may be content with probability) from the extreme scepticism of those who despaired of any reasonable basis for beliefs about the world. Part of his point in doing this was to make it clear that his own method of doubt—his methodological scepticism—was not to be confused with either of these earlier (and indeed, in his day, still current) forms of scepticism. Nor, on the other hand, did he wish to be confused with earlier forms of 'dogmatism' (what, in recent philosophy, has been called 'naive realism') which place too much reliance on the senses. What Descartes sought was a sophisticated dogmatism, i.e. a certainty grounded on taking care of the sceptic's doubts. Methodological scepticism was the road to a reasonable certainty.

Students of the history of philosophy will recognize the method of Descartes, of searching for indubitable foundations recognized by reason and of building on these by demonstrative arguments as what is commonly called 'rationalism'. What was sought was the certainty of geometry:

> These long chains of reasoning, simple and easy as they are, of which geometricians make use in order to arrive at the most difficult demonstrations, had caused me to imagine that all those things which fall under the cognizance of man might very likely be mutually related in the same fashion; and that, provided only that we abstain from receiving anything as true which is not so, and always retain the order which is necessary in order to deduce the one conclusion from the other, there can be nothing so remote that we cannot reach to it, nor so recondite that we cannot discover it. (Haldane and Ross, I 92)

If this was Descartes' ideal of scientific knowledge, his later writings show that he was neither a sceptic nor a rationalist in his scientific methodology. But there is no doubt that in the *Meditations on the First Philosophy* he was a methodological rationalist so far as metaphysics was concerned. He believed, in particular, that it was possible to have certain knowledge both of the essence and the existence of matter. As we have seen this was a major point of difference between Descartes and Leibniz: a point at which Leibniz was a moderate ('Platonic') sceptic and not a methodological rationalist.

This disagreement with Descartes, however, is one which only gradually finds a sharp expression in Leibniz's writings. What immediately impressed Leibniz and Foucher about Descartes' project for a first philosophy was not that it was misconceived but that it conspicuously failed. They believed, in short, that methodological rationalism should be pursued, only with greater caution and rigour. Foucher continued to profess this throughout his career, though he was never satisfied with any attempt to carry out the task of succeeding where Descartes had failed. Leibniz, as I shall try to bring out in the next two chapters, was highly taken with methodological rationalism for a few years but, increasingly beset with difficulties, gradually abandoned it in favour of a methodology more akin to that of the natural sciences.

I use the (regrettably barbaric) expression 'methodological rationalism' to distinguish a substantive seventeenth-century point of view from one with which it might be tempting to confuse it. It was common currency in the seventeenth century that a perfect knowledge of the world would be that which methodological rationalists sought to possess. It was the kind of knowledge actually achieved to some extent in arithmetic and geometry. That, it was very widely assumed, was the kind of knowledge God had of the world, though of course God is able to grasp in one 'intuition' what lesser creatures could only see as a result of laborious demonstration. This was the common currency of so-called 'rationalists' and 'empiricists' alike. Those, like Locke, who advocated an empiricist methodology for science did so because they thought it unrealistic for humans to try to achieve such a perfect knowledge of nature. Such an 'ideal rationalism' can still be traced in Hume.[7] Leibniz makes much more of it but it is important not to treat the rationalist picture he offers of God's knowledge as if there were no distinction between divine epistemology and human epistemology.[8]

Foucher and Leibniz, at least for a while, supported what I have called the 'methodological rationalism' of Descartes. They did not use that phrase, of course, but it corresponds to what they took to be implied in their acceptance of the 'laws' (i.e. methodological rules) of the Academics. Foucher thought that the details of Descartes' metaphysics were often original but quite wrong. Where he was right, he claimed, Descartes was largely unoriginal. In particular Descartes' own methodological rules were, or so Foucher claimed, basically a revival of the laws of the Academics.[9] This is no doubt too much of an attempt to cut Descartes down to size. But it was by no means a baseless charge and one which very probably informed Leibniz's judgement that what Descartes had contributed, apart from restoring the study of Plato, was to add to it 'the doubts of the Academy' (PPL 432, G iv 468). Descartes revived a desire for methodological rigour but, 'he missed the mark because of a certain wavering or license in making assertions and failed to distinguish the certain from the uncertain'. (PPL 432, G iv 469) Hence the judgement, as commonplace amongst philosophers then as it has been since, that Descartes was a sceptic in spite of himself.

Two phrases sum up the context of Leibniz's philosophizing. One is a phrase of Leibniz's—'confusion of disputes'.[10] The other was given currency by R.H. Popkin's important work on sixteenth- and seventeenth-century thought—'sceptical crisis'.[11] Leibniz's project is one he referred to as that of 'escaping from the confusion of disputes'. Finding a thread which would enable the philosopher to make his way out of the labyrinth was his favourite metaphor for the enterprise. But the persistence of the difficulties made it easy for philosophical sects to flourish and made the disputes between them seem interminable. The problem of resolving the difficulties in a satisfactory way was grist to the mill of the sceptics. As we shall see in the next chapter, Leibniz's initial response was to try to meet the sceptics on their own ground. But he later concluded that this was a mistaken strategy. It was only once he had arrived at this conclusion that he was able to move beyond the largely programmatic philosophy of his first decade at Hanover to the constructive philosophy of his *Discourse on Metaphysics*.

Notes

1 *The Principles of Descartes's Philosophy* (1663) was Spinoza's first publication.

2 Leibniz, finding difficulty in publishing his *Critical Remarks on the General Part of Descartes' Principles of Philosophy*, hoped that his own criticisms would be included in a later edition of Huet's book (G i 421). But nothing came of it and Leibniz became hesitant about publishing further criticisms of Descartes after he was accused of trying to build his own reputation on the ruins of Descartes'.

3 By Richard A. Watson in his *The Downfall of Cartesianism*, The Hague, Nijhoff, 1966, Chapter 2.

4 Leibniz's remarks on Berkeley's *Principles* were transcribed by Willy Kabitz in 'Leibniz and Berkeley' in the *Sitzungsberichte der König Preussischen Akademie der Wissenschuften* for 1932. The rest of this short (Latin) review (p.635) reads as follows:

The true substances are monads, or things that perceive. But the author should have gone much further, certainly as far as infinitely many monads out of which, by means of the pre-established harmony, everything is composed. Wrongly, or at least vainly, he rejects abstract ideas, restricting ideas to mental pictures and despising the subtleties of arithmetic and geometry. He is quite wrong to reject the infinite divisibility of extension, if right enough in rejecting infinitesimal quantities.

5 In his *History of Scepticism from Erasmus to Spinoza*, Berkeley, Calif, University of California Press, 1979, Preface, p.xiii.
6 In his Author's Letter which he intended to serve as a Preface to his *Principles of Philosophy*, the work on which his reputation rested most of all in the seventeenth century and to which Leibniz gave closest attention. The passage is quoted from *The Philosophical Works of Descartes*, trans E.S Haldane and G.R.T. Ross (1911) Volume 1, Dover Publications, 1955, p. 206.
7 Thus Hume writes: 'The other scientific method, where a general abstract principle is first established, and is afterwards branched out into a variety of inferences and conclusions, may be more perfect in itself, but suits less the imperfection of human nature ...' (Hume's *Enquiries*, ed. L.A. Selby-Bigge, Oxford, Clarendon Press, 1902, p. 174).
8 Leibniz's metaphysics in the late 1680s may indeed be characterized as a kind of 'transcendental rationalism', i.e. as concerned with how the world must be if such an ideal of knowledge is to be realized in the case of God. His theory of substance (see Part Three of this volume) may be seen as such an exercise in 'transcendental rationalism'. So may Locke's theory of 'real essences' (see Section 11.2 below).
9 In his *Dissertation sur la Recherche de la Verité, contenant l'Apologie des Academiciens*, Paris, 1687, Part III, Article 5.
10 The phrase occurs, for instance, in a passage on § 36, G vii 165, quoted at the beginning of Chapter 6 below. See also G i 382, quoted below in Section 6.3. The spirit and programmatic character of Leibniz's approach of the late 1670s is well encapsulated in the title of a paper apparently written in the hope of securing Louis XIV's patronage: 'Discourse touching the Method of Certitude, and the Art of Discovery, to serve to end Disputes and to make Progress quickly'. (S 46, G vii 174).
11 The reader familiar with Popkin's *History of Scepticism* may be interested to see this and the next two chapters as in part an extension of that work to include Leibniz. Popkin himself has written a paper on 'Leibniz and the French Sceptics' in which he remarks:

... unlike Descartes and Berkeley who may best be understood in terms of their heroic and ingenious efforts to conquer scepticism, Leibniz appears, amongst the sceptics, as a man who has found a happy home among some friends with who he belongs only in a somewhat superficial sense. Leibniz is neither sufficiently dogmatic nor

sufficiently destructive to be *engaged* in the *crise pyrrhonienne* ...
(*Revue Internationale de Philosophie*, 76-7, 1966, p. 248)

It may be exactly because Leibniz was no longer 'engagé' in the
'sceptical crisis' that he was able to take the view (in 1692) that the
dogmatists promised and the sceptics demanded too much (PPL 384, G
iv 356). But, as we shall see in the next chapter, he was sufficiently 'engagé'
in 1675 to take the programme of Cartesian-style 'first philosophy'
seriously himself. It is arguable that Leibniz was indeed prepared to be
thought of as an Academic sceptic even in the *Discourse* period and
differed from his friend Foucher only in his interpretation of the 'laws' of
the Academics. (See G i 390, quoted in Chapter 6, Note 6, below.) The
issue between Leibniz and Foucher is that Leibniz insisted that
Academics should continually try to make progress and that *this* was the
only way out of total suspense of judgement rather than the discovery of
'evident truths'. Leibniz may have become less *worried* because more
confident about making progress in the sciences and in that sense have
ceased to be 'engagé' in the sceptical crisis felt by others. That may have
led him to a way with scepticism which would not have satisfied others
more involved in it. (Foucher, for example, was not tempted by Leibniz's
approach.) But it does not mean that Leibniz's philosophy is
disconnected from the problems posed by the sceptic. In this respect
there are interesting comparisons to be made between Leibniz and
Locke. Both are constructive sceptics who offer an alternative to total
scepticism, though Leibniz thought Locke's alternative led directly to
scepticism (See NEHU 392).

PART TWO

New Directions in Search of a Philosophy (1675–85)

5 The Search for Certainty (1675–79)

I agree with you [Foucher] that it is important once for all to examine all our presuppositions in order to establish something sound. For I hold that it is only when we can prove everything we assert that we understand perfectly the thing being considered .... To the extent that I have read him [Descartes]... it seems to me that I have at least been able to discover what he has not done or tried to do, and among other things, this is to analyse all our assumptions. This is why I am inclined to applaud all who examine even the smallest truth to the end, for I know that it is much to understand something perfectly, no matter how small or easy it may seem. (Letter to Foucher, 1675, PPL 151 and 153, G i 369 and 371)

It was not until the late 1680s that Leibniz began to read Descartes' writings with close attention. But this letter involves several references to the project of Descartes' *Meditations on a First Philosophy*. Leibniz agreed with Foucher that the programme of methodological scepticism embarked on by Descartes was on the right lines. Descartes, he conceded, might have discovered a 'first philosophy' had he been more thorough both in the assumptions he considered and the inferences he drew from them. The *Cogito* was an important truth, though not the only truth of its kind. And Descartes was not rigorous enough in the argument by which he sought to prove the existence of a material world.

Leibniz, in fact, had no intention of merely attempting to tighten up Descartes' metaphysics. Rather he saw in it a project comparable to his own. There are important differences between the two as to the foundations on which a first philosophy could be built. Leibniz was never enamoured, and was later highly critical, of Descartes' appeal to 'clear and distinct ideas'. Leibniz regarded Descartes as an important recent figure who sought 'the road to certainty'.[1] In his own time that road was sought more by geometers, some of whom were engaged in trying to demonstrate Euclid's axioms.[2] But there was one philosopher who was reputed to be engaged in a search for a first philosophy—Benedict de Spinoza (1632–77).

Leibniz had known of his older contemporary for some time. Originally he had taken him for a Cartesian on the strength of Spinoza's first book, an exposition in geometric form of Descartes' philosophy. But he admired Spinoza's *Tractatus Theologico-Politicus* and thereafter respected him as a philosopher in his own right. While in Paris he met one of Spinoza's disciples and through his agency sought access to Spinoza's unpublished writings. At that time, however, Louis XIV of France was planning a military campaign to assert a territorial claim on The Netherlands. Spinoza, although free from religious persecution except from the Jewish synagogue (who had expelled him), was worried about having dealings with a foreigner in Paris, however much they might have in common. Leibniz was not to be deterred. On his way (via London) to his new appointment in Hanover, he stayed in Amsterdam for several weeks. There he not only gained access to Spinoza's unpublished writings (including the *Ethics*) but was even received by the 'master' and had several philosophical discussions with him.

Leibniz is commonly represented as having belonged to the same philosophical 'school' as Descartes and Spinoza—that of 'rationalism'. For a few years, at least, Leibniz's writings conform entirely to the expectation aroused by the label of 'rationalist'. He himself would have objected to the use of the word 'school' because of its association with intellectial sectarianism. But there is no doubt that at least in the late 1670s he saw himself as part of a tradition, going back to Aristotle, which included Descartes and Spinoza among its more illustrious Modern representatives.[3]

5.1 Proof and Understanding

In the passage quoted at the beginning of this chapter Leibniz declared that 'it is only when we can prove everything we assert that we understand perfectly the thing being considered' (PPL 151, G i 369). To demonstrate the truth of something was also to explain it and a 'first philosophy' would derive such an explanation from fundamentals. Nor did Leibniz value only the explanation of grand truths. That is why he approved 'all those who examine even the smallest truth to the end' (PPL 153, G i 371).

Leibniz was taken by the saying of St Augustine: 'Do not permit yourself to think you have known truth in philosophy, unless you can explain the leap in which we deduce that one, two, three and four together make ten' (quoted in S 37, G vii 166). The analysis of such an 'assumption' into its simple components would count as both an explanation and a proof provided that it showed how the truth embodied in it was a fundamental principle in disguise. Here Leibniz's logical and mathematical abilities made him confident that, for necessary (or what he also called 'eternal') truths, the fundamental principle was the principle of contradiction.

What is known as 'Leibniz's Law' is a rule which allows the substitution of 'identicals'. Thus, wherever the '3' occurs '2+1' can be substituted in its place without loss of truth.

By means of this rule Leibniz was able to explain the 'leap' of which Augustine wrote in which we infer that '1+2+3+4=10'. The step-by-step process is the same no matter how high the sum. Only in the case of higher sums it is more laborious. In his *New Essays* Leibniz responded to Locke's suggestion that a proposition such as 'two and two equals four' is a proposition 'known without any proof' by offering a demonstration of it. This is how Leibniz's demonstration runs:

Definitions. (1) *Two* is one and one.
              (2) *Three* is two and one.
              (3) *Four* is three and one.
Axiom. If equals be substituted for equals, the equality remains.
Demonstration. 2 and 2 is 2 and 1 and 1 (def. 1) $2 + 2$
                 2 and 1 and 1 is 3 and 1 (def. 2) $2 + 1 + 1$
                 3 and 1 is 4 (def. 3) $3 + 1$
                                                  4

Therefore (by the Axiom)
2 and 2 is 4. Which is what was to be demonstrated.
(NEHU 413f.)

Leibniz acknowledged that all such truths depended on definitions. He saw that by defining complicated numbers (all those above 1) in terms of simpler numbers and that by defining complicated operations in terms of simpler ones (multiplication in terms of addition, for instance), it was possible to show how the whole of arithmetic was analyzable into simple notions.

Leibniz's rationalism took the form of believing in 'a method of setting up a reasonable philosophy with the same unanswerable clarity as arithmetic' (PPL 223, G vii 187). There was much that was right in Descartes' approach. But he had failed to produce the method which would have given those who philosophized in his manner 'the same sovereignty in the realm of reason as geometry ...' (G vii 187).

The 'realm of reason', as Leibniz saw it, was in a state of anarchy. A right understanding of what it is that gives to the truths of arithmetic the authority they enjoy was the clue to how to proceed in philosophy:

> ... reason will be right beyond doubt only when it is everywhere as clear and certain as only arithmetic has been until now. Then there will be an end to that burdensome raising of objections by which one person now usually plagues another and which turns so many away from the desire to reason. When one person argues, it is usual for his opponent, instead of examining his argument, to answer thus, 'How do you know that your reason is truer than mine? What criterion of truth have you?' And if the first person persists in his argument, his hearers lack the patience to examine it. For usually many other problems have to be investigated first, and this would be the work of several weeks, following the laws of thought accepted until now. And so after much agitation, the emotions usually win out instead of reason, and we cut the Gordian knot rather than untying it. (G vii 188)

Leibniz's thought was the apparently naive one, that if only there were the right symbolism available and clear forms of argument within it, people would no longer become bogged down in disputes but say to another 'Let us calculate, Sir' and 'by taking to pen and ink, we should soon settle the question' (S 15, C 156).

5.2 The 'Alphabet of Human Thoughts'

Leibniz's interest in a logical calculus and in its use in settling arguments is one he had nurtured since his youth. But in the late 1670s his enthusiasm for it reached a new peak. He even went so far as to claim: 'Where this language can once be introduced by missionaries, the true religion, which is in complete agreement with reason, will be established, and apostasy will no more be feared in the future than would an apostasy of men from the arithmetic or geometry which they have once learned' (PPL 225, G vii 188).

What Leibniz had in mind was a device which would afford the same kind of knowledge of other matters as could be achieved in arithmetic. As we saw in the previous section Leibniz held that arithmetical thought could be reduced to certain simple elements. An 'adequate knowledge' of arithmetic involves identifying these elements—the basic language or 'alphabet' of arithmetic—and seeing how the rest of arithmetic can be derived from them by logical operations. The language can be divided into two parts—a basic *vocabulary* (names of simple elements like the number 1) and a *syntax* ('+', '=', etc.) by means of which words are combined into statements and statements are used as the means of deriving further statements. Leibniz's thoughts about the basic vocabulary of such a language are, to our way of thinking, amongst his most foreign. But his thoughts about questions of syntax make him seem much more modern and it is in respect of this work that he is an important figure in the history of symbolic logic.

Leibniz believed that ultimately the world needs to be explained in terms of God's nature. The world is as it is because God is as He is. The simples in terms of which an 'ultimate analysis' of things are to be given must, accordingly, be themselves part of God's nature. They are the divine 'perfections'. God is that being in whom all the perfections reside. An adequate knowledge of the world would be that knowledge which God himself has, namely, of how all things follow from the nature of God.

The question about the limits of human knowledge, couched in seventeenth century terms, is a question as to how far human beings can participate in such knowledge. Not surprisingly, epistemological debates were often theologically motivated. A Calvinist, like Pierre Bayle, could stress the totality of man's fall from grace and adopt a highly sceptical position about human

knowledge. Others, like Leibniz and Berkeley, were motivated
at least partly by their desire to defend the view that man is
made in the 'image of God' to oppose such a far-reaching
scepticism.[4]

Leibniz, as we have seen, did not think that certainty could be
achieved about the material world. But he thought that
demonstrations could be given in metaphysics which had the
same certainty as those of arithmetic. His universal
characteristic would make such demonstrations more rigorous
because it would rid metaphysical argument of confused
notions. He assured Tschirnhaus that 'with the aid of
characters, we will easily have the most distinct notions, for we
will have at hand a mechanical thread of meditation, as it were,
with whose aid we can very easily resolve any idea whatever into
those of which it is composed' (PPL 193, GM iv 452).

If it were not possible to carry out such an analysis then
metaphysics would be beset with its characteristic pitfalls—in
particular, that of using abstract notions of things whose very
possibility might be questioned. An analysis into simples might
clear a complex notion of this suspicion. Equally the attempt to
produce such an analysis might serve to confirm the suspicion
that a notion is an impossible one and that therefore there can
be no such thing as it purports to represent. Thus it could be
shown, to take one of Leibniz's favoured examples, that
(contrary to what we may think) we have no idea of 'the most
rapid motion':

> Suppose that a wheel turns at a most rapid rate. Then anyone can see that if
> a spoke of the wheel is extended beyond its rim, its extremity will move
> more rapidly than will a nail in the rim itself. The motion of the nail [sc. in
> the rim itself] is therefore not the most rapid, contrary to hypothesis. Yet at
> first glance we seem to have an idea of the most rapid motion, for we
> understand perfectly what we are saying. But we cannot have any idea of
> the impossible. (PPL 292, G iv 424)

This process of validating genuine ideas is what Leibniz called
'real definition'. It might seem as if all this process accomplishes
is to distinguish possible notions from impossible ones. But
Leibniz held, and continued to hold, that all possible ideas are
'true'. At one stage he seems to have been tempted to think that
everything that could possibly happen would actually happen.

But his discussions with Spinoza in 1676 left him in no doubt about the deterministic implications of that view. He was later to content himself with the view that though all possibilities exist in the mind of God there are infinitely many possibilities which are not true of the actual world. His retention of the claim that all possible ideas are 'true' in the face of that modification might seem misleading at least. But he continued to hold that all *simple* ideas are 'true' in a stronger sense, namely, of designating the basic elements of any possible universe. They are identified as the 'perfections' or 'attributes' of God but, since the world is ultimately to be understood in terms of them, these perfections must be reflected in the universe God created. Adequate knowledge of the universe would involve an understanding of how everything arises from these simple ideas and would provide the same certainty about it as we can actually achieve by deriving arithmetic from its simple elements.

5.3 Platonic Atomism

Leibniz's thought about simple ideas or 'forms' in the late 1670s belongs to a tradition which, in some respects, derives from Plato and which was revived in the 'logical atomism' of Bertrand Russell.[4] But here we shall consider Leibniz's defence of it in his own context.

Leibniz took it as axiomatic that all demonstration depended on definitions. To demonstrate that $2+2=4$ it was necessary to define the signs involved and, by substituting one definitional equivalent by another by a rule known as 'Leibniz's Law', the statement requiring a demonstration would be reduced to a statement of identity (say, '$2+2=2+2$' or '$1+1+1+1=1+1+1+1$'), i.e. to a statement which it would involve a contradiction to deny. The principle of contradiction was, Leibniz held, the highest principle of such truths and, he went on to claim, of all 'eternal' truths.

Other philosophers of Leibniz's time did not think the principle of contradiction was of much importance. Indeed one of Leibniz's own former heroes, Thomas Hobbes, had gone so far as to assert that definitions were 'arbitrary' and hence that demonstrations accomplished by them resulted in 'truths' which were no less so. In 1677 Leibniz wrote his 'Dialogue on the Connection between Words and Things'—one of the better of his several attempts to write Socratic dialogue—in order to show where Hobbes was wrong.

Leibniz agreed that all demonstration depended on definitions and that all notations were 'arbitrary'. But he pointed out that, while there might be different systems of arithmetic (say the decimal and duodecimal systems), all systems of *arithmetic* embodied certain fundamental ideas which were constant throughout different (arbitrarily) chosen notations. Such ideas as are designated by '1', '0' and '+' would be found in any system. Moreover all the truths of one system could be mapped onto truths in another. Hence, even if 7+5=12 is true in decimal but not in duodecimal, there is a truth (7+5=10) which corresponds to the truth familiarly expressed by '7+5=12'.

Leibniz thus sought to answer Hobbes' criticism by claiming, in effect, that although all nominal definitions are arbitrary, definitions cannot go on for ever and tend to converge on certain indefinables (simple ideas) which are the common property of mankind whatever conventions and languages they may use. Adequate knowledge of arithmetic thus turns out to be the same whatever conventions are involved, i.e. to be a knowledge of how the truths reached can be derived from simple ideas together with the principle of contradiction.

The simple ideas of metaphysics might have included such basic categories as being, perception, having location and so on, to judge from some of Leibniz's examples. But the programme of producing a calculus which would provide a sort of arithmetic of metaphysics ran into difficulties. It became clear to Leibniz that 'ultimate analysis' into absolute simples was humanly impossible and that it would be necessary to accept as simple what was so only relatively to us (humans). In fact this consequence struck Leibniz as not too disastrous for his programme, since it is not necessry to have a complete analysis in order to demonstrate an eternal truth. The analogue with the case of arithmetic would be this: suppose it is impossible to reduce 2+2=4 to 1+1+1+1=1+1+1+1 because we lacked the ability to carry the analysis so far: then it would still be enough to show that 2+2=2+2 to show 2+2=4 is an eternal truth because it would involve a contradiction to deny it.

However, without an analysis into simples, Leibniz was faced with a problem he himself made much of in other contexts—namely, that some uncertainty is introduced as to whether the basic notions are free from contradiction. It is an eternal truth that everything is identical with itself but only of *real* things i.e. those whose notion is possible. Thus if there is no highest prime number because there is always a higher prime than any given one, the notion of the highest prime number is an impossible one. If that is so then 'The highest prime number is identical with itself' could not be defended as an eternal truth. Only those who regard the principle of contradiction as a trivial truth could cheerfully accept as true that the highest prime number is identical with itself. And no philosopher was further removed than Leibniz from those who regarded the principle of contradiction as trivial. The apparatus of Platonic atomism is necessary to give substance to the principle of contradiction, even if humans can only make a limited use of it.

5.4 An 'Ontological' Argument for God's Existence

On his way to take up his new position in Hanover in 1676 Leibniz visited Spinoza in Holland and 'spoke with him several times and for very long'.[6] In a short paper he presented to Spinoza (PPL 167f., G vii 261f.) he pointed out a gap in Descartes' form of ontological argument for the existence of God and produced an improved version of the argument. He claimed to have convinced Spinoza on both points but, if so, Spinoza did not live on long enough to revise his *Ethics* in such a way as to free his version of the argument from the same objection.

Descartes' argument was that God had to be thought of as a being possessed of all the perfections. From this, together with the premise that existence is one of the perfections, he reasoned that it was part of God's essence to exist. Leibniz had no quarrel with either of these premises and disputed only the validity of the argument. Descartes' reasoning about the existence of a most perfect being assumed that such a being can be conceived or is possible. But this assumption needed to be proved. As it stands, according to Leibniz, the argument is incomplete. What was needed was a real definition of 'God' which showed (as a merely 'nominal' definition did not) that the notion we have of God is a possible one.

Leibniz claimed to repair the defect in Descartes' argument by defining a 'perfection' as any 'simple quality which is positive and absolute', i.e. as a 'simple form'. He invoked his Platonic atomism further by claiming that all such *simple* forms are compatible with one another in the same subject. Incompatibility can only occur as between *complex* qualities. Thus, for example, red and green would not be 'simple forms' for Leibniz because a definition of them (in terms of primary qualities) would explain why one and the same thing cannot be both red and green (all over at the same time).[7] The simple forms are logically independent of one another and hence can all inhere in one subject. By identifying God's 'perfections' with the 'simple forms' Leibniz is able to claim that the notion of a most perfect being is possible and thus to join Descartes and Spinoza in holding that it is part of God's *essence* to exist.

Nor is this identification of these Platonic atoms with the perfections of God merely an abstruse device to shore up the Ontological Argument. It offers a philosophical expression to the thought that God is not only the most real being (*ens realissimum*) but the source of all other reality. As we have seen, an 'ultimate analysis', on Leibniz's account, would reveal how everything follows from these simple forms and thus from the nature of God.

5.5 Second Thoughts

Leibniz's thought, in 1675, had much in common with that of Spinoza and it is not surprising that he should have taken the trouble to seek Spinoza out. But he was not to be satisfied with this way of thinking for long. To begin with, if everything in the universe follows from the nature of God, then there is no room for spontaneity (including human freedom) in the universe. Spinoza saw these consequences and accepted them. Leibniz saw them and was appalled. During the next decade or so he tried to find a way of avoiding having to say that everything which is true of the universe is true by a metaphysical necessity (see Chapter 9 below). Not only did Leibniz begin to doubt whether 'ultimate analysis' could be humanly achieved at all. But he began to reflect on the price to be paid for representing it as the model of adequate knowledge.

In the end Leibniz gave up the search for metaphysical certainty, at any rate in matters relating to the physical world. By 1686 he had rejected all the beliefs which characterized his earlier methodological rationalism. He rejected the method of universal doubt, he rejected the need for indubitable foundations in philosophy and allowed to experience an extensive role in validating even the concepts of metaphysics.[8] His view of geometry as providing a model of what should be aimed at in metaphysics remained. But he thought of geometry, not as a completed science whose foundations were already secure, but as depending on axioms that still needed to be demonstrated. Geometry was not any more an example of a science built on unmoveable foundations but an example of the need to make assumptions if progress in the sciences was to be made. (see Chapter 6).

Leibniz continued to share the widespread assumption that the sciences were deductive hierarchies—an assumption which is a corollary of the belief that to explain something is to deduce it from a 'higher' law or principle. But his method, even in metaphysics, is much closer to what is nowadays called the hypothetico-deductive method than to that characteristic of Descartes and Spinoza in metaphysics. In practice Descartes was obliged to make use of hypotheses in physics since he could only deduce the most general physical propositions (e.g. that matter consists of extension alone) from his metaphysics. Thus Leibniz certainly did not invent the hypothetico-deductive method. Nor was he the first to use it in metaphysics. It might be said, indeed, that he was restoring a more Aristotelian conception of metaphysics. However that may be, Leibniz's 'system', as he came to call it, involved a very different methodology from that of Descartes and Spinoza. If there is reason, on the basis of Leibniz's writings in the late 1670s, to treat him as belonging to the same 'school' of philosophy as Descartes and Spinoza, his mature writings show that he abandoned these earlier allegiances.

Notes

1 The phrase occurs at the beginning of a paper on the art of discovery: 'Men have known something of the road to certitude: the Logic of Aristotle and the Stoics is proof of it, but above all is the example set by the mathematicians ...' (S 50, C 185).

2 Leibniz frequently refers to the programme of Gilles de Roberval (1602–75) which seems to have been ridiculed when aired in the Académie des Sciences. Leibniz implies (NEHU 107f., cf. NEHU 407f.) that he intervened in the elderly de Roberval's defence. But Leibniz's support for such a programme was, at all events, unwavering.

3 Leibniz's belief that a 'method of certainty' was needed in order to make progress in the sciences and put an end to disputes was, so far than I can tell, abandoned in the early 1680s (see Chapter 6 below). But it should be acknowledged that there are considerable problems about dating Leibniz's unpublished papers. One paper which I have taken as belonging to Leibniz's period of 'methodological rationalism' refers back to his youthful work on the art of combinations as having been largely completed 'more than twenty years ago'. That might seem irrefutable evidence, since the *Dissertation on the Art of Combinations* was published in 1666, that this paper was written around 1686. This is what Couturat supposed (C 195, cf. S 50). But it is known that Leibniz tended to exaggerate the time which separated his adult work from his juvenilia. For instance, he claimed that he was only fifteen when he was converted to Modern philosophy (PPL 655, G iii 606) whereas it is clear (see PPL 660) that he was actually a few years older than that. The dating of this paper (*Project and Essay for aiming at some certainty to put an end to disputes and to advance the art of discovery*) cannot, therefore, be settled by the simple arithmetic of adding twenty or so to 1666. In any case a fault in the manuscript cannot be ruled out—Leibniz was twenty years old when he wrote his *Dissertation*.

At all events there is a considerable body of internal evidence to date the 'Project and Essay ...' before 1678. Leibniz refers to Spinoza's *Principles of Descartes' Philosophy* (1660) as a recent attempt at giving demonstrations. He would surely have referred to the *Ethics* (posthumously published in 1678) if it had appeared. Moreover his final paragraph implies that he has just received Pascal's work 'the geometrical spirit', which suggests 1676 or 1677, eight or nine years earlier than the date given by Couturat.

The scholarly issues about dating of unpublished papers cannot be settled conclusively at this stage. But, so far as concerns Leibniz's changing attitude towards methodological rationalism, the correspondence with Foucher may be taken as definitive. If Leibniz was sometimes inclined to exaggerate the extent to which he agreed with his correspondents, he was not inclined to exaggerate the differences. Foucher remained steadfast in his profession of methodological rationalism and the increasing intellectual distance between them is owing to Leibniz's desire to produce a positive metaphysics, if only a hypothetical one. Leibniz, to judge from the

Foucher correspondence, had clearly abandoned the 'method of certainty' by 1686 for a different method of settling disputes:

> ... in matters of human sciences we must try to advance and although this can only be by establishing many things on a few suppositions, that remains useful, for at least we will know that all that remains to reach a full demonstration is to prove these few suppositions, and in the meantime we will escape from the confusion of disputes...
> ... It is certain, even, that some truths must be supposed, on pain of giving up any hope of making demonstrations, for proofs could not go on to infinity. You cannot ask for the impossible, otherwise you would be a witness that you were not seriously searching for the truth... (G i 38lf., trans R.N.D.Martin)

At the time of writing 'Project and Essay for Aiming at Some Certainty...' Leibniz believed that the only way to make progress was to produce demonstrations on the basis of what was indubitable. It is most unlikely that this paper would have been written around the time when Leibniz had become so impatient of those (like Foucher) who refused to depart from the method of certitude as to question their sincerity.

4 This is a point rightly brought out by E.J. Craig in 'Philosophy and Philosophies', *Philosophy*, 1983, pp. 193–201. Leibniz's epistemology is influenced by the Platonic Christian thought that 'even in our present state ... we see ... all things as "in a glass" '. The thought that we see as in a glass, *darkly*, is explained one way by Leibniz in adding that this is due to 'the ray of thought being refracted by corporeal bodies' (*System of Theology*, p. 162). Leibniz's most usual explanation is, however, in terms of indistinct and confused perception: ' ... in every state of our existence, our mind is a mirror of God and of the universe; with this difference, that, in the present state, our view is clouded and our knowledge confused' (*System*, p. 73, see also *Discourse* § 9).

5 Towards the end of his lectures on 'The Philosophy of Logical Atomism', Russell remarked:

> One purpose that has run through all that I have said, has been the justification of analysis, i.e. the justification of logical atomism, of the view that you can get down in theory, if not in practice, to ultimate simples, out of which the world is built, and that those simples have a kind of reality not belonging to anything else. (*Russell's Logical Atomism* (1918), ed. David Pears, Fontana, 1972, p.129)

Leibniz made a careful study of Plato's *Theaetetus* and may have derived some of his 'Platonic atomism' from that work, including the famous passage quoted by Wittgenstein in the *Philosophical Investigations* (I 46) where he identifies the 'objects' of his earlier *Tractatus Logico-Philosophicus* (and Russell's 'individuals') as 'primary elements' in Plato's sense. I believe Leibniz's simple 'ideas' or 'forms' are also such 'primary elements'.

6 Letter to Abbé Gallois in 1677, A II i 379, quoted in PPL 167.
7 Leibniz himself gives no examples. I have deliberately chosen one of Wittgenstein's (see *Tractatus* 6.3751).
8 His rejection of universal doubt and therefore the need to find certain foundations is clearly stated in a paper of c. 1680 which is discussed in the next chapter (see S 34–5, G vii 164–5). Leibniz seems to have become convinced by the early 1680s that the project of analysis 'by which we are enabled to arrive at primitive notions, i.e. at those which are conceived through themselves, does not seem to be in the power of man' (PW 8, C 514. See also *Discourse* § 24).

6 An Alternative Method (1680–84)

> ... it is astonishing to me to see that that famous philosopher of our times Descartes, who has recommended so much the art of doubting, has practised it so little in good faith on the occasions when it would have been most useful, contenting himself with alleging self-evidence he claims for ideas which Euclid and other Geometers have very wisely refused to begin with; this is also the way to cover up all sorts of illusory ideas and prejudices. However, I agree that we can and should often be content with a few assumptions, at least while waiting until they can also be made into theorems some day; otherwise we should sometimes be holding ourselves back too much. For it is always necessary to advance our knowledge, and even if it were only to establish many things on a few hypotheses, that would still be very useful. Then at least we should know that there remained only these few hypotheses to be proved in order to arrive at a full demonstration, and in the meantime we should at least have the hypothetical ones which will lead us out of the confusion of disputes. That is the method of Geometers ... (S 35f., G vii 165)

This passage is from a paper some editors entitle 'Precepts for Advancing the Sciences and Arts', designed for the attention of Louis XIV's advisors in the hope of securing patronage for a project Leibniz had for an encyclopaedia. It was evidently written around 1680 and at any rate before 1683 when Leibniz burnt his bridges with Louis XIV by writing a satire (*Mars Christianissimus*—'Most Christian War-God') attacking Louis' military expansionism. This paper represents almost a *volte face* compared with the opinions expressed by Leibniz about Descartes only a few years previously. Whereas Descartes seemed earlier to be following a good method, only not practising it with sufficient rigour, this paper represents him as fundamentally mistaken in his method. By 1680 or so Leibniz had come to believe that the method of universal doubt was unsound and that it was an illusion to hope for certainty from 'clear and distinct' ideas. Indeed the quest for an absolutely certain starting point in philosophy now seemed to Leibniz impracticable, if not Quixotic. The way to make progress was to keep one's basic assumptions to a minimum and to admit them only provisionally, in the hope that they will turn out to be demonstrable from still higher principles.

6.1 The New Strategy against Scepticism

This change of strategy permeates Leibniz's later philosophy. To appreciate it we need to bear in mind that 'philosophers' in the seventeenth century (including those we would now call 'physicists') were at loggerheads with one another about a whole range of matters. This 'confusion of disputes' was an obstacle to cooperative work and hence to scientific progress. Moreover it encouraged some of the more extreme sceptics to doubt whether there was any point in pursuing science when there seemed no prospect of escaping from this 'confusion of disputes'. It is against this background that Descartes sought to provide the sciences with a new start. It is this strategy which Leibniz himself initially favoured in the mid to late 1670s. Hence he could write of Descartes:

> ... had he seen a method of settling up a reasonable philosophy with the same unanswerable clarity of arithmetic, he would hardly have used any other way than this to establish a sect of followers, a thing which he so earnestly wanted. For by applying this method of philosophizing, a school would from its very beginning, and by the very nature of things, assert its supremacy in the realm of reason in a geometrical manner and could never perish nor be shaken until the sciences themselves die through the rise of a new barbarism among mankind. (PPL 223, G vii 187)

The strategy which Leibniz then favoured was to defeat scepticism and to dispel disputes by providing definitive answers which people could no more quibble about than they could quibble about a piece of arithmetic. The strategy had not worked in Descartes' case. Leibniz lost his optimism that he might succeed where Descartes had failed. A new strategy was needed—the cause of reason had to be pursued, so to speak, through diplomacy if it were to succeed where it had failed to compel. It had to be advanced by making assumptions which would readily be granted. Territory had to be ceded to the sceptic and denied to the 'dogmatist'. Scepticism would not be routed but it might be contained. The dogmatist, according to Leibniz, is to be resisted when he claims absolute certainty. We do not have absolute certainty about the world but only of certain eternal truths. That concession made to the sceptics, another kind of certainty may be claimed which is sufficient for the conduct of human life—what Leibniz calls 'moral certainty'. The sceptics who demand a greater certainty are simply living on the fraudulent promises of the dogmatists.

In his *Critical Remarks on the General Part of Descartes' Principles of Philosophy*, Leibniz sums up this attitude as follows:

> About sensible things we can know nothing more, nor ought we to desire to know more, than that they are consistent with one another as well as with rational principles no one doubts,[1] and hence that future events can to some extent be foreseen from past. To seek any other truth or reality than what this contains is vain, and sceptics ought not to demand any other, nor dogmatists promise it. (PPL 384, G iv 356)

Leibniz held that on strict empiricist grounds there would be no basis for even moral certainty about the world. Certain rational principles needed to be invoked in order to provide such moral certainty. For instance, he continued to believe that it was impossible to demonstrate with metaphysical certainty (*pace* Descartes) that life is not one long dream. Yet, as he puts it in a later work, 'this would be as contrary to reason as the fiction of a book's resulting by chance from jumbling printer's type together' (NEHU 375). Metaphysically speaking, in other words, the hypothesis that life is a coherent and prolonged dream is not an impossible one. We may be certain that it is false because, in the first place, there would have to be a reason why life is like that and it would require a very far-fetched hypothesis to explain how it was possible. The rational principle in play in rejecting this possibility as wildly improbable seems to be the principle of preferring the hypothesis which 'has fewer requisites, or, is easier' (PW9, C 515).

The question as to whether there is a material world is independent, for Leibniz, of the problem as to whether there are any other minds. Leibniz, as we shall see, claimed that it was morally certain that a perfect God would create a world in which there were as many substances as possible. But since these are immaterial it does not follow that there is a material world. The hypothesis that life is a coherent and prolonged dream is one that, for Leibniz, has to apply not just to one mind but to all the minds that there are. It would be too great a coincidence if my experiences not only tallied among themselves but with other people and yet those experiences not be of a common material world. Much more probable is the accepted opinion of the reality of the material world.

Leibniz's position here might be seen as a common sense one and indeed Leibniz's account of the status of 'accepted opinions' might be seen as a theory of common sense. Leibniz used the phrase 'common sense' but only in its original meaning of what is common to more than one sense. But he had nonetheless something like our concept of common sense which shows itself in his opposition to a variety of extravagant claims which he terms 'paradoxical': Berkeley's denial of matter, Spinoza's denial of contingency, Spinoza's claim that God is the only (true) substance and Malebranche's claim that God is the only (true) cause, to mention some celebrated examples. That a 'paradoxical' claim—one which is contrary to well-established opinion—is false is something we may *presume* until proof is offered to the contrary.

'Presumption' is a legal term. The accused is *presumed* to be innocent until it is proved otherwise. A received opinion may have in its favour 'something close to what creates a "presumption", as jurists call it' (NEHU 517). This includes some[2] of what have been called 'common sense' beliefs in more recent philosophical literature. Such opinions do not always turn out to be right. But we are entitled to *presume* that they are in the absence of proof to the contrary.

Insofar as Leibniz can be seen as committed to it, his defence of common sense is neither dogmatic nor complacent but dialectical. He himself was willing to propound paradoxes (e.g. *Discourse*, § 9) and undertake to defend them by showing how they followed from principles which were not 'paradoxical'. Moreover he was willing to look carefully at the proofs offered by other philosophers who did likewise. The point of an appeal to 'accepted opinions' is not to settle anything definitely but to secure common points of reference so that discussion is not brought to a halt. The nub of Leibniz's criticism of the sceptics was that they wanted more than 'common points of reference' and brought discussion to a halt by refusing to engage in discussions which used 'undemonstrated principles'. Descartes' strategy only encouraged the demands of the sceptics by promising too much.

To contemporaries who knew their Plato and Aristotle, Leibniz's approach might have seemed merely a 'second-best course'[3] or a reversion to mere 'dialectic'.[4] It might have appeared a great come-down from the ideal of a deductive science afforded by Euclidean geometry. It always seemed that way to Simon Foucher[5] with whose Academic Scepticism Leibniz had closely associated himself.[6] But Leibniz still had his best card to play. The traditional conception of Euclidean geometry as based on indubitable truths was mistaken.[7] Leibniz's new strategy, so far from being a come-down from the geometrical method, was to be seen as an application of it, properly understood. Euclid was right to take what he took as axiomatic even though the project of demonstrating Euclid's axioms had not yet been accomplished:

> I blame Euclid much less for assuming certain things without proof, for he at least established the fact that if we assume a few hypotheses, we can be sure that what follows is equal in certainty, at least, to the hypotheses themselves. If Descartes or other philosophers had done something similar to this, we should not be in difficulty. Moreover, the sceptics, who despise the sciences on the pretext that they sometimes use undemonstrated principles, ought to regard this as said also to them. I hold, in contrast, that the geometricians should be praised because they have pinned down science with such pegs, as it were, and have discovered an art of advancing and of deriving so many things from a few. If they had tried to put off the discovery of theorems and problems until all the axioms and postulates had been proved, we should perhaps have no geometry today. (PPL 384, G iv 355)

6.2 The New Conception of Geometrical Method

In Leibniz's writings of the late 1670s there is much emphasis on the need to demonstrate accepted axioms and thus to improve on Euclid. At this stage Leibniz wanted geometry to be put on a

more certain basis and saw the provision of such a certain basis
as necessary to advancing the sciences. Thus he concludes one
short paper:

> I have been sent a writing of the late Pascal called 'the geometric mind' in
> which that illustrious person observes that Geometers have the habit of
> defining everything which is in the least obscure and of demonstrating
> everything which is in the least doubtful. I should like to have been given by
> him a few indications for detecting what is doubtful or obscure. And I am
> convinced that for the perfection of the sciences it is even necessary to
> demonstrate a few of those Euclid assumed without demonstration. Euclid
> was right but Apollonius was also justified. It is not necessary to do so but
> it still remains important to do it, and necessary to certain views. The late
> Roberval planned a new Elements of Geometry in which he was going to
> demonstrate rigorously several propositions which Euclid took as
> assumed without proof. I do not know whether he completed his work
> before he died, but I know that many people ridiculed it; if they had known
> its importance, they would have judged otherwise. It is not necessary for
> apprentices or even ordinary teachers, but in order to advance the sciences
> and to pass beyond the columns of Hercules, there is nothing more
> necessary. (S 57f., C 181f.)

The programme of de Roberval is one which was taken up by
eighteenth century geometers and led to a very important
negative result, namely, that it was not possible to demonstrate
all of Euclid's axioms. The conception of geometry which is
reflected in the methodology of Descartes and in Leibniz's
writings of the late 1670s became an untenable one. The
assumption that the truths of geometry are eternal truths was
undermined. Different geometries, it turned out, could be based
on incompatible assumptions. Geometry did indeed 'pass
beyond the columns of Heracles' and achieve what before
would have been thought impossible. But not in the way that
Leibniz had in mind. Leibniz, and others who supported the de
Roberval project, expected it to put Euclidean geometry on an
even stronger footing. That was not how it turned out.
Nonetheless, Leibniz's judgement that even geometry was not
yet rigorous enough was vindicated and those who laughed at
the de Roberval project did not laugh last.

Leibniz supported the programme of de Roberval in itself.
But he also believed, in the late 1670s, that metaphysics or 'first
philosophy' should be pursued in the same way. By 1680 or so
he had come to reflect that geometry, if not perfect, had at all

events been able to make progress. If the state of philosophy ought to be compared with that of geometry then philosophy was in a very backward position. It should try to emulate the methods of the earlier geometers and not the programme of de Roberval (excellent though that would be). They made use of certain common assumptions which were not demonstrated but from which they were able to demonstrate many geometrical truths. In the extract from his 1680 paper quoted at the beginning of this chapter Leibniz claims that Descartes would have done better to have adopted the method of the early geometers. In a letter of 1686 to Foucher he makes clear that this is to be his own method. This became Leibniz's point of departure from what I have termed 'methodological rationalism' or what Leibniz knew as 'Academic Scepticism':

> The Philosophy of the Academics, which is the knowledge of the weaknesses of our reason, is good for the beginnings, and since we are always at the beginning in matters of religion, it is certainly suitable for the better subjection of reason to authority, something you have shown very well in one of your discourses. But in matters of human sciences we must try to advance and although this can only be by establishing many things on a few suppositions, that remains useful, for at least we will know that all that remains to reach a full demonstration is to prove these few suppositions, and in the meantime we will escape from the confusion of disputes. It is the method of the Geometers. For example, Archimedes only supposed these few things: that the straight line is the shortest, that of two lines of which one is everywhere concave on the same side, the line included is less than the including line, and on that basis he completes his demonstrations with rigour. (G i 381f., trans by R. Niall D. Martin)

6.3 Progress without 'Full' Demonstration

Leibniz, in his later writings, uses the words 'demonstration' and 'proof' in a modern way, i.e. as assumption-relative. In the above quotation Leibniz appears to pay lip-service to the ideal of a 'full demonstration'. Certainly he continued to believe that, in metaphysics as in the de Roberval programme for proving the axioms of Euclid, it was worth looking for more fundamental assumptions from which to derive those which had previously been taken as 'first principles'. But the context of this letter to

Foucher raises doubts as to whether Leibniz thought this ideal was attainable. For he goes on to argue:

> It is certain, even, that some truths must be supposed, on pain of giving up hope of making demonstrations, for proofs could not go on to infinity. You cannot ask for the impossible, otherwise you would be a witness that you were not seriously searching for the truth. Hence, I will suppose boldly that two contradictions could not be true, and that what implies a contradiction could not be, and consequently that necessary propositions (that is whose contraries imply a contradiction) have not been set up by a free decree, or else we are misusing words. Nothing could be more clear for proving things. You yourself suppose them in writing and reasoning, or else at any moment you could defend the opposite of what you say. (G i 382, trans R.Niall D.Martin)

There is evidently a note of sarcasm in Leibniz's remark, 'I will suppose boldly that two contradictions could not be true . . . .' If the reduction of a statement (like '7+5=12') to a statement of identity which it would be contradictory to deny did not count as a 'full demonstration' for Leibniz, nothing would. But Leibniz had no criterion of indubitable truths which would serve as the starting point (as Descartes' clear and distinct ideas were supposed to do) for a full demonstration. Justification could not go on for ever and hence some assumptions had to be made if demonstrations were to be possible at all. Leibniz appears to be overscrupulous in defending the principle of contradiction. But he is in fact defending the most defensible of several principles which, in accordance with his new conception of geometrical method, he believed would be fruitful for producing demonstrations in metaphysics:

> If we suppose the principle of contradiction, for example, and in addition that in every true proposition the notion of the predicate is included in that of the subject, and *several other axioms of this nature*, and if we could prove many things as demonstratively as the Geometers, would you not find this result of consequence? Indeed we would need to begin this method one day if we are to begin to put an end to the disputes. It would always be a means of gaining ground. (G i 382, italics added)

The axiom that 'in every true proposition the notion of the predicate is included in that of the subject' was Scholastic in origin.[8] Leibniz frequently referred to it in its standard Latin formulation: *praedicatum inest subjecto*. In 'boldly supposing' it, Leibniz knew it had the authority of the Scholastics but that this counted for nothing with the Moderns. There is no doubt that he regarded it as being beyond reasonable contention. Writing to Arnauld, he appealed to it as a 'decisive reason' for holding his metaphysical theory of substance; concluding with evident exasperation: 'Either the predicate is in the subject or else I do not know what truth is' (BW 132, G ii 57).

In later writings Leibniz maintained a rationalist view of the principle of contradiction as an immediate truth (NEHU 362). But that identities are true and contradictions false are the only immediate 'truths of reason'. No such status was ever claimed by Leibniz for the *inesse* principle or for what he at one time took to be its corollary, the principle of sufficient reason. Yet these principles were, at different times, counted by Leibniz as fundamental principles. The *inesse* principle was regarded by him as an axiom which other philosophers either would (in the case of the Scholastics) or should accept and from which demonstrations of other truths could be made.

It was a characteristic consequence of the 'confusion of disputes' which clouded much seventeenth century philosophy that what some philosophers regarded as uncontentious was variously regarded by others as dubious or irrelevant. This is how Leibniz could represent the *inesse* principle as a 'supposition' to Foucher and as 'my fundamental principle, which I think all philosophers ought to agree to' when writing at much the same time to Arnauld (BW 132, G ii 56). The importance of the principle, for Leibniz, lay in its fruitfulness for clarifying and resolving issues in metaphysics and it is on this ground that he sought to recommend it, and the theory of substance he developed from it, to Modern philosophers. Its fruitfulness he held to consist in the fact that, if it and a few other principles are supposed, a rich variety of consequences could be drawn, many doubtful propositions clarified and many problems resolved.

Leibniz did not claim that the *inesse* principle was self-evident or that it could be demonstrated from other principles that were. His adoption of it as a central principle is thus indicative of his departure from a rationalist methodology. From a sceptic's point of view it was a *mere* assumption, having only the authority of traditional philosophy. That is why, writing to

Foucher, Leibniz should have included it as something he was 'boldly supposing'. Though it was certainly no conjecture, so far as Leibniz was concerned, the *inesse* principle had virtues which could be recognized by those who regarded it as no more than that. Philosophy could progress without being founded on what everyone regarded as self-evident. Indeed, had it to depend on such foundations, Leibniz came to see, it might make no progress at all.

6.4 Explanation in Metaphysics

Leibniz's philosophical writings in the early 1680s show a preoccupation with methodological issues. Two of his more important writings are his *Meditations on Knowledge, Truth and Ideas* and a preliminary draft of a book *On the Elements of Natural Science*. The former work—a paper published in the *Acta Eruditorum* of Leipzig in 1684—identifies Leibniz's position in relation to a number of recent debates. One point which Leibniz stressed was that a concept is a 'real' one and an idea 'true' if, and only if, it is possible (does not imply a contradiction). This would be established *a priori*, by 'a perfect analysis of concepts'. Leibniz probably still believed that such an analysis was possible in arithmetic, i.e. that the reality of the concept 'five' could be demonstrated by analyzing it into 1+1+1+1+1. But he here emphasizes his pessimism about knowing that concepts are possible *a priori*. 'For the most part', he insists, 'we are content to learn the reality of particular concepts by experience' (G iv 425). He goes on:

> From this therefore I believe we can understand that it is not always safe to appeal to ideas and that many thinkers have abused this deceptive word to establish some of their own fancies. That we do not always at once have an idea of a thing of which we are conscious of thinking, the example of the most rapid motion has shown. Nor is it less deceptive, I think, when men today advance the most famous principle that *whatever I perceive clearly and distinctly in some thing is true, or may be predicated of it.* For what seems clear and distinct to men when they judge rashly is frequently obscure and confused. (PPL 292, G iv 425)

Leibniz sought to produce more objective criteria of clarity and distinctness. We have a *clear* idea or clear knowledge of something, on his account, if we are able to recognize the thing in question: as we have, say, of redness if we are able to recognize red things in virtue of their colour (PPL 291, G iv 422f.). But our clear ideas are often confused, i.e. we are not able to explain in virtue of what we judge something to be red (or whatever). Where we have a *distinct* idea or knowledge of something, we are able to provide such an explanation or else, in the case of a primitive concept which is 'irreducible and to be understood only through itself', it is neither possible nor required that an explanation be given. By 1684 Leibniz had so little use for such ultimate elements of analysis that 'primitive concepts' receive only a token mention. In practice such absolutely distinct (adequate) knowledge was not humanly attainable (except perhaps in explaining arithmetic) and it was necessary to recognize degrees of distinct knowledge. To that extent our knowledge of things is always partially confused.

Leibniz's stock example of *distinct* knowledge is the kind of knowledge an assayer has of gold, i.e. knowledge of the distinction between real gold and other substances by 'sufficient marks and observations'. But he allows: 'We usually have such [distinct] concepts about objects common to many senses, such as number, magnitude and figure, and also about many affections of the mind such as hope and fear; in a word, about all concepts of which we have a *nominal definition*, which is nothing but the enumeration of sufficient marks' (PPL 292, G iv 423). But, since nominal definitions commonly make use of concepts which are clear but confused, *distinct* knowledge admits of degrees. The process of analysis cannot begin with absolute simples but it can gradually move in the right direction by replacing clear but confused concepts with distinct ones. To that extent progress towards better explanations is possible.

6.5 Requirements for a Metaphysical Theory

Leibniz frequently refers the reader of his *New Essays* back to his 'Meditations..' paper as a definitive statement of his mature position on a number of subjects. Its thought is, as often with Leibniz's published papers, highly compressed. It is sometimes unclear just where Leibniz actually makes the points which he later claims to have argued in the paper. For instance, in response to Locke's complaint that we have no clear idea of substance in general, Leibniz's spokesman replies:

> My own view is that this opinion about what we don't know springs from a demand for a way of knowing which the object does not admit of. A true sign of a clear and distinct notion is one's having means for giving *a priori* proofs of many truths about it. I showed this in a paper about truths and ideas which was published in 1684 in the *Acta* of Leipzig. (NEHU 219)

This point is of considerable importance in view of the centrality to Leibniz's metaphysical system of the concept of substance. Leibniz never claimed to have an absolutely definitive concept of 'substance' but he believed that it was possible to achieve a more distinct concept of substance than was to be found in other philosophical writings of the time or than Locke believed possible. Against Locke he had insisted on the fruitfulness of the concept: 'Several consequences arise from it; these are of the greatest importance to philosophy, to which they can give an entirely new face' (NEHU 218).

Leibniz may not have quite arrived at his new conception of substance by the time[9] of his 'Meditations' but, at least on his own later judgement, he had already arrived at the theory of metaphysical explanation which he was later to put into practice. Explanation has to be given in terms of relatively distinct concepts, i.e. in terms of concepts which are more distinct than those involved in the *explanandum*. The mark of relative distinctness in a concept of X is that it is possible to derive many *truths* about the nature of Xs from it. But, if the explanation does not reach back to primitive concepts, it is only hypothetical. It has to be justified by reference to what nowadays is called 'explanatory power' or what Leibniz called 'fruitfulness'. For the later Leibniz it is almost pleonastic to call a concept 'true and fruitful' in metaphysics. Thus, in his paper 'On the Correction of Metaphysics and the Concept of Substance' (1694) he began with the claim that 'the true and fruitful concepts, not only of substance, but of cause, action, similarity, and many other general terms as well, are hidden from popular understanding' and that a new method of metaphysics was needed to arrive at them. Later he went on to assert:

> The importance of these matters will be particularly apparent from the concept of substance which I offer. This is so fruitful that there follow from it primary truths, even about God and minds and the nature of bodies—truths heretofore known in part though hardly demonstrated, and unknown in part, but of the greatest utility for the future of the other sciences. (PPL 433, G iv 469)

Part of the task of a reformed metaphysics would be to explain how it is that certain things are true about whose truth there nonetheless is some problem. For instance, it was part of a widely accepted view of substance that a substance is a being which 'subsists in itself'. But it was unclear how, if that were so, there could be any genuine substances other than God. Again, and relatedly, it was part of the generally accepted view of substance that substances are able to initiate change. This is reflected in the Scholastic maxim, *actiones sunt suppositorum.* But it was difficult to give a rigorous definition of 'cause' which did not have the consequence that God was the only substance. Spinoza accepted this consequence and made it a cornerstone of his metaphysics. But for Leibniz the denial of human individuality and spontaneity was not only unpalatable but paradoxical. To him it was much more likely that Spinoza's theory of substance was wrong than that the established view that human beings are individuals endowed with the capacity for free action should be wrong. Yet it needed to be explained how the established views could be true. That is part of what Leibniz looked for from a theory of substance.

Leibniz had arrived at a provisional statement of his metaphysical system by early 1686. It is contained in his *Discourse on Metaphysics*, whose articles Leibniz summarized to send out for the opinion of Arnauld. These articles seem to lay out a metaphysical 'Credo'. But that was not how Leibniz intended them to be taken. In a covering letter he described what he had written as offering 'new points of approach fitted to clear up great difficulties' (BW 67, G ii 11). The *Discourse* was an attempt at reducing the 'confusion of disputes', of replacing what was obscure and controversial by what was at least relatively clear and solid. It was not entirely successful in this respect. At least in the judgement of Arnauld it was in certain important respects itself obscure and controversial. Leibniz accordingly sought to explain, defend and eventually to amend his system and it was only after nine years that he was prepared to see even part of it published. This period of Leibniz's mature philosophizing, and the problems which Leibniz sought to solve in it, will be the focus of attention in the next part.

Notes

1 Loemker here gives 'rational principles that cannot be doubted' but the Latin is *'rationibus indubitatis'*. Apart from the fact that Leibniz could have used the stronger adjective *'indubitabilis'* if he had meant *'cannot* be doubted', the context makes it clear that Descartes' promise of indubitability is partly to blame for the continuing dispute between dogmatists and sceptics. Leibniz has in any case no criterion of indubitability other than reducibility to a statement of identity. The 'rational principles' involved here are principles which are not derivable from the principle of contradiction. The principle of preferring the hypothesis with 'fewer requisites', referred to in the text, is a 'principle of topical knowledge', i.e. is a starting point for dialectical reasoning which begins from assumptions disputants are expected to allow. It is a principle which may be *presumed* to be true in contrast with one which is proved or merely conjectured (see NEHU 457). The onus of proof lies with whoever favours the more elaborate hypothesis (see PW8, C 514, NEHU 438).

2 It also includes established axioms and principles in philosophy which have not been demonstrated. For instance, the missing premise in the Ontological Argument (see Section 5.3 above) of which Leibniz offered a proof to Spinoza, is later reduced to the status of a *presumption*, thus changing the status of the conclusion of the argument to that of mere *moral certainty*: 'We are entitled to assume the possibility of any being, and above all of God, until someone proves the contrary; and so the foregoing metaphysical argument does yield a *moral* conclusion' (NEHU 438, italics added).

3 Leibniz's hypothetical method may well have been influenced by the 'second-best course' of Plato's *Phaedo*, a work which he had read very thoroughly and much admired. But since Leibniz carried the acknowledgement of intellectual debts to excess it would be surprising if this were a conscious influence, since Leibniz does not acknowledge it. In any case Leibniz's 'second-best course' is not *merely* hypothetical but involves an emphasis on what we are entitled to assume which reflects his own strong background in jurisprudence. It would be more apt to describe

Leibniz's method as 'provisional' than as a 'second-best' since it involves steps in the direction of 'full demonstration'.

4 Leibniz tends to underplay the influence of Aristotle on his thought—probably to avoid being suspected of still being under 'the bondage of Aristotle'—but the reader interested in pursuing the question how far Leibniz was restoring 'dialectic' will find much of relevance in the *New Essays*, especially in the helpful English edition prepared by Peter Remnant and Jonathan Bennett (see, e.g., NEHU 372, and the editors' notes under the heading 'Topics').

5 Foucher criticized Leibniz's *New System* because of Leibniz's departure from the Academic method and failure to take things back to 'first principles':

> To such an extent it is true that we must observe the laws of the Academics, of which the second forbids bringing into question things—such as those of which we have been speaking—that we can well see cannot be decided; not that such questions are absolutely insoluble, but that they are only [soluble] in a certain order, that requires philosophers to begin by agreeing on the infallible criteria of truth, and to subject themselves to demonstrations based on first principles... (G iv 490, trans R.Niall D.Martin)

6 Leibniz was so tactful about his qualifications regarding Academic Scepticism that they were not taken up by Foucher in their earlier correspondence. In 1687 he roundly declared that he had found Foucher's interpretation of the Academics entirely to his liking: 'The laws of the Academics that you express by the words of St. Augustine are those of the true logic.' But he went on to express what seems a minor qualification: 'All I find to add is that in beginning to practise them we must not only regret what is poorly established, but also try to establish solid truths bit by bit' (G i 390). Leibniz's point, repeated elsewhere in the correspondence, is that progress can be made gradually by establishing many things on a few assumptions so that only these assumptions remain to be proved (see, e.g., G i 381).

7 It is quite possible that Leibniz's new conception of geometrical method reflects his own uncertainties about the basis of his infinitesimal calculus, details of which he first published in 1684. Being unable to prove the reality of infinite and infinitesimal lines, he nonetheless wanted to suppose it and to justify his calculus by its fruitfulness. In a later letter Leibniz remarked that 'infinites and infinitesimals are grounded in such a way that everything in geometry, and even in nature, takes place as if they were perfect realities' (PPL 544, GM iv 94). Indeed Leibniz saw the role of his sceptical critics regarding the calculus as comparable to that of earlier sceptics regarding algebra and geometry. 'I even find that it means much in establishing sound foundations for a science that it should have such critics' (PPL 544, GM iv 95). But neither should the progress of the sciences be held up while these foundations are discovered. It may thus be no coincidence that Leibniz's new methodology for geometry and metaphysics was evolved at

much the same time as he must have been worrying about the absence of acceptable foundations for his infinitesimal calculus.

8 But Leibniz's use of it involves a crucial generalization to apply to all truths and not just abstract truths (see below, Section 8.7). One way of stating the *inesse* principle is to say that every truth does have an 'ultimate analysis' (see Sections 5.1 and 5.2 above) even although (as Leibniz came to accept in the early 1680s) we can reach it only in a few rare cases. The importance of the *inesse* principle for the Leibniz of the *Discourse* period is that it constitutes a supposition about God's knowledge of the world from which Leibniz then believed he could derive much of his theory of substance.

9 But, as we shall see in Chapter 11, certain remarks Leibniz makes in the *New System* imply that he had by about this time found his theory of the *nature* of substances, though not his theory about the *communications* between them.

7   The Construction of a Philosophical Agenda (1679–85)

I approve most heartily these two propositions which you advance: that we see all things in God and that strictly speaking, bodies do not act upon us ... (To Malebranche, 1679, PPL 210, G i 330)

Perhaps if the Revd. Father Malebranche were himself to consider what I have said, he will find it reasonable. It can perhaps be said that it is not so much a reversal as a development of his doctrine and that it is to him that I owe my foundations in this subject. (GM ii 299)

Malebranche became the centre of much philosophical attention when Leibniz was in Paris. He had published his best-known work (his *Recherche de la Vérité*) by 1675 and Leibniz's friend Foucher wrote a critique exposing its 'dogmatic' assumptions. Leibniz was evidently attracted by Malebranche's doctrine that we see all things in God. For he was prompted to offer a clarification and defence of it in notes he wrote on one of Foucher's contributions to the ensuing debate:

Idea can be taken in two senses; namely, for the quality or form of thought, as velocity and direction are the quality and form of movement; or for the immediate or nearest object of perception. Thus the idea would not be a mode of being of our soul. This seems to be the opinion of Plato and the author of the *Recherche*. For when the soul thinks of being, identity, thought, or duration, it has a certain immediate object or nearest cause of its perception. In this sense it is possible that we see all things in God and that the ideas or immediate objects are the attributes of God himself. (PPL 155)[1]

The suggestion that we see all things in God may seem initially to be a strange one. But it is connected with the not so unfamiliar thought that we are immediately dependent on God for everything. Leibniz followed Malebranche in considering this suggestion not just as an expression of piety but as something which could be said in strict metaphysics.[2]

7.1 The Problem about Causality

There were at least three good reasons in currency in the late seventeenth century why material things could not be the causes of our ideas. One was that matter was 'inert' and therefore lacking in the power to produce our ideas. Another was that material things and mental things had nothing in common and hence there could be no interaction between them. There was thus a kind of negative way to the thought that only God could produce those ideas which are not dependent on our wills—a way of arguing which Berkeley was to develop fully some years later.[3] Malebranche himself made use of a positive argument for saying that God is the only 'real and true cause' of what happens, which he expounded in the *Recherche* as follows:

> ... when we examine our ideas of all finite minds, we do not see any necessary connection between their will and the motion of any body ...

> But when one thinks about the idea of God, i.e. of an infinitely perfect and consequently all-powerful being, one knows ... that it is impossible to conceive that He wills a body to be moved and that this body be not moved.

> ... when a ball that is moved collides with and moves another, it communicates to it nothing of its own, for it does not itself have the force it communicates to it. Nevertheless, a ball is the natural cause of the motion it communicates. A natural cause is therefore not a real and true cause but only an occasional cause, which determines the Author of nature to act in such and such a manner in such and such a situation. (*op. cit.*, p. 448)

Leibniz agreed 'heartily' with Malebranche in 1679 that 'strictly speaking, bodies do not act on us' and that we see all things in God. He had reasons of his own for coming to some of the same conclusions as Malebranche, as we shall see in Part Three. Indeed Malebranche's metaphysics might have been acceptable to him if it had been freed of certain difficulties.

Central among these, as is clear in Leibniz's *Discourse*,[4] is that of distinguishing the actions of God from those of the creatures. Leibniz sided with Malebranche in wanting to oppose those who asserted a total independence of humans from God both in respect of their cognitive powers and in respect of this capacity for action. But he came to regard Malebranche's metaphysics as going too much to the other extreme. This led him first to see a number of difficulties in Malebranche's philosophy and then, through a solution of these, to his own 'system'.

7.2 The Problem of Interaction

The view that we see all things in God is one which, as presented by Malebranche, involves denying that we have ideas of our own. It was contested by the celebrated Antoine Arnauld and there ensued a protracted and eventually bitter controversy between them.[5] Leibniz wanted to agree with Malebranche that we see all things in God but to accept Arnauld's claim that we have ideas of our own. Ideas do not just exist in the mind of God but also in our minds. This Leibniz annexed to the familiar thought that human souls are made in the image of God and that therefore we may expect to find in them, however faintly delineated, traces of the attributes of God.

Malebranche's use of the word 'idea' may seem retrograde to those more accustomed to that of Descartes. But Descartes' use of the word had problems of its own in the context of Cartesian metaphysics. Descartes found it difficult to explain how ideas could be produced by material substance or, for that matter, how something corporeal and mechanical could interact with what was neither. Malebranche's theory denied that there was true causality between souls and bodies or, for that matter, even between bodies. And, at least for a while in the early 1680s, Leibniz was of the opinion that Malebranche's theory was the only one which could solve these problems. In his so-called *System of Theology*, Leibniz presents his own modified Malebranchism in just this light:

> God is the sole immediate object of the mind, outside of itself; ... it is only through the medium of God our ideas represent to us what passes in the world; for on no other supposition can it be conceived how the body can act on the soul, or how different created substances can communicate with one another ... (*op. cit.*, p. 73)

But, although a Malebranchist account could provide some answer to the mind-body problem and to the problem of the communication between substances generally, it was not one with which Leibniz was long satisfied. There were, for Leibniz, two main areas of difficulty. He was concerned, in the first place, that such an account made God the source of all action and therefore denied effective action to creatures. He was also concerned at the implications of making every event effectively miraculous, partly for the same reason but also because it seemed to detract from the orderliness of God's providence and therefore, in Leibniz's eyes, from His wisdom. Both these problems are prominent in the early sections of the *Discourse* and this has led scholars,[6] rightly in my opinion, to stress the Malebranchian provenance of Leibniz's first mature essay on metaphysics.

7.3 Order, Reason and the Arbitrary Will

It is difficult for many twentieth century readers to enter sympathetically into the heated debates of seventeenth century theology. But some of these debates become more accessible once it is realized that there is a tendency in Christian theology *both* to stress the majesty of God and so the vast difference between God and man *and* to stress an affinity between the two on the ground that man is made in the image of God. There are doubtless dangers to piety in either emphasis. But Leibniz was more conscious of the risks which resulted from stressing the distance between God and man. At a cognitive level, since God's knowledge is a perfect knowledge, such an emphasis tended to promote scepticism about human powers. A number of seventeenth century sceptics known to Leibniz, including Pierre Daniel Huet and Pierre Bayle, professed to be pious men. On the other hand, such an emphasis on the distance between man and God also led to a stress on human autonomy and therefore encouraged free-thinking. From a post-Enlightenment stance free-thinking seems entirely natural and proper. But Leibniz was quite typical of his age in the particular horror he felt of it.

L.E. Loemker refers to this as 'the moral problem of the [seventeenth] century':

> A revolution threatened Europe; the moral order of the *homme honnête* who found his true freedom in obedience to higher order, political,

ecclesiastical, and 'natural', was threatened by the *libertin*, whose freedom recognized no higher order than his own thinking. (*op. cit.*, p. 453)

Loemker rightly identifies one of the philosophical problems which relates directly to this moral problem—namely, of giving an account of human freedom which does not imply that God's knowledge of power is limited. (Leibniz's attempt to solve this problem is discussed in Chapter 9 below.) But there is a related problem, affecting the account given both of the divine and the human wills, namely, the question whether it can be free if it is wholly determined by reason. One defence of freewill common in Leibniz's time required that agents were only free insofar as they enjoyed 'a liberty of indifference' as between the courses of action open to them. Leibniz wished to defend the view that the existence of reasons determining the will in no way detracted from human freedom. Relatedly, in the case of God, he wished to insist that God is a perfectly rational being who is to be praised for doing what is best. This required him to insist that the laws of goodness and justice are eternal truths which are independent of God's will.

Leibniz thus took one side over a classical problem which was discussed in one of Plato's dialogues and so has come to be known as 'the Euthypho problem': 'Does God do what he does because it is best? Or is it best because it is what God does?' On the other side from Leibniz were those who emphasized the majesty of God, insisted that God's will was inscrutable to us and that we must accept as good whatever accords with 'the divine will'. According to this view (known as 'voluntarism') it is God's will which makes moral truths true. Philosophers, like Descartes, who adopted a thoroughgoing voluntarism, made all necessary truths (i.e. those, like mathematical truths, that seem necessary to us) dependent on God's will.

This theological debate can, as I believe Leibniz saw it, be summed up in the question: Is God an *homme honnête* writ large or is He a *libertin* writ large? Voluntarism was in effect an encouragement to the *libertin* and so indeed was any theology which exhibited God's actions as 'arbitrary'. Leibniz noted with what we may take to be satisfaction that Malebranche claimed, in his *Traité de la Nature et de la Grace*, to be refuting the *libertin*.[7] Malebranche was right, in Leibniz's view, to allow that there are laws of Grace. But Malebranche did not go far enough. Having said that, so far as the order of nature is concerned, God's intervention to produce the usual effect of any particular cause is on the basis of His general will, Malebranche found himself unable to give a satisfactory account of miracles. He was obliged to say that miracles were due to the *particular* volitions of God. From Leibniz's point of view this was tantamount to making God 'arbitrary' in respect of miracles and this seemed to Leibniz to detract from God's perfection:[8]

> As for me, I should rather believe that everything that takes place through wisdom takes place through general laws, that is, through rules or principles, and that God always acts wisely. So miracles [are] themselves entirely in the general order, that is, in general laws.

This is one point at which it seems true that Leibniz was building on 'foundations' laid by Malebranche, where Leibniz's philosophy is a 'development' rather than a 'reversal' of Malebranche's metaphysics (GM ii 299). It might even be claimed that Leibniz's *Discourse on Metaphysics* was in part an attempt to purge Malebranche's *Treatise of Nature and of Grace* of its last voluntarist traces. Leibniz himself gave his 'little discourse' a title different from that by which it is universally known. Leibniz's title—*Traité sur les Perfections de Dieu*—stresses what he has in common with Malebranche—namely, an emphasis on the principle that God always does what is best. Many of Leibniz's disagreements with Malebranche are over what is implied by this principle.[9] We shall consider some of these implications in Chapter 12.

7.4 God and Human Individuality

A further dimension of the problem posed by the *libertin* has to do with the extent to which human beings are independent of God. The 'man of honour' (*homme honnête*) like Malebranche and Leibniz acknowledged a total dependence of man on God. But this poses what is perhaps the central problem of Leibniz's *Discourse*:

It is rather difficult to distinguish the actions of God from those of creatures; for there are some who believe that God does everything, and others imagine that all he does is to conserve the force he has given to creatures: the sequel will show how far the one or the other can be said. (§ 8)

Malebranche was inclined to the view that God does everything and there is little doubt that the Leibniz of the *System of Theology* was inclined in this direction too. But, as we shall see, such a view was for Leibniz effectively a denial of human individuality. For it was, as it seemed to Leibniz, essential to something's being an individual substance that it be capable of 'action', i.e. of initiating change. Malebranche's view, so far as Leibniz was concerned (see Section 8.1 below) was practically the same as that of Spinoza on this point. Commentators on Leibniz have long noted the tendency of his philosophy towards Spinozism.[10] But it is just this tendency which Leibniz sought to correct by showing how, although God is in a sense the only true cause, there are other *true* substances, i.e. individual things capable of action. Leibniz's tendency towards monism (the view that there is only one substance), like his tendency towards determinism, was a real one. But it by no means follows that Leibniz was 'at heart' (or *au fond*) either a monist or a determinist. For his commitment to apparently contradictory doctrines is no less real.

It may be argued indeed, as Loemker seems to argue,[11] that Leibniz was above all concerned to defend a particular view about human beings. They are made in the image of God and are therefore capable (subject to divine grace) both of action and of knowledge. Indeed Leibniz even went so far in the *Discourse* as to claim that *all* substances imitate the infinite wisdom and omnipotence of God as far as they can. (§ 9) Lesser substances form the lower end of a great chain of being in which the divine attributes are traced more and more faintly.[12] But towards the higher end of this chain are human substances. We are right to expect, therefore, that other substances will be at least distantly analogous to human substances. There are, that is to say, strong theoretical links between what is said about God, what is said about man, about other animals and indeed the physical universe. This means that Leibniz's view of man needs to be defended at many levels. But that view, on Loemker's account, plays a pivotal role in Leibniz's theorizing.

Although I am inclined to agree with Loemker's view that the key to Leibniz's metaphysics lies in his desire to defend a particular moral point of view (namely, that of the *homme honnête*), I have not assumed that interpretation in what follows. In the next part I shall simply present it as a fact that the theory of the individual substance is the cornerstone of Leibniz's metaphysical system, that his treatment of the problems proceeds on the basis of certain assumptions (I shall also call them 'requirements') about the nature of substance and that he was looking in particular directions for answers to these problems. The questions as to why a philosopher should be concerned with certain problems, make the assumptions he makes or look for solutions in a particular direction are always worth asking. But answers to them are almost bound to be more speculative and contentious than accounts which merely identify what is assumed without argument. Happily it is quite possible to separate out an exposition which simply notes that certain assumptions are made from a theory as to why they are made. I shall return, in Part Four, to further considerations about what motivated Leibniz's philosophizing. In the meantime we shall be considering how Leibniz addressed certain central problems on his agenda in the *Discourse* and in the period leading to the publication of his *New System* in 1695.

Notes

1 Translated from a manuscript published by F. Rabbe in *L'Abbé Simon Foucher*, Paris, Didier, 1867, p. 301.

2 In the *Discourse* Leibniz acknowledges that 'in rigorous metaphysical truth there is no external cause which acts on us except God alone and he alone communicates himself to us immediately by virtue of our continual dependence' (§ 28). He goes on in the next section to distinguish his position on ideas from that of Malebranche.

3 In his *Principles of Human Knowledge* Berkeley was critical of those of 'the modern philosophers'—amongst whom he would have included Malebranche—who allowed matter to exist even although it could not produce our ideas:

... that they shou'd suppose an innumerable multitude of created beings, which they acknowledge are not capable of producing any one effect in nature, and which therefore are made to no manner of purpose, since God might have done every thing as well without them, this I say thô we shou'd allow it possible, must yet be a very unaccountable and extravagant supposition. (§ 53)

The Malebranchian context of both their philosophies is one reason for the curious convergence between the metaphysics of Leibniz and Berkeley. The convergence is discussed in part in Section 10.4 below.

4 Leibniz appears to get down to real philosophical business in *Discourse*, § 8 by outlining the Cartesian and Malebranchian views on this subject and remarking that it will be apparent from what follows how far one or other of these views can be maintained. This much can be said in defence of G.H.R. Parkinson's editorial decision, in his *Leibniz: Philosophical Writings*, to cut out §§ 1-7. Even if we begin from § 8 the Malebranchian (and Cartesian) context is clear. But the importance of that context is even clearer if the opening sections are taken into account. A. Robinet, in his invaluable *Malebranche et Leibniz*, has produced a comparative table aligning Malebranche's *Traité* with Leibniz's *Discourse*. (*op. cit.* p. 140) The correspondence is particularly striking with respect to the first seven sections of the *Discourse*.

5 Arnauld's main contribution to the controversy was *Des Vraies et des Fausses Idées* of 1683, a work whose full title indicated it was directed against the author of the *Recherche*. Leibniz first publicly addressed himself to the controversy in his 'Meditations on Knowledge, Truth and Ideas' in the *Acta Eruditorum* for November 1684 (PPL 291-4, G iv 422-6). The importance of the controversy for Leibniz's philosophy is discussed in L.E. Loemker's paper 'A Note on the Origin and Problem of Leibniz's Discourse of 1686', *Journal of the History of Ideas*, 1947, pp. 452-8. Loemker's paper has an interesting supplement containing translations of unpublished notes Leibniz wrote on the controversy.

6 Including L.E. Loemker in the paper cited in Note 5 and A. Robinet in his *Malebranche et Leibniz*.

7 See the supplement to Loemker's paper, *op. cit.*, p. 462.

8 Cf. *Discourse* §§ 5-7.

9 Thus it is appropriate that Leibniz, in seeking to pursue a public discussion with Malebranche, should entitle a 1687 paper: 'Letter of Mr Leibniz on a General Principle useful in explaining the Laws of Nature through a Consideration of the Divine Wisdom ...'. Leibniz's point, with which he hoped Malebranche would agree, was that 'the true physics should in fact be derived from the source of the divine perfections' (PPL 353, G iii 54).

10 Perhaps the most influential commentator in the English literature who makes much of this tendency is Bertrand Russell in his *Critical Exposition*.

11 *Op. cit.*, p. 453. See also Loemker's introduction to his edition of Leibniz's writings, PPL p. 3f. The view that it is a central thought of Leibniz's philosophy that man is made in the image of God is (I think plausibly) argued by E.J. Craig in 'Philosophy and Philosophies', *Philosophy*, *58*, 1983, pp. 193ff.

12 The great chain of being is further discussed in Section 12.2 below, though I have probably underplayed its importance in spite of A.O. Lovejoy's influential *The Great Chain of Being*. Although, for Leibniz, there is even greater variety in nature than we can conceive of, things are fundamentally the same. That is why a unitary theory of substance has some point for Leibniz. In a striking passage in the *New Essays* he underlines this view:

> The foundations are everywhere the same; this is a fundamental maxim for me, which governs my whole philosophy. And I conceive unknown and confusedly known things always in the manner of things that are distinctly known to us. This makes philosophy very easy, and I really believe that this is how it should be carried on. (NEHU 490)

In the *New Essays* Leibniz puts into the mouth of Theophilus this praise for his 'system': I find in it an astounding simplicity and uniformity, such that everything can be said to be the same at all times and places except in degrees of perfection.' (NEHU 71) That indeed is to be expected if every created thing is to bear the marks of its Creator. Nor is it surprising, in view of the relatively distinct conceptions we have of ourselves as substances, that Leibniz puts forward as the fundamental theoretical element of his universe something whose conception must resemble 'our ordinary notion of *souls*' (PW 117, G iv 479). But, as we shall see in Chapter 10, Leibniz did not arrive at this view until some time after writing his *Discourse*.

PART THREE

'New Points of Approach Fitted to Clear up Some Great Difficulties':
A Metaphysical System Tried Out
(1685–95)

8 The 'System' of the Discourse on Metaphysics

... I have not taken sides on important matters without having first considered and reconsidered many times and having examined again the arguments of others .... The greater part of my opinions were arrived at after a twenty year deliberation. For I began to meditate when I was very young. I was only fifteen years old when I went on long walks in a wood to make up my mind between Aristotle and Democritus.[1] Yet I changed and rechanged my mind because of new insights. It is not more than about twelve years since I found myself satisfied and had arrived at demonstrations of matters which had not seemed to be demonstrable at all ... (Letter to Thomas Burnett, 1697, G iii 205)

In the winter of 1685–86 Leibniz penned what is, by common consent, the first statement of his mature philosophy. He referred to it in correspondence as 'a little discourse on metaphysics' and it has come to be known as the *Discourse on Metaphysics* even although the manuscript does bear a title—*Traité sur les Perfections de Dieu*. What Leibniz later referred to as his 'system' differs in a number of respects (as we shall see) from the metaphysics of the *Discourse*. But the long period in which Leibniz 'changed and rechanged' his mind was over. He now had a theory in which a number of principles could be securely fitted. He now had a 'system'.[2]

Leibniz did not call his *Discourse* a 'system' and indeed it is not organized as such. It was Foucher who seems to have been eager to foist the word on Leibniz. But Foucher was not sent the *Discourse*, only given to expect that Leibniz had organized a body of metaphysical propositions which were deducible from certain 'suppositions'.[3] The *Discourse* is written more in accord with the contemporary conventions for a theological treatise than those for a scientific work. If the *Discourse* itself is a piecemeal work, Leibniz was already organizing many of its fundamental thoughts in a 'systematic' manner. This was about the time at which he was satisfied that he 'had arrived at demonstrations of matters which had not seemed to be demonstrable at all...' (G iii 205). If the *Discourse* was not conceived as a 'system' it was soon to admit of systematic reorganization.[4]

8.1 The Context of the *Discourse*

The *Discourse on Metaphysics* appears to be partly a response to Malebranche's *Traité de la Nature et de la Grace*. Leibniz, like Malebranche (and in contrast with Descartes), did not separate metaphysics from theology. The *Discourse* has a strong theological content and is comparable with his so-called *System of Theology*, a work of the early 1680s. The *System of Theology* was written in pursuance of Church unity. It is likely that the *Discourse* was intended to serve the same purpose as the '*System*'. Both put forward a set of doctrines Leibniz (and perhaps any reasonable Lutheran) could accept in good conscience and which, so far as Leibniz could see, were also ones a Catholic would be allowed to believe.

Leibniz had earlier intended to involve Antoine Arnauld in his project of reconciliation. When he had gone to Paris on a diplomatic mission in 1672 he carried with him letters from the ecumenical Baron von Boineburg to Antoine Arnauld. Leibniz, with this introduction, was to approach Arnauld with his opinions about how members of his own Church might be able to approve the declarations of the Council of Trent. This involved controversial problems of interpretation but the assumption was that Arnauld's opinions 'could carry great weight' in the Catholic Church and that therefore his approval of Leibniz's interpretations might provide a diplomatic breakthrough. Unfortunately, von Boineburg died before Leibniz could make these overtures to Arnauld. He did indeed meet Arnauld in Paris, but this delicate matter was not broached.

The immediate use to which Leibniz intended to put the *Discourse* seems to have been to further his ecumenical project. Arnauld was to play a key role. Once more a Catholic nobleman was to act as the intermediary, this time Count Ernst von Hessen-Rheinfels. Leibniz wrote to von Hessen-Rheinfels in

February 1686 telling him rather casually that 'being at a place lately for several days with nothing to do' he had written a discourse on which he would be 'very glad to have the opinion of Arnauld'. He promised that 'the questions in regard to grace, in regard to the relations of God with created beings, in regard to the nature of miracles, the cause of sin, the origin of evil, the immortality of the soul, ideas, etc. are discussed in a way which seems to offer new points of approach fitted to clear up great difficulties' (BW 67, G ii 11). The intention was evidently to secure Arnauld's favourable judgement on Leibniz's 'new points of approach'.

Leibniz seems to have decided not to make too much of what Arnauld was being asked to do. He sent a summary of the articles contained in the *Discourse* and asked that Arnauld be requested 'to look it over and give his judgement upon it'. He gave as an excuse for not sending the whole *Discourse* that he had not had time to make a clean copy. But it is most improbable that this was his reason. Arnauld never received a full copy of the *Discourse*. Leibniz's strategy was almost certainly the one he adopted on other occasions, namely, of revealing only part of what he thought and awaiting a favourable response before revealing more.[5] That way he would not be caught having played his hand.

The strategy was a risky one and nearly proved a disaster. Arnauld's religious sensibilities were shocked by what he read. His reaction was summed up bitterly by Leibniz in the Latin adage 'Touch the mountains and they erupt'. But Arnauld's eruption was short-lived. He had obviously not been able to understand much of Leibniz's point of view from the short headings he had been given. This provided Leibniz with the chance to explain himself more fully and the result was a highly fruitful correspondence which, if it contributed little or nothing to the cause of Church unity, stimulated Leibniz both to amplify and modify the details of his new philosophical perspective.

8.2 The *Discourse* and the Schism in Philosophy

Many of the Modern philosophers, including the Cartesians

and, later, Locke and Berkeley, referred to Scholasticism only to abuse or dismiss it. They thought philosophy needed to be begun again, as if earlier philosophy had achieved nothing. Leibniz, though in some respects a radically Modern philosopher, took a different view. He allied himself with philosophers who valued both the Moderns and earlier philosophers, including the Scholastics. He believed that philosophy would continue to be bogged down in muddle and controversy unless there was a proper though critical appreciation of the Ancients and Scholastics. Indeed he was later to claim for his new perspective that it provided the means to just such an appreciation.

Leibniz's position in relation to the division between Scholastic and Modern philosophy and in relation to the fragmentation of philosophy in the seventeenth century helps to explain his frequent invocation of 'authorities' like Aquinas and his appeal to Scholastic maxims in the *Discourse*. Leibniz saw it as the mark of a freethinker to reject such appeals out of hand and shared the common moral horror at such a rejection of tradition for novelty. (See Section 7.3 above.) Leibniz thought we ought to accept what is received on good authority, at least provisionally.[6] But he also thought that beliefs should be organized in a scientific way and, where possible, shown to follow from higher principles. He sought, therefore, to transcend the appeal to authority characteristic of Scholastic argumentation. To that extent the *Discourse* is a slightly misleading work. But the *Discourse* itself shows examples of Leibniz's arguing from higher principles (e.g. from §§ 5 and 6 to §7 and from §8 to §9). The authority of the Ancients was ultimately to be supported by the project which Leibniz characteristically describes as giving a 'good sense' to what they had to say (see, e.g., *Discourse* §28).

The *Discourse* thus exemplifies the new method of doing metaphysics which Leibniz came to profess in the early 1680s (see Chapter 6 above). But it does so imperfectly. Metaphysics, as Leibniz practised it, is certainly based on 'suppositions'. Like geometry, metaphysics is concerned to deduce things which we are inclined to believe anyway. But what we are inclined to believe in a pre-theoretical way in metaphysics is a very mixed bag in which are included things everyone takes for granted, at the one end, and special convictions of our own, at the other. Many of Leibniz's starting-points fall somewhere in between. Many of Leibniz's contemporaries might have accepted Leibniz's basic requirements for a theory of substance. But not everyone. So, even supposing the theory was free of internal problems, there are other theories of substance which it would not so much supplant as pass by. How far that is so is too large a question to be addressed here. It is sufficient to note that Leibniz's problems about substance only arise if certain assumptions are made. We shall approach his theory by looking at what those assumptions appear to have been and how the main problems the theory addresses arise out of making them.

8.3 Problems about Substance

In a letter to Count Ernst von Hessen-Rheinfels, Leibniz drew attention to the 'new points of approach' in his 'short discourse on metaphysics', claiming they were 'fitted to clear up some great difficulties' (BW67, G ii 11). These 'difficulties' included several relating to the nature of individual created substances. Leibniz mentioned two which were on the recognized agenda for those concerned with problems relating to religion and metaphysics. One was the problem as to how to allow that God is the ultimate cause of everything while still allowing that created things could be genuine causes, specifically, that humans can really initiate and so be held responsible for what they do. The other was the problem as to whether the soul is immortal.

Such problems only arise on certain background assumptions. The problems they give rise to will be *solved* only if, at the end of the day, these assumptions can be retained. They will, however, have been clarified, e.g. it will be clearer in just what sense both God and created substances can be said to be 'causes'. Amongst these assumptions are five about the 'nature' of substance—requirements, from Leibniz's point of view, of something that is to count as a substance. Leibniz appeals to them as accepted maxims rather than as theses which require argument. They are assumptions that are nowhere questioned in Leibniz's writings.

Leibniz's assumptions about substance are:

1   *Unity.* A substance must be a genuine unity and not a
    merely accidental one. It must, in the Scholastic jargon,
    be an *unum per se* and not an *unum per accidens*, as a
    collection of things is. Thus, in *Discourse* § 34, Leibniz
    begins: 'Assuming that the bodies which constitute an
    essential unity (*unum per se*), such as man, are
    substances ...'.
2   *Identity.* Substances are individuals which remain the
    same through change. Leibniz, as we saw earlier
    (Section 2.2.1), took the Scholastic problem of finding a
    principle of individuation seriously and indeed wrote a
    student dissertation on it.
3   *Autonomy.* Leibniz, in an early work, defines
    'substance' as 'being which subsists in itself' (PPL 115,
    A VI i 508). Some such requirement he took to be
    common ground and, on the strength of this, he (and
    others) accepted that, in a full sense, only God is a
    substance. This left him with the problem as to the sense
    in which there are other substances at all.
4   *Agency.* Leibniz, again in an early work, defines
    'substance' as 'whatever moves or is moved' (PPL 73, G
    iv 32). Related to this is the Scholastic maxim *Actiones
    sunt suppositorum*—that agency, or the capacity to
    initiate change, pertains to *supposita* or individual
    substances—which Leibniz once referred to as 'that
    most widely accepted principle of philosophy' (PPL
    502, G iv 509).
5   *Completeness.* An individual substance is 'a complete
    being' (*Discourse* §8), i.e. one which is wholly
    determinate. We may refer to something as 'a ring' but,
    if it is an individual substance, it will be a particular
    ring, say, the ring of Gyges, of which things are true
    which are not true of rings *in general.* An individual
    substance is unique in that its total qualities specify it as
    different from other substances of the same kind.

There are problems arising from these assumptions which it was
a central aim of the *Discourse* to resolve. These are exacerbated

by Leibniz's commitment to the total 'interconnection of things' (§ 8). Leibniz, in admitting that it is 'difficult enough to distinguish the actions of God from those of the creatures' (§ 8), is alluding particularly to the implications of Malebranche's view that God is the only 'true cause'. But he must have been aware that full autonomy and total interconnection are difficult to reconcile with a plurality of substances. Indeed a total interconnection might more readily be construed as implying that ultimately the universe is a single whole whose parts are mere aspects endowed with none of the requisites of substance. Some such view had been adopted by Parmenides and Plotinus amongst the Ancients and by Spinoza amongst the Moderns. Leibniz did not address it in the *Discourse*, though (replying to the erudite Bayle) he later made it clear that he could, in his 'system', accommodate 'the one and the whole of Parmenides and Plotinus, yet without any Spinozism' and 'the Stoic connectedness, which is yet compatible with the spontaneity held to by others' (PPL 496, G iv 523).

Some of Leibniz's basic assumptions about individual created substances are not obviously comparable with one another. Others are clearly interrelated, as is true of *unity*, *identity* and *completeness*. Since, however, Leibniz himself associated each of these assumptions with different (though interconnected) problems, it will make for ease of exposition if they are considered one by one.

8.3.1 *Unity and Substantial Forms*
In the draft of the *Discourse* § 9 Leibniz remarks that 'if bodies are substances, it is not possible that their nature should consist solely in size, figure and movement, but that something else is needed.' By themselves these qualities do not explain, for instance, what constitutes the essential unity of an organism. It is partly for this reason that Leibniz thought there was a case for rehabilitating a reformed theory of 'substantial forms'. This is one problem inadequately treated in the *Discourse* but discussed in Leibniz's correspondence with Arnauld. As a result of Arnauld's criticism of this aspect of Leibniz's theory of substance, it is substantially modified in later writings (see Chapter 9 below).

8.3.2 *Identity and Individuation*

An account of substance needs to provide a principle of individuation. Leibniz's account accords to each individual substance its own substantial form. Each individual substance is a 'lowest species' (*infima species*) and it follows that there are no two substances which are exactly alike and differ only numerically. This, Leibniz points out (*Discourse* §9), is an extension to substances generally of a doctrine put forward by Aquinas about angels and intelligences (see above, Section 2.2.1.).

8.4 Autonomy and Creation

Autonomy is a feature of substance much emphasized by Descartes and by philosophers like Malebranche and Spinoza. Leibniz thought there were difficulties in the definitions of substance given by these philosophers and addressed them in a dialogue written late in life (1711) to provide a popular exposition of how his own thought related to that of Malebranche. The account of substance is outlined by a fictitious disciple of Malebranche, in the following terms:

> Whatever one can conceive by itself, without thinking of anything else, or without using the idea which represents something else, or better, whatever one can conceive by itself as existing independently of anything else, is a *substance*. And whatever one cannot conceive alone, or without thinking of some other being, is a mode of being, or a *modification of substance*. This is what we mean when we say that a substance is a being which subsists in itself. (PPL 620, G iv 581)

The spokesman for Leibniz in the dialogue replies:

> This definition of substance is not free from difficulty. In the end only God can be thought of as independent of any other being. Shall we say then, as does a certain innovator who is only too well known, that God is the only substance and that created beings are only his modifications?

Leibniz had been rebuked by correspondents for so much as mentioning the notorious Spinoza by name. But there is no doubt that his reader was expected to take the phrase 'innovator who is only too well known' to be an oblique reference to Spinoza. Leibniz's dissatisfaction with Spinoza's account of substance is expressed in the notes he made about the *Ethics* when it was (posthumously) published in 1678. But he was well aware of the problem to which Spinoza gave such a drastic solution: how can there be *created* substances if substance is that which subsists in itself? Leibniz looked for a solution along the lines of saying that a 'substance' is 'a concrete being independent of every created concrete being' (PPL 620, G iv 586). But if substances are capable of interacting with one another, this would not be a viable solution. For, insofar as substances act upon each other, they cannot be independent of one another.

8.5 Action and Interaction

The context in which Leibniz outlines his theory of substance in the *Discourse* is the problem of distinguishing the actions of God from those of the creatures. We saw earlier (Chapter 3) how Leibniz, like other Modern philosophers, was struck by the fact that matter as defined in the mechanical philosophy did not contain within itself the capacity to initiate changes in motion. From this it would follow, by the principle that actions pertain only to substances, that there are no material substances. Moreover it would require God's action to initiate and conserve motion in the universe. Thus, for a Modern philosopher, it was tempting to conclude either that God is the only true substance, or that God is the only true cause, or both.

Spinoza pressed these conclusions home by denying to human beings either the individuality or the freedom commonly believed to be distinctive of them. The Cartesian dualism of mental substances and material substances would have provided a way of avoiding such subversive consequences. But it did so at a price. How could minds act on bodies, or vice versa, if minds and bodies are essentially different? Leibniz, as we saw in Chapter 3, had long agreed with Malebranche's conclusion that, strictly speaking, 'bodies do not act upon us' (PPL 210, G i 330). In the 1680s he came to see that there was, as indeed Malebranche had maintained, just as much of a problem about

how minds can act on bodies. Leibniz came to agree with
Malebranche that the interaction supposed by Descartes was an
impossibility.

Malebranche's scepticism about causation had a decisive
influence not only on Leibniz but also on Berkeley and Hume.
Leibniz freely acknowledged his debt to Malebranche's sense of
the problem about causation. Malebranche and other
likeminded 'disciples' of Descartes 'have gone a great way in
regard to this problem by showing what cannot possibly take
place' (*New System* § 13).

Leibniz accepted the negative part of Malebranche's account
of causation, viz. that what we ordinarily call causes are not
'real and true' causes. As he himself put it: 'What we call
"causes" are, in metaphysical rigour, merely concomitant
requisites' (PW 90, C 521). There is, to put it Hume's way, no
more to what we judge to be the 'cause' of a phenomenon than
an event which we have found in experience to be of a kind
which is 'constantly conjoined' with the phenomenon in
question. Hume's scepticism about 'necessary connexions'
between phenomena is one entirely shared by Malebranche and
Leibniz. Where they differed from Hume was in using this
scepticism as a base from which to launch a metaphysical quest
for *true* causality.

Malebranche's conclusion was that God is the only true cause
because only in God's case is there a necessary connection
between willing and action. Ordinary causes are no more than
'occasions' and the necessary connections between ordinary
causes and their effects exist only by courtesy of divine
intervention.

Leibniz did not accept Malebranche's account of true
causality partly because it had the consequence that human
beings did not genuinely act and partly because it offended
against his principle of sufficient reason. Leibniz took that
principle to mean not simply that everything is comprehensible
by God but that the ordinary course of nature is in principle
intelligible to human beings. In the *Discourse* Leibniz insists
that everything takes place 'in conformity with the general
order'. Even miracles do so, though we cannot understand why
they happen in the way we can understand the laws of the
common natural order from which they depart. Thus the

principle of sufficient reason, as applied to phenomena, implies that miracles should not be multiplied beyond necessity. A philosopher should not resort to a *deus ex machina* to get out of difficult situations any more than a playwright. If God is to be brought into the story let it be, Leibniz frequently urges, to solve a problem worthy of him and not to explain the everyday course of events.[7]

Accordingly Leibniz sought what he believed to be a very different solution to the problem about causality from Malebranche, one which attempted to make sense of ordinary causal transactions while still maintaining the strict causal independence of each created substance from all the others. Commenting on Foucher's reply to Desgabet's *Critique de la Critique de la Recherche de la Vérité*, Leibniz wrote (in 1686):

> I feel also you are right ... to doubt that bodies can act on minds and vice versa. On this matter I have an agreeable opinion, which appears to me necessary and is very different from that of the author of the *Recherche*. I believe that every individual substance expresses the whole universe in its manner and that its following state is a consequence (though often free) of its previous state, as if there were only God and it in the world; but since all substances are a continual production of the sovereign Being, and express the same universe and the same phenomena, they agree with each other entirely, and that makes us say that the one acts on the other, because the one expresses more distinctly than the other the cause or reason of the changes, rather in the way we attribute motion to the vessel rather than to the whole of the sea ... (G i 382f., trans R Niall D Martin)

What Leibniz introduced to Foucher as an 'agreeable opinion' is nothing less than a condensed statement of what he later referred to as his 'system of pre-established harmony'. In describing it as 'une plaisante opinion' it is likely that Leibniz was aiming to disarm Foucher who, if philosophically severe, was nonetheless a pious man. In the *Discourse* itself Leibniz had not hesitated to stress the 'utility of these principles in the matter of piety and religion' (§ 32) and indeed was later to claim that he owed to St Theresa 'the fine thought that the Soul should conceive things as if there were only God and itself in the world' which he employed in one of his 'hypotheses'.[8]

By itself, however, an 'agreeable opinion' is no substitute for sound philosophy. It is necessary to make this view of substance intelligible. In particular it is necessary to explain why it should be thought that the later states of a substance should be understood as a consequence of its earlier states rather than as an effect of other substances.

8.6 Completeness and the Identity of Indiscernibles

The requirement of *completeness* is one which Leibniz introduces when he is within sight of a theory of substance.[9] It is closely connected with that of *identity*, as is clear in Leibniz's explanation. Whereas *unity*, *activity* and *autonomy* are requirements for anything to be a substance of *a certain sort* (e.g. *a* ring, *a* king or whatever) *completeness* and *identity* are requirements for something to be an *individual* substance. Of course a substance has to be *an individual* to be an individual *of a certain sort*. But we may consider its individual and its generic character in abstraction from one another. Thus we may consider the quality of being a king 'which belongs to Alexander the great' as something 'abstracted from its subject'. So considered, being a king is not 'sufficiently determinate for an individual' (*Discourse* 8). In a more modern idiom we may say that it describes Alexander but it does not *definitely* describe him.

Here, as on many other points, Leibniz explains himself more fully in response to the difficulties raised by Arnauld:

> ... the concept of the sphere in general is incomplete or abstract, that is to say we consider only the essence of the sphere in general or theoretically without regard to the particular circumstances, and consequently the concept does not involve that which is required for the existence of a certain sphere. The concept of the sphere which Archimedes had put upon his tomb is complete and should involve all that pertains to the subject of this kind ... (BW 108, G ii 39)

The complete concept of the individual sphere referred to must contain what is necessary and sufficient to identify it as that particular individual. If individuals have such complete concepts then there are no two individuals which differ *solo numero*: and vice versa. In this way *identity* and *completeness* are interrelated.

The identity of indiscernibles seemed to Leibniz, at least

when writing the *Discourse*, to be a 'paradoxical' principle. Accordingly he sought 'higher ground' in the attempt to justify it. As things turned out, it required a good deal of explanation to convince Arnauld of Leibniz's justification of the principle and none to persuade him of the principle itself, with which he did not disagree. Partly for this reason, perhaps, Leibniz was later to defend the identity of indiscernibles in a different way. But his defence of it in the *Discourse* and for a time thereafter is important because of the way it integrated Leibniz's formulation of a theory of substance. The principle which—apparently to Leibniz's surprise[10]—Arnauld found objectionable is one which is cited in the *Discourse* as an 'agreed' one. It is that in every true proposition the predicate is contained (expressly or implicitly) in the subject—what the Scholastics had known by the adage '*Praedicatum inest subjecto*' but which I shall refer to simply as 'the *inesse* principle'. It is this principle (supposition) which Leibniz initially believed to provide the key to solving the problems about substance to which his metaphysics was particularly addressed.

8.7 Leibniz's Generalization of the *Inesse* Principle

The *inesse* principle was a legacy from the Scholastics (sometimes referred to as the 'common' philosophers or even as 'the Philosophers') and, as applied to what philosophers since Kant have called 'analytic' truths, has continued under other names to impress philosophers of different traditions. Applied, for example, to the proposition '4=2+2' the principle can be understood as saying that the predicate 'is the sum of two and two' is contained in the subject 'four'. The relation of 'containing' was taken by Leibniz to cover cases where the concept of the predicate is identical with that of the subject as well as cases where it only forms part of the concept of the subject, as in 'All sisters are female', 'A square is a bounded figure' and so on. It seems to have been part of the received wisdom that the *inesse* principle held good for 'abstract truths' generally and indeed that the principle of contradiction was the highest principle of such truths.

The fundamental breakthrough, as it seemed to Leibniz,

consisted of the thought that the Scholastic *inesse* principle could be generalized so as to apply to all truths. Only a few years before (in his paper 'Of Universal Analysis and Synthesis') he had supposed that the principle had only restricted application, to abstract truths and not to truths of experience. He had then favoured a sharp dichotomy between two sorts of truth, which he variously referred to as *a priori*, abstract, necessary and eternal, on the one hand, and as *a posteriori*, empirical and contingent, on the other. He did not use the word 'empirical' in this context but his reference to 'matters of fact, i.e. contingent matters, which do not depend on reason but on observation and experience' (PW 15, G vii 296) is clearly a reference to what others have termed 'empirical' matters.

Leibniz claimed no originality for this distinction and seems initially to have made use of what he regarded as an established dichotomy. The Scholastic principle of *inesse*, to which he refers with approval, is one he took to be applicable only to abstract truths:

> ... what are commonly regarded as axioms are reduced to identities, i.e. are demonstrated, by the analysis either of the subject or of the predicate, or of both, so that if one supposes the contrary they appear at the same time to be and not to be. It is evident, therefore, that in the last analysis direct and indirect proof coincide, and *it was rightly observed by the Scholastics that all axioms*, once their terms have been understood, *are reduced to the principle of contradiction.* And so a reason can be given for each truth; for *the connection of the predicate with the subject is either self-evident, or it has to be displayed, which is done by the analysis of terms.* This is the unique and highest criterion of truth *in the case of abstractions*, which do not depend on experience: namely, that it should either be an identity or reducible to identities ... (PW 14f., G vii 295 f., italics added)

This dichotomy between abstract *a priori* truths (depending on the principle of contradiction) and empirical (*a posteriori*) truths has remained a plausible one.[11] The *inesse* principle (that the predicate *is contained* in the subject of true propositions) is also plausible, taken as applying to *a priori* truths. It is plausible to suppose, for instance, that all the properties of the number 5 could be shown to be contained in the concept '5'. That the number 5 is the square root of 25, the sum of 2 and 3, the only prime number between 3 and 7, and so on, may thus be shown to be reducible, through definitions and by a series of steps, to the principle of contradiction. Whether or not Leibniz was right in supposing that all *a priori* truths are demonstrable in this way is by no means certain. But it is a position which is familiar and intelligible to students of twentieth century philosophy.

Leibniz himself, however, could not rest content with this dichotomy. In his paper 'Of Universal Synthesis and Analysis' it is clear that by adopting it he made his overall philosophical position incoherent. For Leibniz sought to make intelligible how God could know everything but without supposing that God has senses to know about contingent matters: '... all things are understood by God *a priori*, as eternal truths; for he does not need experience, and yet all things are known by him adequately' (PW 15, G vii 296). This statement left Leibniz with a dilemma: *either* all things are known by God *a priori* as eternal truths and there are no genuinely contingent truths, since all truths after all 'depend on reason': *or else* there are genuinely contingent truths (*pace* Spinoza) and so God's knowledge of *them* must be different from his knowledge of eternal (necessary) truths. Leibniz was aware of this problem but failed for some time to come to grips with it. A unitary theory of truth was needed which allowed God to know all truths *a priori* but which left room for some of those truths to be genuinely contingent. Leibniz believed, at the time of writing the *Discourse*, that he had managed to produce such a theory of truth. Eternal truths are true independently of the divine will but contingent truths are true only in virtue of God's free decrees. God knows contingent truths *a priori* but not as eternal truths.

Leibniz's accounts of the distinction between necessary and contingent truths merit a separate chapter. As we shall see, there were problems left unresolved in the *Discourse* account. I mention these problems now since they explain why Leibniz needed a unitary theory of truth at all (namely, to make sense of God's knowledge of the world) and why the theory should have been introduced in *Discourse* § 8 in the context of solving the difficulty of distinguishing 'the actions of God from those of creatures'.

The unitary theory of truth proposed by Leibniz involves at once an extension of the *inesse* principle to apply to contingent as well as necessary truths. To do this Leibniz had to show how the principle could be extended to 'existential propositions', i.e. propositions about individual existents. Scholastic philosophers would have been deterred from making such an extension by the thought that many of the things which are true of individual existents are purely accidental, are purely 'extrinsic denominations'. The disciple Peter would still have been Peter if he had not denied Jesus of Nazareth three times. Indeed it may seem as if it could not be essential to Peter's being Peter that he did this and still be a contingent fact about him or something he was free to do or not to do. But to suppose this, Leibniz insisted, is to confuse what is *certain* (since God has foreknowledge of it) with what is *necessary* (*Discourse* § 13). God has a 'complete notion' of Peter from which He is able to foresee everything that Peter will freely do as well as everything that happens to him. But that did not mean, he insisted, that Peter's actions are necessary in themselves.

I shall return, in the next chapter, to the question whether this answer is compatible with Peter having been genuinely free—a question raised in Leibniz's subsequent correspondence with Arnauld. But, even if it were satisfactory, this answer supposes that sense can be made of there being a 'complete notion' of any given individual substance from which everything that is true of it could be deduced. If this did make sense then the Scholastic problem about the principle of individuation (discussed in Section 2.2.1 above) would be based on a misunderstanding. For that problem arises only on the assumption that individuals might resemble one another completely and differ only numerically. Leibniz, in adopting his principle of the identity of indiscernibles, denied that assumption. In denying it he was committed to the view that every individual is a 'lowest species' (*infima species*), i.e. is the only one of its kind (*Discourse* § 9).

Leibniz's argument in *Discourse* § 8 for his new conception of the individual substance is thus based on a curious blend of radically Modern and Scholastic ideas. For instance, when he observes that 'it is agreed that every true prediction has some basis in the nature of things', he is appealing to Scholastic thought. But a Scholastic would have taken this as implying, for example, that to truly predicate of gold that it is fusible is to say something about the nature or essence of gold. If we knew enough about the nature or essence of gold we should be able to deduce all the properties of gold. Leibniz took a radical nominalism which denied such natures or essences for granted.[12] The world does not contain 'natural kinds' but only particulars. Leibniz's account of the individual substance is a nominalistic counterpart of the Scholastic realist thought that everything that is true of gold can be deduced from its essence. Every different kind or species of thing has a different essence. So, if every individual is an *infima species*, this must be in virtue of there being a different essence or what Leibniz calls a 'complete notion' for every individual substance. As he puts it, 'it is the nature of an individual substance, or complete being, to have a notion so complete that it is sufficient to contain, and render deducible from itself, all the predicates of the subject to which this notion is attributed' (*Discourse* § 8).

8.8 The Incompleteness of the *Discourse*

Partly because of its theological context no doubt, there are a number of gaps in the *Discourse*. They are indeed just the gaps which the proper title of the work—*Treatise on the Perfections of God*—would lead one to expect. There is no argument for the existence of God and indeed a number of assumptions are made about what follows for the nature of the world from the supposed fact that it has a perfect Creator. Amongst these assumptions is that everything is connected with everything else and hence that each thing is a microcosm of the whole universe. Although every substance is unique, everything is fundamentally the same, a tension which Leibniz purports to resolve by saying that each substance expresses the universe from a slightly distinct point of view. Since, moreover, every effect expresses its cause and God is the cause of everything in the universe, the universe—indeed each of the individuals who comprise it—must be regarded as a 'representation of his work' and indeed as a 'mirror of God' (*Discourse*, § 9).

The gaps in the 'system' of the *Discourse* can be filled in by reference to other writings of that period. But the effect of filling in those gaps is to bring in question the principle which is the cornerstone of the *Discourse* system, namely, the *inesse*

principle. Leibniz thought that the principle that there is
nothing without reason was simply a corollary of the *inesse*
principle (PW 88, C 519). But the *inesse* principle, once
generalized, becomes too vague to generate the implications
Leibniz wished to draw from the principle of sufficient reason.
It is that richer principle (that God always acts with the *best*
reason) which informs the earlier parts of the *Discourse* and
which must come into play in order to develop the theory of
substance. It may be partly for this reason that Leibniz later
elevated the principle of sufficient reason to the position he
accords in the *Discourse* to the *inesse* principle and ceased to
make much mention of the latter principle at all.[13]

8.8.1 *Mirrors of God*

Leibniz, as we saw earlier (Section 5.3), was once convinced that
the ontological argument could be made into a sound proof of
God's existence. But later he was inclined to think that it
presumed that God's existence was possible and that, while this
was a reasonable presumption, the ontological argument could
provide no more than moral certainty of God's existence.
Leibniz offered, at one time or another, several different
arguments for the existence of God. Most of these depend on
the principle of sufficient reason but perhaps none is more
characteristically Leibnizian than what is commonly known as
'the argument from contingency'. Leibniz, in a paper written
within a year or so of the *Discourse*, stated this argument as
follows:

> If there were no necessary being, there would be no contingent being; for a
> reason must be given why contingent things should exist rather than not
> exist. But there would be no such reason unless there were a being which is
> in itself, that is, a being the reason for whose existence is contained in its
> own essence, so that there is no need for a reason outside it ....(PW 75, G
> vii 310)

The explanation for the universe has to be found, Leibniz goes
on, in the attributes of God. Moreover the universe, as the effect
of divine creation, must bear the traces of it cause (as all effects
must). Thus Leibniz concludes: 'Each substance has something
of the infinite insofar as it involves its cause, God, i.e. it has

some trace of omniscience and omnipotence' (PW 77, G vii 311).

By such reasoning Leibniz fills a gap in the argument of the *Discourse*, which assumes the existence of a Creator but includes among the 'notable paradoxes' which 'follow' from the theory of substance that 'every substance is like an entire world and like a mirror of God, or of the whole universe' (§ 9). Each substance reflects the whole universe from a particular point of view so that everything that is true of the whole universe could be derived from the complete notion of a single individual substance. But each substance expresses the universe differently, some aspects of it more distinctly than others, 'very much as one and the same town is variously represented in accordance with different positions of the observer' (§ 9). Since our ideas are often confused, this represents only a faint trace of divine omnipotence, but a trace nonetheless.

Moreover, according to Leibniz, every substance bears a trace of divine omnipotence. For everything which is done by any one substance has an effect on every other: 'as all other substances express that substance in their turn and agree with it, it can be said that it extends its power over all others, imitating the omnipotence of the Creator' (§ 9). Strictly speaking, however, the imitation of divine omnipotence is more apparent than real. For substances cannot strictly act on one another at all but rather 'each substance is like a world apart, independent of every other thing, except for God'. (§ 14) Indeed 'God alone brings about the liaison or communication between substances, and it is by him that the phenomena of any one tally with and agree with the phenomena of others ...' (§ 32).

Leibniz sought to distinguish minds or 'rational souls' from created substances generally and, in the *New System*, describes these as 'little gods, made in the image of God, and having in them some glimmering of Divine light' (§ 5). This 'glimmering' consists in such knowledge of eternal truths as humans are able to achieve. But, if in a lesser way, all created substances are made in God's image all can to some degree be described as 'little gods'. Thus Leibniz could allow that in a way God can be said to be the only true substance. For only God enjoys the full autonomy *and* power to cause changes which are characteristic of a true substance. Created substances enjoy a full autonomy in relation to one another (see 7.2.1 above) but they are only the cause of their own phenomena and do not strictly act on one another at all (see 7.2.2 above).

Leibniz agreed with other philosophers of his time that there is a sense in which God is the only true substance. As we have seen, Descartes was prepared to concede this. But, after Spinoza's insistence that there are no other substances than God at all, it became necessary for Leibniz to explain much more carefully how there could be created substances. This problem was of a piece with the problem of distinguishing the actions of God from those of the creatures. Created substances had to be shown to enjoy genuine autonomy and agency if they were to have any standing as substances. Thus the alternative to Spinoza's theory of substance offered by Leibniz required an explanation of how created substances could be the cause of their own phenomena and, in the case of souls, be said to act freely. In the next chapter we shall consider Leibniz's attempts to provide such an explanation.

8.8.2 *Perfection and 'the Interconnection between Things'*
I suggested in the previous section that every created substance, according to Leibniz, must bear the marks of its Creator and be, in a sense, a 'mirror of God' as well as 'the whole universe'. Sometimes he is content to argue that this is because every effect 'expresses' its cause (*Discourse* § 9) and therefore 'has some trace of omniscience and omnipotence' (PW 77, G vii 311). But his more settled view seems to be that only minds or spirits properly show the traces of divine omniscience through their capacity to discover eternal truths (*Discourse*, § 34). If that is so then other created substances must reflect the universe in virtue of something other than possessing traces of divine omniscience.

This further consideration is another fundamental assumption Leibniz takes for granted. It is that everything in the universe is thoroughly connected with everything else. Like a number of Leibniz's other principles this one corresponds to a vague though widely-shared belief about the world. Leibniz incorporates it in varying formulations sometimes as a more and sometimes as a less fundamental assumption within his explanations. Sometimes it seems to be as much a physical as a metaphysical assumption, for instance in the formulation 'Every change of any body propagates its effect to bodies at any distance; i.e. all bodies act on all bodies and are acted on by all' (PW 86, G vii 317, cf. PW 90, C 521). But in the *Discourse* it makes its appearance only as a metaphysical assumption:

> ... when one considers properly *the connection between things*, one can say that there are in the soul of Alexander, from all time, traces of all that has happened to him, and marks of everything that will happen to him - and *even traces of everything that happens in the universe*—though no one but God can know all of them. (§ 8)

The point, as becomes clear in the correspondence with Arnauld, is that God, in creating a particular individual, only does so after considering the implications for the universe as a whole. If any truth about, say, Alexander the Great, had been different, the universe as a whole would have been different. Thus, although the complete concept of Alexander contains everything that is ever true of that king, a full explanation of why just those things are true of Alexander would need to refer to the universe as a whole. Every truth about the universe is more or less distantly connected with every other truth. In giving the cause of what happened to Alexander on a particular occasion we should, for practical reasons, confine ourselves to what is immediately relevant. But if our thoughts turned to the 'cause' in the largest possible sense we should need, or so Leibniz thought, to refer to the universe as a whole. The complete being known as Alexander, as the effect, must therefore bear traces of the universe as a whole.

This way of thinking may seem strange to us but its strangeness is in part the same as that of the thought that everything in the universe gravitationally attracts and is attracted by everything else. And that thought was being put forward by Newton in the same decade as that in which Leibniz wrote the *Discourse*. Leibniz was an opponent of gravitational theory—not because it postulated an interaction between everything in the universe but because it postulated 'action at a distance'. Leibniz, like the Cartesians, believed that the universe was a *plenum* and that therefore gravitation would require a medium.

It may seem that Leibniz's view that everything in the universe is connected with everything else flatly contradicts his denial of strict interaction between substances. But there is no inconsistency since, in talking about 'the interconnection between things', Leibniz is referring to a pre-established harmony which underwrites the correspondence between what is true of different substances without requiring a strict interaction. That is how he can write *'Every created individual substance exercises physical action on, and is acted on by all others'* and then write a few sentences later that *'no created substance exercises on another a metaphysical action or influx'* (PW 90, C 521). In 'metaphysical rigour' what we call 'causes' are, he goes on to explain, 'merely concomitant requisites'. Substances are strictly autonomous. Talk of their 'influencing' or 'acting on' one another belongs to a looser language—justifiable in its proper place (like talk of the sun 'rising') but not in strict philosophy.

Leibniz's theory of substance was not fully worked out in the *Discourse.* He was soon to realize that much more needed to be said to reconcile 'the interconnection between things' with human freedom. In the *Discourse* he did not set out to decide whether, in metaphysical exactness, it was admissable to speak of 'corporeal substances'. His consideration of these questions, as we shall see in the next two chapters, was to lead him to make significant modifications in his theory.

Notes

1 That is, between substantial forms and Modern philosophy (see Chapter 3 above). Leibniz had been very much taken with Gassendi's atomism. The reference to the ancient Greek atomist Democritus is an instance of a tendency highly typical of Leibniz to disown any temptation to novelty. A distaste for novelty was expected of an *homme honnête* (see section 7.3 above).

2 In his 'Leibniz and the Concept of a System', Nicholas Rescher has noted that the word 'system' was taking on new meanings in the late seventeenth century. He suggests that Leibniz's understanding of 'system' marks ' . . . a new turning. For him, the ideal model of a cognitive system was provided not by the geometry of the ancient Greeks but the physics of 17th century Europe' (*Studia Leibnitiana 13*, 1981, p. 122). If that is true then Leibniz had not made the turning openly in 1685–86. The sense in which he had a

'system' then was that of an organized body of knowledge and the 'official' paradigm for Leibniz at that time was Euclidean geometry. In the mid-1680s Leibniz was, as we saw in Chapter 6, still defending his own practice by reference to Euclidean geometry, but offering a novel interpretation of it.

3 See Section 6.3 above. Leibniz claimed to be able to offer a large number of 'demonstrations', i.e. rigorous deductive arguments, 'all demonstrated hypothetically from a few suppositions by the simple substitution of equivalent characters. The most important would be about cause, effect, change, action, time, where I find that the truth is very different from what people imagine; for although a substance can with reason be called the physical and often the moral cause of what happens in another substance, nevertheless, speaking with metaphysical rigour, every substance (in conjunction with the concourse of God) is the real immediate cause of what happens within itself ...' (G i 391). It is notable in this letter and elsewhere (see PW 79, G vii 312f.) how Leibniz at this time was willing to invoke experimental evidence in support of what he has demonstrated. This suggests that his metaphysical practice was running ahead of his 'official' methodology and that he was already producing in the 1680s what he was later to claim as a new 'system'. See previous note.

4 I have been unable to sort out a chronology for several undated writings and so do not know whether the *Discourse* was produced before the more 'systematic' writings of this period. If Leibniz's claim to Burnett in May 1697 that it was 'not more than about 12 years' since he had managed to find these demonstrations were taken as reliable, that would suggest some of these 'logical' writings pre-date the *Discourse*. But it may not have been until after writing the *Discourse* that Leibniz made much link between his logical work and his metaphysics. Systematic writings such as 'Primary Truths' (PW 87–92, C 518–23) and the 'Specimen of Discoveries...' (PW 75–86, G vii 309–17) seem to contain qualifications or modifications which reflect the correspondence with Arnauld. A detailed chronology of Leibniz's writings of the mid-1680s could throw a good deal of light on the fraught controversy over the connection between Leibniz's logic and his metaphysics. It will be apparent that I agree with G.H.R. Parkinson (*Logic and Reality in Leibniz's Metaphysics*) over against Couturat and Russell in taking Leibniz's metaphysics as largely independent of his logic. That this is so may be seen from a study of the so-called *System of Theology*. From this work it may be seen that many of Leibniz's metaphysical directions were firmly established before he found he could produce 'demonstrations' of them. Many of his claims about human minds in the *System* became claims about substances *in general* in the *Discourse*. Much of *Discourse* § 9, for instance, is anticipated on p. 73 of the *System*, only generalized for all substances. It is significant, however, that the principle of the identity of indiscernibles is new, since that 'paradox' (unlike the others in *Discourse* § 9) is a consequence of the generalized *inesse* principle. See Section 8.5.

5 This was also Leibniz's strategy in publishing the 'New System', which gives only a partial introduction to the whole system. As Leibniz explained to Foucher in 1695:

You will have seen that the whole of my system is founded on the consideration of the real unities that are indestructible and *sui juris*. Each expresses the universe in its own manner and by the laws of its own nature, while receiving no external influences besides that of God who has caused it to subsist, since he created it by continuous renewal ... *If the public receives these meditations well, I will be encouraged to give in addition some rather singular thoughts I have*, aimed at removing the difficulties *de fato et contingentia*, and to clarify an essential difference we can conceive between material forms and intelligences or spirits ....
(G i 423 italics added)

These additions relate to parts of Leibniz's system which are included in the *Discourse* (respectively, in §§ 13 and 34).

6 Leibniz may have been led to this view by his reading of Augustine. At all events he frequently quotes Augustine's *On the Usefulness of Believing* in support of accepting authority. He is particularly clear on this point in the *New Essays*, where he opposes Locke's claim that arguments from authority should always be rejected. He goes on, in one context, to say:

As for 'received opinions': they have in their favour something close to what creates a 'presumption', as the jurists call it; and although one is not obliged always to adopt them without proof, neither is one permitted to destroy them in the minds of others unless one has proofs against them. (NEHU 517)

7 In his *Confession of Nature against the Atheists* (1668) Leibniz took it as a maxim for Modern philosophy that 'in explaining corporeal phenomena we must not unnecessarily resort to God or to any other incorporeal thing, form, or quality ... but that so far as can be done, everything should be derived from the nature of body and its primary qualities—magnitude, figure and motion' (PPL 110, G iv 106). In support of this he cited the Roman poet Horace '*Nec Deus intersit, nisi dignus vindice nodus inciderit*'. ('And let no god intervene, unless a knot come worthy of such a deliverer') (*Arts poetica*, 191) See PPL 119.

8 In a letter to André Morell, 10 December 1696 (*Grua* 103). This is cited and explained in a footnote in the English edition of the *Discourse on Metaphysics* prepared by Peter G Lucas and Leslie Grint for Manchester University Press, 1953, p.55.

9 See note 4 above. These requirements, except that of completeness, all appear in the *System of Theology*, though unity is only required of souls there (p. 159), not of substances in general. Identity (p.115) and autonomy (p. 73) are implicitly assumed and agency specifically required (p. 16) for substances generally.

10 Arnauld himself had defended the Scholastic view that the *inesse* principle was true of maxims. What he resisted was Leibniz's generalized version of it to cover all truths, including contingent ones.

11 It is very similar to one of the two 'dogmas of empiricism' identified by W.Quine in a paper in his *From a Logical Point of View* (1953). Leibniz,

unlike twentieth century empiricists who have maintained that all necessary truths are reducible to the principle of contradiction, held such truths to be eternally true and therefore regarded knowledge of them as substantive. Although I say this is a 'plausible' position it is one which is widely rejected in view of scepticism about carrying out the programme of reduction.

12 In 1670, for instance, he had written:

> The hypothesis of any astronomer who can explain the celestial phenomena with few presuppositions, namely, with simple motions only, is certainly to be preferred to that of one who needs many orbs variously intertwined to explain the heavens. From this principle the nominalists have deduced the rule that everything in the world can be explained without any reference to universals and real forms. Nothing is truer than this opinion, and, nothing is more worthy of a philosopher of our own time. (PPL 128, G iv 158)

Leibniz agreed with the nominalists against the Aristotelians but opposed Hobbes' extreme nominalism which yielded the conclusion that all truth, being dependent on arbitrary definitions, was arbitrary (see Section 5.2 above). But Leibniz's Platonism about abstract entities is consistent with and doubtless reinforced his continued rejection of the Aristotelian theory of universals.

13 Arnauld was impressed by Leibniz's use of this principle and Leibniz seems to have thought of making more of it about ten years later, when he was thinking of publishing the correspondence with Arnauld (see PW 135, C 10). But generally Leibniz's later defence of the principle of the identity of indiscernibles is by an appeal to the principle of sufficient reason. *Inesse* ceases to play its role of the mid- to late-1680s. It is referred to in the *New Essays*, in connection with Leibniz's theory of demonstration *de continente et contento* (of the container and the contained) and this may provide the clue as to another reason why Leibniz ceased to use it as a fundamental principle for his theory of substance. For that theory is one about *how* statements are to be reduced to identities, namely, by showing that the subject either contains the predicate or is identical with it as in propositions like '5=2+3'. If the *inesse* principle was equivalent to the principle that all true propositions are demonstrable *de continente et contento*, then it is diluted by the thought that in the case of contingent propositions it is only possible to see the direction of the analysis and not to complete it (see PW 107ff., F de C 179). In the *New Essays* Leibniz seems to have returned to this earlier view that the *inesse* principle is valid only for abstract truths (see NEHU 486). With the dropping of the *inesse* principle Leibniz also dropped the completeness requirement. Unity becomes the fundamental requirement for substances in the later writings. See G i 423, quoted in Note 5 above. This shift is discussed below in Chapter 11.

There is some doubt as to the form in which Leibniz later accepted the *inesse* principle. My contention is that at all events it ceased to play the fundamental role it had in the *Discourse* period. In this I disagree with most other modern commentators. C.D. Broad, for instance, claims that 'there is no reason to think that Leibniz ... ceased to think it of fundamental importance' (*Leibniz: An Introduction*, p. 6). Broad writes that Leibniz was happy to have his theory of substance considered as an explanatory hypothesis. 'But it is in fact *necessary*, for reasons he had developed in his *Letters to Arnauld*' (*op. cit.*, p. 6). Leibniz did (in the *first* and not, as Broad says, the *second* reply to Bayle) imply he could demonstrate his system: 'Perhaps I shall not claim too much if I say I can demonstrate all this, but for the present the question is merely to maintain it as a possible hypothesis for explaining phenomena' (PPL 493, G iv 518). But, although Leibniz did indeed have *a priori* reasons for his theory of substance in the 1690s they were not the same as they had been before. Broad simply assumes that they would have been. In fact, as is clear from Leibniz's reply to Foucher's critique of the *New System*, these *a priori* reasons have to do with his 'view of unities' (PW 126, G iv 494). Moreover it is not that the system is necessary in a rationalist sense, as Broad assumes. Leibniz's point is that his is no 'arbitrary' hypothesis but one to which he was led by *a priori* reasons and 'my whole contention stands or falls together'. The new *a priori* basis for Leibniz's theory of substance is discussed below in Chapter 11.

9 Necessity and Freedom (Review, 1671–89)

> For my part, I used to consider that nothing happens by chance or by accident, except with respect to certain particular substances; that fortune, as distinct from fate, is an empty word; and that nothing exists unless its individual requisites are given, and from all these taken together it follows that the thing exists. So I was not far from the view of those who think that all things are absolutely necessary; who think that security from compulsion is enough for freedom, even though it is under the rule of necessity, and who do not distinguish the infallible—that is, a truth which is certainly known—from the necessary.
>
> But I was dragged back from this precipice by a consideration of those possibles which neither do exist, nor will exist. For if certain possibles never exist, then existing things are not always necessary....(PW 106, FdeC 178)

It is not certain how close Leibniz had come to openly denying that there are no contingent truths. In a letter of 1671 he already maintained that 'God wills the things which he understands to be the best and most harmonious and selects them, as it were, from an infinite number of all possibles' (PPL 146, A II, i, 117). But there is nothing in that letter to suggest that these unrealized possibilities could really have existed. That they are possibilities only appears if they are considered in abstraction from the nature of God. Given the nature of God this is the only possible world. 'Since God is the most perfect mind ... it is impossible for him not to be affected by the most perfect harmony, and thus to be necessitated to do the best by the very ideality of things' (PPL 146, A II, i, 117).

This, Leibniz went on to insist, 'in no way detracts from freedom. For it is the highest freedom to be impelled to the best by a right reason. Whoever', he adds, 'desires any other freedom is a fool.' He does not seem to have advanced much beyond this position as a result of his discussions with Spinoza, continuing to believe that it is sufficient to preserve contingency to insist that there are possibles which do not exist. His notes (2 December 1676) give weight to the principle that 'whatever can exist and is compatible with other things, does exist' (PPL 169, C 530). But this yields the result that many things which are possible in themselves are not actually possible (because not compossible with other actual things). So if the thought that there are 'possibles which neither do exist, nor will exist' dragged Leibniz back from the precipice, it did not drag him to complete safety. For the result is that 'existing things are not always necessary' *in themselves*, only seen in the context of the universe as a whole.

This thought, that what is contingent is what is not necessary *in itself* was to be further clarified in Leibniz's notes of 1678 on Spinoza's *Ethics*. A necessary being is one whose essence involves existence, i.e. whose existence can only be denied on pain of contradiction. A contingent being is one which is not necessary. Leibniz, complaining of the absence of a definition of contingency in Spinoza's book, wrote: 'I use the term "contingent", as do others, for that whose essence does not involve existence' (PPL 203, G i 148). Now, in this sense of 'contingent', not only are individual created things contingent but so is the totality of created things. For it is not possible to explain the existence of the universe, on Leibniz's account, except by reference to something outside it. The universe is not, that is to say, a self-explanatory[1] thing. God, by contrast, contains within His own nature the reason for His existence.

For a while Leibniz seems to have thought that it was sufficient, to avoid the conclusion that 'all things are absolutely necessary', to distinguish what is necessary from what is contingent along these lines. Everything, on this account, is certain, i.e. will happen infallibly, but no event is in itself necessary. This view is reflected in the *Discourse* where Leibniz insists that 'one must distinguish between what is certain and what is necessary' (§ 13). And this distinction is put forward as in accordance with a generally held view: 'Everyone agrees that future contingencies are certain, since God foresees them, but it is not thereby admitted that they are necessary.' However Leibniz goes on to acknowledge that, in view of what he has said about the notion of an individual substance, it is necessary for him to say more:

But, it will be said, if some conclusion can be deduced infallibly from a definition or notion, it will be necessary. Now, we maintain that everything that is to happen to some person is already contained virtually in his nature or notion, as the properties of a circle are contained in its definition. So the difficulty still remains. To give a satisfactory answer to it, I assert that connexion or sequence is of two kinds. The one is absolutely necessary, whose contrary implies a contradiction; this kind of deduction holds in the case of eternal truths, such as those of geometry. The other is only necessary by hypothesis (ex-hypothesi), and so to speak by accident; it is contingent in itself, since its contrary is based, not on ideas pure and simple, and on the simple understanding of God, but on his free decrees and on the sequence of the universe. (§ 13)

The emphasis in the *Discourse* is on distinguishing contingent truths as at least partially dependent on God's 'free decrees'. In opposition to Descartes, he had insisted that eternal truths are independent of the will of God (§ 2). His view in the *Discourse* is thus very different from that he himself had previously adopted. Whereas earlier, for instance in the 1671 letter referred to above, he had claimed that it was 'impossible' for God 'not to be affected by the most perfect harmony and thus to be necessitated to do the best', his later view stresses God's spontaneity in relation to contingent things.

But, even if this change preserved God's freedom, it remained unclear that it helped in any way to preserve that of human beings. It became apparent to Leibniz 'as a result of his correspondence with Arnauld' that there were still problems. Arnauld accepted the distinction between metaphysical and hypothetical necessity and claimed that the problem remained how, on Leibniz's account, he (Arnauld) could have chosen to marry and be a physician rather than be a celibate theologian. If everything that is true of the individual Arnauld is contained in his full concept then evidently it is part of that full concept that he would become a celibate theologian. It is necessary for him to become a celibate theologian in order to be the individual Arnauld in question. It seemed to Arnauld that this consequence showed that there was something fundamentally wrong with Leibniz's apparatus:

... we must conclude ... that since it is impossible for me not to always remain myself whether I marry or whether I live a life of celibacy, the individual concept of me has involved neither the one nor the other of these states. (BW 95, G ii 30)

In short there cannot *be* a complete notion of Arnauld consistent with his being free to marry and become a physician. The point was well taken by Leibniz and led him to a new phase of thinking about the subject.

9.1 Fatalism and the *Inesse* Principle

Once I had recognized the contingency of things, I then began to consider what a clear notion of truth would be; for I hoped, not unreasonably, to derive from this some light on the problem of distinguishing necessary from contingent truths. However, I saw that it is common to every true affirmative proposition—universal and particular, necessary or contingent—that the predicate is in the subject, or that the notion of the predicate is in some way involved in the notion of the subject, and that this is the principle of infallibility in very kind of truth for him who knows everything *a priori*. For if, at a given time, the notion of the predicate is in the notion of the subject, then how, without contradiction and impossibility, can the predicate not be in the subject at that time, without destroying the notion of the subject? (PW 107, F de C 179)

Leibniz's uncharacteristically obscure phrase 'destroying the notion of the subject' is not to be understood literally. The thought seems to be that, for example, 'Arnauld was a physician' is not simply false but involves a contradiction. Being a physician is something which could not have been true of the individual Arnauld in question since Arnauld would not have been Arnauld, if he had been a physician, but someone else. If Arnauld was free to be a physician then, since it was part of his complete notion that he would be a theologian instead, he could not have become a physician without 'destroying' that notion. Thus freedom appears to be excluded by Leibniz's model of divine knowledge. For a freely acting individual might become different from what God had in mind in including him among actual existents.

Leibniz seems initially to have supposed that the nub of this problem lay in its seeming that being a theologian is as essential to a particular individual's being Arnauld as being the square root of 25 is essential to a number being the number 5. Accordingly he sought a solution by distinguishing between contingent truths and necessary truths. A contradiction is involved in supposing that a necessary truth is false. But no contradiction is involved in supposing that a contingent truth is false.

He elaborated this solution by suggesting further that the mark of contingent truths is that they require an infinite analysis and hence that, although their predicates are in their subjects, this cannot be demonstrated. He put forward an analogy between surds and rational numbers. Truths about surds cannot be demonstrated because they inolve an infinite number of steps. Thus the decimal expansion of π involves an infinite series which no finite mind can grasp. Yet this conforms to the *inesse* principle. Something analogous is true, Leibniz suggested, in the case of contingent truths.

But this analogy does not help. For, in the first place, the impossibility of demonstrating everything which occurs in the decimal expansion of π does not in any way detract from the fact that whatever does occur in the sequence does so necessarily. Moreover, as Leibniz himself recognized (PW 111, F de C 184), it is possible to produce demonstrations of infinite series. So the fact that the analysis of something generates an infinite series is no guarantee of contingency.

Leibniz's attempt to show that the *inesse* principle applies equally to contingent as well as to necessary truths does not answer the problem posed by Arnauld. A more promising answer is that found in the reply given to Arnauld directly.

9.2 A Possible Escape from Fatalism

In one of his major letters to Arnauld, drafted in May 1686 but not sent till July, Leibniz distinguished between two different ways of thinking about individuals. An individual, say Adam, can on the one hand be thought of as one of several possible Adams all of whom satisfy the description 'was the first man', 'was set in a pleasure garden', and so on. To think of an individual in this way is to think of him *sub ratione generalitatis*, to think of him in a general or at least not wholly determinate way. This, Leibniz takes it for granted, is the way in which we ordinarily do think of people, including ourselves. Indeed it is the only way in which we can think of them in a temporal context. There was a time at which Adam had not yet taken the apple Eve offered him.

Once he has accepted it, however, he has become a more determinate Adam. If we think of his choice as a free one we are alluding to *his* part in, so to speak, writing the book of his life. While the book is not yet written or insofar as we consider alternative ways in which it might have been written we are thinking of a particular individual *sub ratione generalitatis*. This is the way we think of ourselves when we deliberate over choices available to us.

In turning to God's knowledge we do not simply change from partial to total knowledge but from knowledge which is time-limited to knowledge which is *a priori* and time-independent. God alone is able to think of Adam *sub ratione possibilitatis*, from the standpoint of the region of eternal possibles. From this standpoint every individual is totally determinate. Each has a complete notion from which its full story can be derived. That Adam freely accepts the apple offered by Eve is part of his complete (atemporal) notion. This and all other notions have been before God's mind for all eternity and God created the world containing certain individuals knowing exactly what is involved in the complete notion of each of them.

From this latter standpoint everything that is true of an individual substance is determined and it is in relation to the individual so considered (*sub ratione possibilitatis*) that Leibniz remarks that, were he to have failed to make a journey he did in fact make, this 'will destroy my individual or complete concept' (BW 126, G ii 52). *Sub ratione possibilitatis* any change of biography is a change in personal identity. This is what Arnauld was unable to accept, as is clear from his remark: 'we must conclude, it seems to me, that since it is impossible for me not to always remain myself whether I marry or whether I live a life of celibacy, the individual concept of me has involved neither the one nor the other of those two states' (BW 95, G ii 30). But, in the light of Leibniz's distinction, it is possible to see how their two positions might be reconciled. For Leibniz can allow, and indeed is committed to allowing, that when Arnauld was contemplating matrimony or considering what it would have been like for *him* to have been married, he was thinking of himself *sub ratione generalitatis*. Leibniz's claim that an individual could not have been different in any way without 'destroying' his individual concept is a claim made *sub ratione possibilitatis*.

It is clear that, depending on which perspective is adopted on human action, there are two quite distinct problems of personal identity. One is the problem of identifying a given individual at two different times as the *same* individual. That is the problem with which Arnauld was concerned and the sense in which he could not fail to be the same person whether he married or remained single. There is another problem of personal identity which presupposes that every individual is absolutely unique and concerns the nature of this uniqueness. Leibniz was more concerned with this problem which, according to him, can only be answered *sub ratione possibilitatis*. Now, although we cannot regard ourselves exclusively *sub ratione possibilitatis*, we can do so insofar as we look at our lives in retrospect. Arnauld might, in this light, have been willing to reflect that he would not have been who he was if he had married or become a physician. Nor would his willingness to reflect on his life in this way involve him in being inconsistent. For the sense in which he *would* have been the same person is different from the sense in which he would *not* have been.

The sense of my own identity which I have is based, according to Leibniz, on 'my inner experience'. It is the sense of being something which persists through change. But what this produces is something which is, in the nature of the case, far from being completely determinate, especially in relation to the future. That perspective on myself is *sub ratione generalitatis*. In that sense Leibniz could have conceded, writing in 1686, that he would presumably remain the same person whether or not he ever revisited Paris. For he would retain that sense of the continuity of his life whether things turned out as he planned or not, whether he regretted some of his decisions or not. In this sense Leibniz is in no way committed to denying that someone remains the 'same person' more or less whatever the future holds for him.

Leibniz did not quite draw the distinction between these two perspectives as I have done. He frequently refers to God's perspective as involving *prior* knowledge rather than an atemporal knowledge. But this is, as I understand it, a confusion. There is no time unless there is a created universe. Yet, on Leibniz's own account, God would still have known everything involved in the complete notion of every possible existent. To consider an individual *sub ratione possibilitatis* is to look at things from outside the temporal order rather than, as Leibniz sometimes implies, from an earlier standpoint in it. It is this confusion which invited Arnauld to believe that, for Leibniz, it was not at any time an open question whether or not Caesar would cross the Rubicon. Reasoning in this way it would be natural to infer that Caesar had no real choice in the matter.

However, if thinking of Caesar from a standpoint prior in time to his crossing the Rubicon is thinking of Caesar *sub ratione generalitatis* then it can remain up to Caesar whether he does so or not. It is only *sub ratione possibilitatis* that he would not be Caesar unless he did. To suppose that an individual is not free to do anything except what is contained in his full concept or complete notion, according to Leibniz, is to confuse these two perspectives or ways of considering a given individual. The ability to act freely, as well as the ways in which this freedom is exercised, is contained in the full concept of certain individual substances though not in all. God might have chosen to create a world in which freedom was not exercised at all. The freedom of Caesar to decide against crossing the Rubicon should not be regarded as compromised from all eternity by the fact that *sub ratione possibilitatis* he would not have been *this* Caesar unless he did indeed choose to cross. He would not have been unless he had chosen freely.

A human being can only regard himself exclusively *sub ratione possibilitatis* on his deathbed. Otherwise, in deliberation, he must regard himself *sub ratione generalitatis*, as a being about whom not everything is yet determined. Leibniz does not merely ascribe to substances certain powers of self-determination. He holds the extreme view that substances are wholly self-determining, i.e. that everything that is true of an individual substance is in some sense a consequence of his own being. The peculiarity of human beings is that they are prompted to act in accordance with what they take to be the best. Humans, therefore, have *their own* reasons for what they do. In the Leibnizian sense in which it can be said that Caesar was fulfilling his particular 'destiny' in crossing the Rubicon, it cannot be taken as an alternative explanation to one in terms of his motivation. By the same token it is no alibi for Judas Iscariot that it was part of his 'destiny' that he should betray Christ since its being so does not mean that he did not do it out of greed, ambition, or whatever. Fatalism, in short, is based on a confusion between two different ways of looking upon an individual.

9.3 God's Freedom

Leibniz, I have suggested, can reconcile his insistence that every individual has a unique destiny with allowing that human actions are free. But he can only do this for created substances, e.g. for beings which are subject to destiny or providence. Only in the case of contingent beings does the distinction between what is regarded *sub ratione generalitatis* and *sub ratione possibilitatis* make any sense. The question remains whether God has an individual 'nature' from which, in accordance with the *inesse* principle, everything that is true of God can be inferred. And, if the *inesse* principle applies to truths about God, then there arises the same problem about God's freedom as arose about human beings. If God is not free to choose to act in the most perfect way possible, then praising Him for his works is out of place.

In the *Discourse* Leibniz shows a willingness to accord a limited place to God's will. There were those, like Descartes, who made so much out of God's will that even eternal truths and therefore all metaphysical necessity were subject to it. That view was unacceptable to Leibniz. If God's will determined the standards of goodness and perfection then there would be no objective basis for praising his works. Those standards would be arbitrary. But once eternal truths were made independent of God's will then, given that God is essentially good, just, wise, and so on, all His actions would appear to arise out of the necessity of God's nature. God's will, as in Spinoza's philosophy, drops out of the picture entirely. Leibniz was never greatly drawn to this extreme but his picture in the *Discourse* of a God freely choosing to act in accordance with independent (eternal) standards of what is best was not obviously consistent with a generalized *inesse* principle. For God would seem resigned to fulfilling His own predictions as to how He would act. He would, that is to say, if God's knowledge of himself were based on knowledge of a full concept, like His knowledge of any *created* substance.

9.4 God's Self-Knowledge and Knowledge of the World

Perhaps no other philosopher has ever attempted to go as far as Leibniz in explaining the kind of knowledge God has of the world. One reason for Leibniz's preoccupation with this problem is his concern with a traditional problem of how to reconcile human freedom with divine foreknowledge. But no less important is a more purely philosophical thought that divine knowledge of the world would be a perfect knowledge. Leibniz's *inesse* principle should not be seen merely as an attempt to speculate on matters that a more cautious philosopher might leave for theologians but as an attempt to provide a model for what a completed science would look like, what would count as a perfect understanding of the world. A perfect understanding of any truth, according to the *inesse* model, consists in seeing the connection between the notion of the subject and that of the predicate.

Leibniz, like his contemporaries (including those commonly labelled 'empiricists'),[2] took mathematical knowledge as a paradigm of perfect knowledge. Perfect knowledge would therefore be *a priori*. But, as we have seen, he could not rest content with the obvious implication of this, that 'all things are understood by God *a priori*, as eternal truths' (PW 15, G vii 296). God's knowledge must be *a priori*. But what He knows, Leibniz was forced to conclude, must be truly contingent. Contingency must not, as in Spinoza, have its basis in human ignorance but correspond to God's knowledge of things. From this in turn it follows that God's knowledge of the world must be importantly different from His knowledge of eternal truths. It must depend in a critical way on the knowledge He has of His own Will. This is hinted at, though not sufficiently explained, in the following passage:

...contingent or infinite truths ... are known by him, not by a demonstration indeed (for that would imply a contradiction) but by an infallible vision. But this vision that God has must not be conceived as a kind of experiential knowledge, as if he saw something in things which are distinct from himself, but rather as *a priori* knowledge (through the reasons for truths). For he sees things which are possible in themselves by a consideration of his own free will and his own decrees, of which the first is to do everything in the best possible way and with supreme reason. (PW 111, F de C 184)

God's knowledge of the world is not knowledge of something outside Himself since the world is exactly as He intended it to be. It is therefore no kind of *a posteriori* knowledge. Neither is it knowledge of eternal truths, which are independent of God's will. In saying that God 'sees existent things by the consideration of his own free will and his own decrees', Leibniz extends *a priori* knowledge to include a certain sort of self-knowledge. It may be compared therefore with our knowledge of what we do intentionally or, better, deliberately. That I succeeded in standing on someone's toe is something I need experience to know about. But my knowledge that I did it *deliberately* (or, if I failed to do it, that I *meant* to do nonetheless) is not based on experience. God's self-knowledge is a limiting case, since nothing counts as God's not succeeding in carrying out His intentions. Hence God's knowledge of the world is *a priori* in the curious way that (taking *a priori* to refer to whatever is known independently of experience) our knowledge of our intentions is.

Leibniz, in claiming that God's knowledge of the world is *a priori* in this way, does not forget that it is nonetheless a scientific knowledge 'through reasons for truths'. But this is consistent with divine knowledge of the world being a limiting case of the kind of knowledge we have of our own intentions. For our knowledge of our intentions is, in general, a knowledge of our motives or reasons for acting in the ways we do. I say 'in general' since it is clear that we often know that we did something intentionally even when we do not know what our motive or reason was. It seems reasonable to suppose, however, that these cases are departures from the norm and that we would not ever know that we did something intentionally unless we normally knew our reasons for behaving as we did. In a normal case where I know that I meant to stand on someone's toe, then, I will know my reasons for doing so.

Here too God's self-knowledge is a limiting case, since none of these qualifications is needed in the case of a being whose knowledge is unlimited. God's knowledge of His own intentions constitutes an 'infallible vision' not only of His reasons for making the world the way it is but, of course, for its being the way it is. But it does depend critically on His motives or what Leibniz calls His 'free decrees', of which, as Leibniz puts it, 'the first is to do everything in the best way and with supreme reason' (PW 111, F d C 184).

Leibniz tends to represent God's decrees as separate acts of will, thus creating problems about how specific decisions relate to his 'primary decrees'.[3] The difference is not one of quasi-temporal priority but simply of generality, as is made more clear by rephrasing Leibniz's distinction in terms of 'motives' or 'intentions'. Just as we may explain the intention with which someone acts on a particular occasion by reference to a wider intention, so knowledge of our own intentions in doing something may be based upon our knowledge of our more general intentions. Intentions readily form a hierarchy so that it is possible to construct what 'must have been' our intention in doing something by reference to more general intentions. Our general intentions provide us, at least to some extent, with policies, practices, habits, and so on. In the limiting case of a perfectly rational being, particular intentions would all be intelligible in the light of more general ones.

As well as general reasons for the world being as it is there are, of course, reasons why every detail is as it is. God has to be supposed to have engaged in a kind of thought experiment in which the consequences of varying the details of the universe in every possible way are considered. The thought experiment has to be conceived of as constrained both by God's general motives and by constraints (the eternal truths) which are independent of God's will. Among the constraints which are not self-imposed are the standards of goodness and perfection themselves. Leibniz took a robust stand, in the dispute over whether things are good because God wills them or whether He wills them because they are good, on the latter side. Since God's intention was to create the best possible universe, He could not consistently choose to create a universe which failed to conform to those standards as well than an alternative possible universe.

This is a brave view and one which incurs the onus of explaining how the existence of evil is possible in a world that meets the standards of perfection better than any other. This is the project of Leibniz's *Theodicy*. It is sufficient to note that, for Leibniz, the fact that this is not an absolutely perfect universe must be taken as evidence that the constraints which are not subject to the will of God are considerable.

9.5 Metaphysical and Hypothetical Necessity

Leibniz, according to his own account, shifted from his position of the 1670s, where he was close to the Spinozistic view that everything that takes place happens by a metaphysical necessity.[4] That is, I have suggested, the view to which he remained committed so long as he held that God knows everything *a priori* as eternal truths. A new account of God's *a priori* knowledge of the world was needed, which allowed for genuine contingency. This was what Leibniz sought to provide in his account of 'hypothetical necessity'.

This account may be divided into two parts. One part is God's knowledge of hypothetical *necessities*, i.e. of what is involved in the full concept of any possible existent. These possibles exist in God's understanding and He knows about them by an 'infallible vision'. God's knowledge of actual things includes his knowledge of them *sub ratione possibilitatis* but also His knowledge of His own decrees. He knows existent things not merely as hypothetical things but as thing whose existence He has decreed. His knowledge is not just of the form 'If *p* then *q*' but of his decree that *p* and hence His knowledge that *q* is a mixture of two kinds of knowledge, only one of which is dependent on His will.

As we should expect, this change in Leibniz's representation of God's knowledge of the world corresponds to his changed conception of metaphysical knowledge of the world. God's decrees are like the suppositions of the metaphysician. They are few in number but rich in their consequences. The metaphysician is attempting, albeit fallibly, to reconstruct the plan of the universe. The hypothetico-deductive method is thus the method for discovering the hypothetical necessities which govern the universe. This can only be done in general terms. In this connection the principle of sufficient reason plays a critical role.

In the period when Leibniz's attention was focussed on the kind of necessity, if any, involved in everything which is true of a given substance following from its nature, the *inesse* principle became of paramount importance for Leibniz. The principle of sufficient reason was at that stage seen as no more than a consequence of the *inesse* principle. But in his later writings the *inesse* principle is scarcely mentioned and then only as a principle governing abstract truths.[5] A possible factor in this change is Leibniz's unwillingness to extend the *inesse* principle to God's knowledge of Himself, insofar as that is knowledge not only of objects in His understanding but also of His 'free decrees'. As Leibniz puts it: God 'sees existent things by the consideration of his own free will and his own decrees, of which the first is to do everything in the best way and with supreme reason' (PW 111, F de C 184).

Notes

1 Leibniz does not use this phrase but talks instead of a being which is '*in itself*', by which he means 'a being the reason for whose existence is contained in its own essence, so that there is no need for a reason outside it' (PW 76f., G vii 310). The phrase 'self-explanatory being' is used in a modern version of Leibniz's argument produced by J.F. Ross in his *Philosophical Theology*, Indianapolis and New York, Bobbs-Merrill Company, 1969, p.173ff.

2 Locke, for example, holds that if we *did* know what the real essence of any substance was, we should have a complex idea of it such that 'the properties we discover in that body would depend on that complex idea, and be deducible from it, and their necessary connexion with it be known; as all properties of a triangle depend on, and, as far as they are discoverable, are deducible from the complex idea of three lines including a space' (*Essay*, II.xxxi.6). The difference between the two philosophers here is that between the Leibniz's nominalism and Locke's esentialism (see above, Section 7.2.3).

3 It is necessary, for instance, for Leibniz to insist that God 'does not decree because he *has* decreed' (PW 104, C23).

4 For a fuller account of Leibniz's various positions on this subject, see G.H.R. Parkinson's *Leibniz on Human Freedom*, Wiesbaden, 1970. See also R.A. Adams, 'Leibniz's Theories of Contingency', *Essays on the*

Philosophy of Leibniz, Rice University Studies, Vol. *63*, No. 4, 1977, pp. 1–41.

5 It seems that Leibniz continued to accept the *inesse* principle in his later writings but demanded less of it than in the *Discourse*. See, for instance, PW 135, C 10: G iv 475. It may be that, once Leibniz realized that *spontaneity* in substances was not a consequence of the *inesse* principle (see Chapter 11 below), its importance dwindled in favour of a dynamic principle governing the change from one perception in a monad to another.

10   Substance and the Material World

> There is another important thing in my philosophy which will give it access to the Jesuits and other theologians. This is my restoration of substantial forms, which the atomists and Cartesians claim to have exterminated. It is certain that without these forms and the distinction that exists between them and real accidents, it is impossible to explain our mysteries.... (Letter of 1679 to John Frederick, Duke of Brunswick-Lüneburg, PPL 261, A II i 482?)

> I know that I am putting forward a great paradox in claiming to rehabilitate ancient philosophy to some extent, and to restore the rights of citizenship to substantial forms, which have practically been banished. But perhaps I shall not readily be condemned when it is known that I have thought very carefully about modern philosophy, and that I have devoted much time to physical experiments and to geometrical demonstrations. I was for a long time persuaded of the emptiness of these entities, and was finally obliged to take them up again despite myself, and as it were by force... (*Discourse* § 11)

Leibniz's employer, in 1679, was a Catholic convert who quite probably shared the suspicion of Modern philosophy widespread amongst Catholic theologians. The apparatus of substantial forms had been employed in articulating the orthodox explanation of the Christian ritual of the Eucharist, in which bread and wine are identified with the body and blood of Christ. The orthodox explanation was that of *transubstantiation*, i.e. that the *matter* of the bread and wine remains the same but that its *form* is changed, thus making it into a different substance, namely, flesh and blood.

Without some theory of substantial forms it seemed difficult, if not impossible, to accommodate the orthodox thought that Christ is really present in the bread and wine of the Eucharist. Leibniz, as we saw earlier (Section 3.3 above), had sought to do just this and so to reconcile Modern philosophy with Christian faith. It is unlikely that he really believed that 'without these forms ... it is impossible to explain our mysteries'. But such was the common belief amongst Catholics and is partly why the teaching of Cartesianism was frequently banned. Leibniz's restored doctrine of substantial forms is a reformed one which would not in fact explain transubstantiation as neatly as the Scholastic doctrine had done. For the *Discourse* version of substantial forms makes them that feature of *individual* substances in virtue of which each has a 'complete notion' different from that of every other individual. It is not a doctrine about what makes a lump of matter a piece of flesh rather than bread.

Leibniz, as a Lutheran, had no particular attachment to the doctrine of transubstantiation. His interest in at least appearing to accommodate it relates to the service he wished to perform in reconciling the different Churches and in preserving the credibility of Christianity in the face of Modern philosophy. That is the context both of his letter to John Frederick and of the *Discourse*.

10.1 From 'Substantial Forms' to 'Monads'

In his later writings Leibniz ceased to use the phrase 'substantial form', at any rate except in a rather incidental way. The reason for this is at least partly that it had become a term of abuse, as Leibniz makes clear in his response to the highly derogatory tone in which Locke wrote about these supposed entities in his *Essay*:

It seems that 'substantial forms' have recently acquired a bad name in certain qurters in which people are ashamed to speak of them. However, this is perhaps more a matter of fashion than of reason. When particular phenomena were to be explained, the Scholastics inappropriately used a general notion, but this misuse does not destroy the thing itself. The human soul somewhat shakes the confidence of some of our modern thinkers. Some of them acknowledge that it is the form of the man, but add that it is the only substantial form in the known part of nature. M. Descartes speaks of it in this way; and he reproved M. Regius for challenging the soul's quality of being a substantial form and for denying that man is *unum per se*, a being endowed with a genuine unity. Some believe that this distinguished man did so out of prudence. I rather doubt that, since I think he was right about it. But the privilege should not be restricted to man alone.... (NEHU 317)

Leibniz's theory of substance in the *Discourse* was intended to accommodate the fact that living things generally are regarded as having an essential unity which cannot be explained on the assumption that the essence of corporeal substance consists of extension alone. Descartes' theory had the consequence that people are essentially thinking substances whereas other kinds of living thing are mere machines. His disciple, Henricus Regis (1598–1679), was doing no more than stating what the main line of Descartes' philosophy pointed to, in denying that even human souls are substantial forms. For the union of soul and body, even if Descartes wished to insist upon it, is left a mystery by his philosophy. Leibniz had aimed to provide a more adequate account in the *Discourse* by means of his restoration of substantial forms:

> Assuming that the bodies which constitute an essential unity (*unum per se*), such as man, are substances and that they have substantial forms; assuming, too, that the beasts have souls, one has to admit that these souls and these substantial forms cannot entirely perish, any more than the atoms or ultimate particles of matter that are believed in by other philosophers. (§ 34)

The *Discourse*, however, embodies a confusion (or at least a fusion) of two problems about the 'essential unity' of substance. One of these, which we may label the 'Aristotelian' problem,[1] is to explain the nature of organic unities. The other, which we may label the 'Platonic' problem,[2] assumes that only beings which are indivisible and indestructible are true beings. The two problems come together as problems posed by the mechanical philosophy for belief in corporeal *substances*. For, if bodies are mere machines, then their unity consists in nothing more than their parts being interrelated with one another to a much greater extent than they are interrelated with other bodies. Again, in virtue of being divisible into parts, a body is merely an *unum per accidens* and not an *unum per se*.

Leibniz had long been struck by the 'Platonic' problem and, even in his atomist phase, he had seen that there was no reason why atoms should not be further divisible. He then thought that it could be supposed that God provided a guarantee, so to speak, of the indivisibility of material atoms.[3] But he came to disapprove of such *deus ex machina* reasoning in *natural philosophy* and to believe, accordingly, that material atoms were contrary to reason. In his *New System* he makes it seem as if the 'Platonic' problem were the main one and that he was converted from belief in material atoms to belief in immaterial ones on account of it:

> At first, when I had freed myself from the yoke of Aristotle, I had believed in the void and atoms, for it is this which best satisfies the imagination. But returning to this view after much meditation, I perceived that it is impossible to find *the principles of a true unity* in matter alone, or in what is merely passive, since everything in it is but a collection or accumulation of parts *ad infinitum*. Now a multiplicity can be real only if it is made up of *true unities*... to find these *real unities* I was constrained to have recourse to what might be called a *real and animated point* or to an atom of substance .... (§ 3)

In the *Discourse*, however, it is the 'Aristotelian' problem which Leibniz seems mainly concerned to solve. The transition from the 'substantial forms' (principles of substantial unity) of the *Discourse* to the 'monads' (immaterial atoms) of the later writings may be partly a change to a less objectionable terminology. But it also reflects a change in priorities and indeed a significant modification of Leibniz's system. For, whereas the author of the *Discourse* attempted to explain how there could be material substances, Leibniz later came to believe that, strictly speaking at least, there were no such substances.[4] The Aristotelian problem was not forgotten, and was discussed at some length with the Jesuit Des Bosses.[5] It is, however, the Platonic problem whose solution is proposed in Leibniz's monadology.

10.2 The Problem about Material Substances

Leibniz's mature philosophy is characterized by a determination only to reject established opinions where they could be proved false. In the absence of a programme for a fully demonstrated metaphysics such a strategy provided him with starting-points.[6] In the *Discourse* and in his correspondence with Arnauld in 1686 Leibniz seemed anxious to preserve the established view that there are material substances. He continued to disapprove of those who, like Berkeley, rejected material substances with insufficient reason. Leibniz dissociated himself from those who, as it seemed to him, were out to win a reputation for themselves by putting forward 'paradoxes'.[7] His 'mean' between those who rejected intellectual authority entirely and those who adhered to it slavishly was to regard established opinion as presumptively true, i.e. to accept the onus of proof in departing from it.

This is the force of the 'must' in Leibniz's assertion in a draft reply to Arnauld (late 1686) that 'we must maintain that bodies are substances and not merely true phenomena like the rainbow' (BW 152, G ii 70). Since that is so, he reasoned, there must be more to matter than extension, since what is extended is infinitely divisible:

> Consequently, we shall never find a body of which we can say that it is really one substance; it will always be an aggregate of several. Or rather, it will not be a real being, for the beings which result from an aggregation have only as much reality as there is in their ingredients. Whence it follows that the substance of a body, if it has one, must be indivisible; whether we call it soul or form makes no difference to me. (BW 154f., G ii 72)

In his actual letter to Arnauld, however, Leibniz's argument involves the hypothetical claim that *if* there are corporeal substances then bodies must have real principles of unity i.e. substantial forms. But, so cast, the argument might readily be turned on its head by someone who was not interested in the Aristotelian but only in the Platonic problem. That was just what happened at the hands of Arnauld, an Augustinian (Christian Platonist) who took up Descartes' philosophy as a congenial alternative[8] to Scholastic Aristotelianism:

> This merely serves to make evident what is worth while pointing out, as St. Augustine has done, that the substance which thinks, or a spiritual substance, is through this fact much more excellent than extended or corporeal substance. The spiritual substance alone has a true unity and a true ego, while the corporeal substance does not have them. It follows from

this, that this fact, that the body has no true unity assuming its essence is extension, cannot be put forward to prove that extension is not of the essence of the body; for, perhaps, the essence of the body is to have no true unity, as you grant in the case of whatever is not united to a soul or to a substantial form. (G ii 87)

This line of thinking was already very familiar to Leibniz (see Chapter 4 above). And indeed, although he always preserved a certain detachment from Augustinianism, he was too imbued with Plato's thought to be anything but receptive to it.[9] In this way he was drawn, willy-nilly, closer to the Descartes of the early sections of *Meditations*. That there were material substances at all became doubtful and, at all events, less certain than the existence of the 'I' which thinks.[10] In Leibniz's later writings the self as conscious subject becomes the paradigm of substantial unity. For instance he held, as against Locke, that 'reflection enables us to find the idea of substance within ourselves, who are substances' (NEHU 105) In the *New System* he had said that it is by means of a soul or form that there exists a true unity in organic things 'which is analogous to the *I* in us'. (§ 11)

Leibniz's later view is brought out well in the way he contrasts his position with that of Berkeley:

...there is no need for us to say that matter is nothing. It is sufficient to say that it is a phenomenon like a rainbow. Nor need we say that it is substantial: rather that it is the result of substances. (See Chapter 4, Note 4 above)

Leibniz remained willing to countenance talk of material *substances*, at any rate in the case of organisms. (See, for instance, PW 175, C 13f.) But generally he regarded matter as a 'well-founded phenomenon', well-founded because although, like a rainbow, it was no more than a phenomenon, it was an appearance which reflected underlying realities. The comparison with the rainbow is significant. For metaphysics would explain how matter is 'the result of substances' just as physics explains how rainbows result from the passage of light through a particular kind of medium.

The comparison with the rainbow is significant in another way. For it marks the extent to which Leibniz retreated from his assumptions about matter in the *Discourse* and for a few years later. At that time he presented rainbows as *mere* phenomena from which bodies must sharply be distinguished if they are to be regarded as substances (see, for instance, BW 135, G ii 58). It seems as if he then believed that corporeal substances could meet the conditions of substantiality. Whereas a rainbow had only an apparent unity, 'the reality of a corporeal substance consists in a certain individual nature; that is, not in mass, but in a power of acting and being acted on' (PW 81, G vii 314). Not only could material body have unity, identity and agency. It could also enjoy relative autonomy: '*A corporeal substance can neither arise nor perish except by creation or annihilation*' (PW 92, C 523).

Material things could not be credited with any of these properties if the essence of matter were supposed (following Descartes) to consist of size, figure and motion. For, as we saw earlier (Chapter 3), material bodies so construed would only be able to receive and transmit motion impressed on them from outside. But, in the first place, this account assumed (as Leibniz believed) that the phenomena could be accommodated by a physical theory postulating the conservation of a total quantity of *motion*. Whereas it was necessary, to explain the phenomena, to suppose that it was the total quantity of *force* which was conserved. According to Leibniz, this meant that the prevailing view of 'dead matter" was incorrect. In any case, as we saw before (Section 8.4), Leibniz thought that causal interaction between substances was not strictly intelligible. Moreover size, figure and motion were relative to a perceiver and could not provide an adequate basis for judging that something remained the same through change. That basis, Leibniz concluded, had to be sought in the 'individual nature' of the substance in question.

The view which Leibniz sought to defend in the *Discourse* was that the sorts of thing we should think of as substances were people, animals and, perhaps, plants as well. 'I do not venture to maintain', he once wrote to Arnauld, 'that animals alone are living and endowed with substantial forms. Perhaps there is an infinity of degrees in the forms of corporeal substances' (G ii 92).

This is, in a way, a theory about the relation of souls and bodies. But it is a monistic theory.[11] Souls are not substances as such. Nor are bodies. What makes a body a substance is its being 'endowed with' a substantial form. This was the 'established' view and, leaving aside problems about the way it was dressed up in Scholastic terminology, probably impressed Leibniz with much the same force as, in a more democratic age, would the standpoint of common sense. Leibniz's strategy of presuming opinions received on good authority to be true until proved otherwise is readily translatable into a strategy for defending what we call 'common sense'. His attempt to rehabilitate substantial forms was thus more than a strategy of intellectual diplomacy. It was an attempt to defend something he was strongly inclined to believe and remained tempted to believe in spite of the difficulty he found in reconciling it with his other beliefs.

The difficulties posed for his defence of substantial forms were considerable and, by the end of his correspondence with Arnauld, he abandoned it. The abstract of his views sent to Arnauld in 1690 contains marked changes in content from the *Discourse* and the letters of 1686–87. The 'abstract' begins with the assertion:

A body is an aggregation of substances, and is not a substance, properly speaking. Consequently, in all bodies must be found indivisible substances which cannot be generated and are not corruptible, having something analogous to souls. (G ii 135)

Leibniz had arrived at his later view of true substances and it only remained for him to adopt the word 'monads' to refer to them. The transition in his view of material substances corresponds to other changes and can be seen very largely as an attempt to make his theory of what true substances are fully consistent with the implications of his requirements for substantiality. The cost of doing so was to reduce material substances to the status of 'well-founded phenomena'. They became like rainbows instead of being contrasted with them. The benefit, apart from gains in coherence, was that Leibniz was forced to enrich his theory with doctrines some of which are of enduring interest.

10.3 Substances and Spatiality

The belief that there are material substances has the consequence that substances can be spatial. But, if this is so, there arises the old problem (Section 2.2.2 above) concerning the composition of the continuum.[12] For whatever is spatially extended seems to be infinitely divisible and the 'Platonic' requirement for something being a real being—namely, that it be a true unity (*unum per se*)—is not met. If that requirement is not met, then there is nothing substantial in the visible world. Leibniz sought to meet this problem by saying that 'there is no portion of matter which is not actually subdivided; so the parts of any body are actually infinite' (PW 98, C 19). Hence 'there is no portion of matter so small that there does not exist in it a world of creatures, infinite in number' (PW 108, F de C 180).

That answer, however, gives rise to two quite different problems. In the first place it does not help with the 'Aristotelian' problem about how living things like man, animals and plants are substances. For on this account living things will themselves contain 'a world of creatures, infinite in number' and it is not clear how the macroscopic things will have a substantial unity. In the second place, even if there is a world of true substances to be found in every particle of matter, this is just as true of rainbows and the non-living world as of organisms.

Leibniz seems to have given the second problem a priority over the first—partly, perhaps, because he became more interested in questions of mechanics and what he called 'dynamics' than in biology. But, though he addressed the 'Aristotelian' problem in his correspondence with Arnauld, his accounts were never free of obvious difficulties. He had been struck by the fact that living organisms could undergo a virtually total transformation, as caterpillars did in turning into butterflies. They retained their identity as substances in spite of being totally transformed. It seemed to Leibniz plausible to suppose that when an animal died a similar transformation would take place. But, as Arnauld was quick to point out, there is no comparison between the transformation which takes place when a caterpillar changes into a butterfly and when it is changed into ashes as a result of fire. Whatever is preserved as a result of reducing a caterpillar to ashes it is not that individual substance. Leibniz was reduced to saying:

> I know that many assure us that the generative powers remain in ashes in such a way that plants can be produced from them but I do not wish to employ doubtful experiments. Whether these small organised bodies produced by a kind of contraction[13] from larger bodies that have become destroyed, are, as it seems wholly out of the series of generation, or whether they can come back to the theatre of action in due time, is something which I am unable to determine. These are secrets of nature where men must acknowledge their ignorance. (BW 227, G ii 122)

Leibniz continued to believe that ashes could contain organized bodies, at least in germ, but the transformations he continued to allow represent a shift in his theory. For, although he continued to insist that substances were naturally undestructible and that, accordingly, the total quantity of substances was always conserved, he ceased to believe in substantial forms tied to particular parcels of organized matter. He came to regard true substances as analogous to souls which were always attached to *a* parcel of organized matter but not necessarily the very same one. Much as a hermit crab must inhabit a shell though it occupied different shells at one time from another, so these quasi-souls can organise different bits of matter.

Leibniz's attempt to address the 'Aristotelian' problem and the 'Platonic' problem simultaneously did not work and, although he continued to give some thought to the 'Aristotelian' problem, he evidently found the 'Platonic' problem both more urgent and more tractable. The view, suppressed in the *Discourse*, that perhaps in metaphysical strictness there are no corporeal substances as such became, by 1690, his acknowledged opinion. But his thoughts about the composition of the continuum were taking him even further in the direction of making his ultimate entities not merely non-material but non-spatial also.

The corporeal substances of the *Discourse* occupy objective space. So do the innumerable creatures contained in every particle of matter. But, if each of these creatures is indivisible, then space itself must be divided into points. And if space itself is divided into points then a number of problems arise associated (for Leibniz as well as ourselves) with the name of the ancient Greek philosopher, Zeno.

10.4 Problems of Space and Time

There are many paradoxes associated with the name of Zeno but the central difficulty, so far as Leibniz was concerned, was that if space were divided into an infinite number of points it would be impossible to go from one place to another. For it would be necessary to traverse the infinite number of points between one place and another. The impossibility of doing this is illustrated by the fact that the series $1/2 + 1/4 + 1/8 + 1/16 + 1/32 + 1/64$ appears to converge closer on the number 1 without ever actually reaching it. But the same argument applies also to time. Someone waiting for a period of time to elapse has to wait through all the intervening points of time. And if time is divided not only into seconds but into all the infinitely small fractions of seconds as well, it may seem as if it is impossible for a period of time actually to elapse.

The argument is less convincing in the case of time since it is tempting to think of time as a mere phenomenon and of its infinite divisibility as an abstraction. We can conceive a part of space devoid of matter (a vacuum) more readily than we can conceive a part of time as devoid of events, as Leibniz acknowledged (G v 142). For we could measure a vacuum in space if there were one but could not measure a vacuum in time. It is therefore tempting to think of time as nothing more than the order of events, i.e. of phenomena insofar as they are related to one another as prior, contemporaneous and successive. Leibniz, like many other philosophers, thought of space and time as analogous. But whereas he at one stage (certainly as late as 1682 and probably in the *Discourse* as well) conceived of space as a container of matter and constructed time in quasi-spatial terms, he later shifted to a conception of space modelled on that of time. This later view is clearly expressed in a letter to Des Bosses of 1712:

> I consider the explanation of all phenomena solely through the perceptions of monads functioning in harmony with each other, with corporeal substances rejected, to be useful for a fundamental investigation of things.

> In this way of explaining things, space is the order of co-existing phenomena, as time is the order of successive phenomena, and there is no spatial or absolute nearness or distance between monads. And to say that they are crowded together in a point or disseminated in space is to use certain fictions of our mind when we seek to visualize freely what can only be understood. In this conception, also, there is involved no extension or composition of the continuum, and all difficulties about points disappear. (PPL 604, G ii 450)

Leibniz's changing views about matter, space, time and the labyrinth of the continuum after he wrote the *Discourse* are difficult to trace in detail. He found various interim solutions. But the tendency of his thought is in what can be called a 'phenomenalistic'[14] direction, i.e. to explain matter, space and time in terms of the perceptions of monads. Material substances are reduced to well-founded phenomena as also are space and time. The tendency is brought out succinctly in his review of Berkeley's *Principles*, quoted earlier (Chapter 4 and Note 4):

> Many things that are here seem right to me. But they are expressed rather paradoxically. For there is no need for us to say that matter is nothing. It is sufficient to say that it is a phenomenon like a rainbow. Nor need we say that it is substantial: rather that it is the result of substances. Nor need we say that space is more real than time: It is sufficient to say that space is nothing but the order of co-existing things and time the order of successive things. The true substances are monads, or things that perceive.

Leibniz did not study Berkeley's *Principles of Human Knowledge* with anything like the attention he gave to Descartes' *Principles of Philosophy*, Malebranche's *Search after Truth*, Spinoza's *Ethics* or Locke's *Essay*. It may therefore be wondered whether he simply failed to notice that Berkeley did not merely deny the reality of matter. It might be claimed that Berkeley was just as much concerned to defend the reality of sensible things as Leibniz:

> That the things I see with my eyes and touch with my hands do exist, really exist, I make not the least question. The only thing whose existence we deny, is *that which philosophers call matter or corporeal substances*. (*Principles* § 35, italics added)

Berkeley, it may be claimed, was not concerned to attack the commonsense belief in material things but the philosophical theory that claimed to articulate it. (Leibniz himself had tried to defend the hypothesis of 'corporeal substances' and found the task beyond him.) But it was only in strict metaphysical usage that Leibniz came to think it was incorrect to talk of material *substance*. He was just as happy to talk of bodies as 'substances' in a theoretically uncommitted way as he was to talk of bodies causing things to happen in other bodies. That he regarded as part of the language of practice, like talking of the sun 'rising' in the morning. Metaphysical language needs to be reconciled to such language by providing an account of the phenomena to which it relates. Otherwise metaphysics will be misunderstood.

Thus far there are no important differences between Leibniz and Berkeley. Nonetheless there are crucial differences. Whereas, for Berkeley, the only substances are *spirits*, Leibniz's monads are supposed to exist wherever there is any kind of organized matter. Berkeley's philosophy thus has a tendency to idealism where Leibniz's tends to what is called 'panpsychism'. Moreover, Berkeley had (by his own standards) only weak (inductive) arguments for supposing that there are any other spirits than God and himself. Leibniz by contrast thought that a perfect God not only would not create the world of phenomena just for one soul but would not have created it just for humans and that therefore it must be as full of souls of every kind as it is possible for it to be. (We shall explore his account of God and the creation in the next chapter.) Even before writing the *Discourse* he was prepared to say:

> I believe that there is in every body a kind of sense and appetite, or soul, and furthermore, that to ascribe a substantial form and perception, or a soul, to man alone [a view attributed by Leibniz to Descartes] is as ridiculous as to believe that everything has been made for man alone and that the earth is the centre of the universe. (PPL 289, from the unpublished manuscripts in Hanover, XXXVII, iv, 6)

That there is, in some sense, an external world was, for Leibniz, a moral certainty. There is infinitely more to the world than is contained in my experience of it—infinitely more, come to that, than is contained in the sum total of the experiences of the human race. The word 'external' is a spatial one and the denial of space as an objective thing outside phenomena means that belief in an 'external' world needs, in strict metaphysics, to be articulated in a way that avoids the objectionable implications of the word 'external'.

In the *Discourse* Leibniz appears to have taken the view that every individual substance has a unique position in space and accordingly expresses the universe from a particular point of view 'very much as one and the same town is variously represented in accordance with different positions of the observer' (§ 9). But his later modifications led him to deny that his substances are strictly in space at all. The universe must accordingly be reduced to the sum total of the substances comprising it and its unity to the interconnection between their phenomena. Not only the 'town' in Leibniz's explanation needs to be taken metaphorically but also the 'one and the same'. Space, insofar as it transcends the relations of simultaneous phenomena in one individual's 'perspective', is a construct rather than an independently existing thing.

Our conception of objective space results from the way in which spatial relationships remain constant within our phenomena. Thus a tree can obscure our view of a house from one point of view but, at a later time, be seen as standing to the side of it or again at the back of it. 'But the mind, not being contented with an agreement, looks for an identity, for something that should be truly the same; and conceives it as being extrinsic to these subjects: and this is what we here call place and space. But this can only be an ideal thing; containing a certain order, wherein the mind conceives the application of relations' (G vii 400).

10.5 'Well-founded Phenomena'

Space, time and matter are what, in Leibniz's later theory, are called 'well-founded phenomena'. They are 'well-founded' in that, unlike *mere* phenomena, they result from substances. A 'corporeal substance' is a phenomenon produced by monads and is not to be understood simply in terms of my perceptions. Some of the properties commonly ascribed to corporeal substances, such as colour and even size, figure and motion are at least partly 'imaginary and relative to our perceptions' (*Discourse* §12). But corporeal bodies also possess properties, like resistance to change, which need to be understood, according to Leibniz, in terms of underlying substances.

That corporeal bodies possess such properties was, Leibniz believed, demonstrable by experiment. Leibniz was much occupied, in the late 1680s and early 1690s, with attempting to launch a new branch of science (called 'dynamics') concerned with various types of forces.[15] The existence of such forces he gave as evidence both that matter could not be understood in terms of size, figure and motion alone and that the world could not be made intelligible solely in terms belonging to physics.[16] Physics, it seemed, had to assume certain properties in matter which, by the standards of the mechanical philosophy, were 'occult'. Some basis was needed, Leibniz assumed, for distinguishing between those cases where physicists needed to reconsider their theory[17] and others where these quasi-occult concepts could be tolerated. This, as Leibniz saw it, was one role which metaphysics could play even in relation to an increasingly autonomous physics. Metaphysics could validate certain physical concepts by explaining them in terms of its own concepts. This process would show the property in question to be either 'occult' or 'well-founded'.

Leibniz first argued that force is essential to matter as a phenomenon (as investigated in physics) and then invoked the maxim that 'activity' is something which pertains to substances. This was compatible, as he realized in the *Discourse*, with there being corporeal substances as such. But, as we have seen in this chapter, he was obliged (in view of other constraints on what could be counted a 'substance') to reject the assumption that there are corporeal substances. The doctrine of 'well-founding' is an alternative solution to the problem of the apparently 'active' character of matter. Ultimately this character is to be explained in terms of what Leibniz is constrained to refer to metaphorically as the 'diffusion' of non-spatial substances 'throughout' the universe. This diffusion makes the force supposed to be inherent in matter 'well-founded'. For ultimately it is referred to the 'activity' of these monads.

Leibniz's monadology has often struck philosophers of subsequent generations as singularly bizarre and even speculative to the point of unintelligibility. Hume spoke for many when he remarked, doubtless with Leibniz's as well as

Descartes' type of philosophy in mind: 'Men are now cured of their passion for hypotheses and systems in natural philosophy, and will hearken to no arguments but those derived from experience.'[18] But Hume was content to regard Nature as essentially mysterious and even invoked 'occult qualities' in a way which Descartes and Leibniz would have seen as retrograde. For Leibniz it was a cardinal matter, definitive of the project of Modern philosophy, that the natural order is completely intelligible. If he was mistaken about this or in the criteria he adopted for deciding what was more and what was less intelligible, it would not be wholly surprising if some of Leibniz's metaphysics was itself unintelligible. Before considering whether this is indeed so it will be instructive to consider in greater detail the nature of the explanatory project which resulted in Leibniz's 'system'.

Notes

1 It is this problem which makes the use of the (Scholastic) Aristotelian phrase 'substantial form' appropriate.

2 That Leibniz himself might have been willing to label this problem as 'Platonic' is clear from a number of passages, most clearly from these remarks in a letter to Arnauld;

> Substantial unity calls for a thoroughly indivisible being, naturally indestructible since its concept involves all that must happen to it. This characteristic ... can be found ... in a soul or a substantial form, such as the one called the me. These latter are the only thoroughly real beings as the ancients recognized and, above all, Plato, who showed very clearly that matter alone does not suffice for forming a substance....
> (BW 161, G ii 76)

3 In his 'Confession of Nature against Atheists' (1669) Leibniz notes that 'no reason for cohesion and indivisibility appears within these ultimate corpuscles' and concludes: 'In explaining the atoms, we may therefore rightly resort to God, who endows with firmness these ultimate elements of things' (PPL 112, G iv 109).

4 In the abstract of his system at the end of his exchange with Arnauld, Leibniz roundly declares: 'A body is an aggregation, and is not a substance, properly speaking' (BW 244, G ii 135).

5 Some of Leibniz's Scholastic Aristotelian critics pursued the objection that his monadology could not explain the unity of corporeal substances. In the correspondence with Des Bosses (1709–15) Leibniz was drawn into developing the idea of a 'substantial bond' linking the monads which

constitute a body. Students of Leibniz differ as to the importance of this correspondence. Russell, for instance, maintains that Leibniz was simply trying 'to persuade Catholics that they might, without heresy, believe in his doctrine of monads' (*Critical Exposition*, p.123). Rescher, by contrast, holds that this correspondence 'is of fundamental importance for an understanding of this aspect of his metaphysics' (*op. cit.* p.122).

6 That there are corporeal substances is an *assumption* of the *Discourse*, is explicit in DM 34 which opens: 'Supposing that bodies which make *unum per se*, like man does, are substances...'. It is significant that, in an earlier draft, this same section began:

> I do not [yet] undertake to determine whether bodies are substances, to speak with metaphysical rigour, or whether they are only *true* phenomena, like the rainbow ... But supposing that bodies ... are substances ... (see *Leibniz: Discourse on Metaphysics*,ed. P.G. Lucas and L Grint, Manchester University Press, 1953, p.57)

Leibniz had deleted the assertion that 'bodies are not substances in strict metaphysics (which was indeed the sentiment of the Platonists)' from *Discourse* § 12. He seems to have suppressed the Platonic problem in favour of the Aristotelian problem in putting the finishing touches to his *Discourse*. Part of the explanation seems to have been his desire to avoid being unnecessarily 'paradoxical' (See Note 7).

7 In a letter to Des Bosses, Leibniz wrote: 'The Irishman who attacks the reality of bodies seems neither to offer suitable reasons nor to explain his position sufficiently. I suspect he belongs to the class of men who want to be known for their paradoxes...' (PPL 609, G ii 492). But privately, as is clear from his review of the *Principles of Human Knowledge*, he was much less dismissive of Berkeley than these remarks make it appear, there saying: 'Many things here seem right to me, but they are expressed too paradoxically' (See Chapter 4, Note 4 above).

8 As one of the Church Fathers, Augustine of Hippo (354–430), was an established court of appeal for those who, for one reason or another, wished to escape from the Aristotelian framework. Augustine made some elements of Plato's thought religiously acceptable and so provided alternatives in philosophy and theology to Aristotle and Aquinas. Descartes' philosophy was generally condemned by those who favoured the latter but was welcomed by those who favoured the former. For this reason Cartesianism had as fellow-travellers priests like Malebranche and Arnauld. Arnauld's religious sect (the Jansenists) referred to themselves as 'the Disciples of Augustine' and indeed Arnauld sometimes capped his arguments against Leibniz with appeals to the support of Augustine. For Leibniz's attitude to Augustinianism, see Note 9 below.

9 Leibniz would not entirely take Arnauld's side in the famous controversy Arnauld engaged in with Malebranche about the nature of ideas. In a letter of 1715 he expressed his opinions about a 'refutation' of (Father) Malebranche in this way:

... the Father may be excused and even praised for having ... given to ideas a more exalted signification, in distinguishing them from notions and taking them for perfections in God which we participate in by our knowledge ... It seems that Plato, speaking of ideas, and St. Augustine, speaking of truth, had kindred thoughts, which I find very remarkable; and this is the part of Malebranche's system which I should like to have retained ... And far from saying with the author of the *Refutation* ... that the system of St Augustine is *a little infected with the language and opinions of the Platonists*, I would say it is thereby enriched and set in relief. (S 557, E 737)

10 Leibniz rejected Descartes' appeal to 'clear and distinct ideas' and took the *Cogito* to be a 'primary truth of fact' based on inner experience (NEHU 367). Leibniz was often less than generous to Descartes, sometimes giving the impression that where he was right he was unoriginal. Leibniz was in the habit of pointing out that the ontological argument, for example, was to be found in Anselm and that the *Cogito* derived from Augustine.

11 Russell, in his *Critical Exposition*, rightly identifies another theory which *is* dualistic. The account in the *Discourse* is not wholly worked out and shows the marks of Leibniz's superadding the assumption of corporeal substances and suppressing his tendency towards Platonic scepticism. In an earlier draft Leibniz had toyed with the possibility that 'Spirits are the only substances which are present in the world, in which case bodies are only real/true phenomena' (§ 35, deleted from copy B). Leibniz tended to dismiss such an idealism as objectionably anthropocentric and this (see Section 9.4) is also a point of departure for him from Berkeley's philosophy. But the ghost of it haunts the *Discourse* and, together with the supposition of material substance, makes it look a dualist theory. Whether Leibniz succeeded in exorcising this ghost will be considered in Section 12.6 below.

12 See Section 2.2.2 above. It was not long after writing the *Discourse* that Leibniz returned to this problem, referring to it as one of the 'two labyrinths of the human mind' (PW 107, F d C 180).

13 Leibniz thought that bodies were capable of contracting to a tiny size and expanding to many times their actual size. So his theory about this matter goes further than a fancy based on observations about butterflies. (He also has more to say on butterflies, see PPL 557, G vi 533f.) Leibniz wrote an interesting 'Appendix on the Resurrection of Bodies' which outlines the theory:

'... I am almost of the opinion that all bodies, as well those of men as those of beasts, vegetables, and minerals, have a seminal principle of subtance .... This seminal principle is so subtle, that it remains even in the ashes of the substance when consumed by fire, and has the power, as it were, of collecting itself in an invisible centre ... I believe, further, that this seminal principle of the whole body neither increases nor diminishes, though its clothing as covering is in constant fluctuation, and at one time is evaporated, at another is again enlarged by the air or by food.' (Quoted in *System of Theology*, p. 164ff., notes.)

14 This point has been argued by Montgomery Furth in his 'Monadology', *Philosophical Review*, Vol. 76, 1967.

15 Useful accounts of Leibniz's work in this area include Pierre Costabel's *Leibniz and Dynamics*, trans R.E.W.Maddison, Paris, Herman; London, Methuen, 1973 and David Papineau's 'The *Vis Viva* Controversy', *Studies in History and Philosophy of Science*, 8 (1977), pp. 111–42, reprinted in R.S Woolhouse, (ed.) *Leibniz: Metaphysics and Philosophy of Science*, Oxford University Press, 1981, pp. 139–56.

16 Leibniz makes the point, in his *New System* for instance, that 'use must also be made of the notion of *force*, which is fully intelligible, although it falls within the sphere of metaphysics' (§ 2).

17 Notoriously, Leibniz joined with the Cartesians in attacking Newton's theory of gravitation. See PW 172, C 11 f.

18 *An Enquiry Concerning the Principles of Morals*, Section 1, Oxford, Clarendon Press, ed. L A Selby-Bigge, 1902, pp. 174f.

11 Mind and Body: The System of Pre-established Harmony

> Once I had established these things, I thought I had reached port; but when I set myself to reflect on the union of the soul with the body, I seemed to be cast back again into the open sea. For I could find no way of explaining how the body causes something to happen in the soul, or vice versa, nor how one created substance can communicate with another. (*New System* § 12)

Leibniz wrote his *New System* in 1695, apparently because he feared he had not long to live and wanted to leave a statement of his system to posterity.[1] In it he concerned himself primarily with two problems, of which the first was the problem as to what fundamentally there is in the world—the problem of what is to count as a 'substance'. Here his account is essentially that of his later monadology, as outlined in the previous chapter. It is in virtue of having 'established these things' about substance that, according to the *New System*, Leibniz thought he had 'reached port' until he realized he had not solved the second problem, about the 'communication' of substances.

Leibniz's choice of the autobiographical mode of presenting his 'system' for the readers of the *Journal des Savants* seems to have been an imitation of Descartes. But, unlike Descartes, he had no philosophical reason for adopting it.[2] Nonetheless it would be surprising if there never was a time when Leibniz had come to his mature view about the *nature* of substances and yet found himself at a loss over the problem of how one substance can *communicate* with another. There is no obvious reason why Leibniz should admit to having been 'cast back again into the open sea' if it were not true.

Yet, if it is true, there is a puzzle as to when Leibniz should have been in this situation. There is more change between the *Discourse* and the *New System* as to the *nature* of substance than there is over how substances can *communicate* with one another (see Chapter 10 above). It seems most improbable, therefore, that Leibniz was stuck over the problem of 'communication' any time between 1686 and 1695. That could only have happened if the hypothesis of concomitance (as Leibniz earlier called his system of pre-established harmony) had been temporarily undermined. More probable is that the time referred to was in the early 1680s and that Leibniz, in the *New System*, represents his theory of the nature of substance as more finished that it actually was.

But even this view would only be plausible if Leibniz's theory of substance existed in essentials prior to late 1685 or early 1686. It cannot be later than that since the doctrine of pre-established harmony is clearly stated in the *Discourse* even although the rationale for it is different in the *New System*, as we shall see later in this chapter. Moreover it is likely that Leibniz was in a quandary over the 'communication' between substances at some time *after* writing the *System of Theology*. For in the *System*, as we have seen (Section 7.2 above), Leibniz thought that a slight variation on Malebranche's theory was the only way to explain how one body can act on another. If 1683 is accepted as the date of the *System* then it would seem reasonable to suppose that Leibniz thought he had reached port in 1683 and was 'cast back into the open sea' at some stage subsequently. This conjecture is supported by the fact that Leibniz makes it seem as if he was led to his system of pre-established harmony through dissatisfaction, firstly, with Cartesian interactionism (Section 8.4 above) and then with occasionalism.

11.1 Leibniz's Quandary over the 'Communication' of Substances

It is possible to discover, in writings of around 1683, the four main assumptions about substance which Leibniz makes in the *Discourse* and in later writings (see Chapter 8 Note 9 above). Leibniz was already inclined to argue that all substances were analogous to souls and indeed that everything is animated. Moreover Leibniz was already inclined to say that all substances are true unities and are therefore indestructible.

(PPL 279)[3] He was not yet clearly of the opinion, however, that each substance enjoyed *total* autonomy (causal independence) from every other substance. Nor, correspondingly, did he claim that each substance was totally spontaneous, i.e. totally responsible for what is true of it. He was a long way, then, from the view of the *New System* that 'God first created the soul, and every other real unity, in such a way that everything in it must spring from within itself, by a perfect *spontaneity* with regard to itself, and yet in a perfect *conformity* with things outside' (§ 14). The most that Leibniz demands for substances in the *System of Theology* is *some* degree of spontaneity: 'The individual essence of a thing', he writes, '... or that "which causes it to be that thing, and to remain the same through manifold changes" consists in a certain power, or actual faculty or capacity of action ...' (p. 115). To be an individual substance it is not required that a thing be perfectly autonomous and spontaneous.

The trouble with Malebranche's account, however, is that it left no room for any spontaneity in individual substances. As Leibniz explained in a later writing:

> ...the doctrine of occasional causes... is fraught with dangerous consequences... So far is this doctrine from increasing the glory of God by removing the idol of Nature that it seems rather, like Spinoza, to make out of God the nature of the world itself, by causing created things to disappear into mere modifications of the one divine substance, since that which does not act, which lacks active force, and which is despoiled of all distinctiveness and even of all reason and ground for subsistence can in no way be a substance (PPL 506, G iv 515)

Some degree of self-sufficiency and agency must be established for created things if they are to count as individual substances with their own 'distinctiveness', able to retain their identity through time. They must therefore have *some* spontaneity, i.e. be capable of being 'true causes', of sometimes containing within themselves the explanation for what is true of them. They must therefore enjoy a *degree* of autonomy, subject only to divine concurrence, within the natural order. That much is needed to defend a plurality of substances.

The difficulty is that there is no way of allowing partial autonomy and spontaneity to an individual substance without supposing that substances interact with one another. If interaction is excluded as unintelligible (see Section 3.2 above) then the issues are polarized. There is no half-way house between denying any spontaneity to created substances and allowing that each of them is perfectly spontaneous. It is because of his insistence on this point that Leibniz could justifiably claim that his position was quite different from that of Malebranche.[4] It is indeed the doctrine of spontaneity which is really original in Leibniz. Apart from it the doctrine of a pre-established harmony would have been a commonplace. But spontaneity is such a preposterous doctrine that it is difficult to imagine that Leibniz would have toyed with it seriously before he had a theory in terms of which it could be presented as credible. In the *Discourse* period the linchpin of this theory is the *inesse* principle.[5] But, as we shall see, the *inesse* principle does not underwrite spontaneity and in the *New System* it is argued for in a different way.

11.2 The *Discourse* Argument for Spontaneity

In the *Discourse* and in writings for a few years thereafter the complete autonomy and spontaneity of substances in the natural order was claimed by Leibniz to follow from the notion of an individual substance. An individual, Leibniz supposed, was unique: 'a certain individual is *this* one, whom I designate either by pointing or by adding distinguishing marks. For although there cannot be marks which distinguish it perfectly from every other possible individual, there are however marks which distinguish it perfectly from other individuals which we meet' (LP 51, C 360). We can identify an individual by pointing or by identifying him as 'the person who...' and then listing a set of features which, taken together, apply only to him. But such a list of 'marks' does not suffice to capture what distinguishes him from any other *possible* individual. For that we should need a complete notion of the individual concerned which would contain everything that is true of him.

According to the *Discourse*, this complete notion must have a basis in the individual concerned, in his individual nature or *haecceitas* ('thisness'). Hence 'it is the nature of an individual substance, or complete being, to have a notion so complete that it is sufficient to contain, or render deducible from itself, all the predicates of the subject to which this notion is attributed' (§ 8). From this in turn it is soon inferred that 'a substance can begin only by creation, and perish only by annihilation, ... that therefore the number of substances is neither increased nor diminished naturally, though substances are often transformed' (§ 9). Individual substances are wholly *autonomous* with respect to the rest of the natural order because, it seems, they are wholly *spontaneous*. They are wholly spontaneous because everything that is true of them can be deduced from their individual natures.

This line of argument is neither clear nor compelling. Indeed as I suggested earlier (Section 8.7), it seems to trade on a residual fund of good will for belief in *essences* in nature. Modern philosophy, or so Leibniz assumed, had swept away explanations in terms of general essences or natures from the natural sciences. But the objections to *general* essences did not apply against *individual* essences, since discussion of these belonged to metaphysics and not to the natural sciences. Supposing that to be so, the *inesse* doctrine could be extended to individual essences, making whatever is true of an individual essence follow from its nature in just the way that the properties of gold were formerly supposed to be derivable from the essence of gold.

That point might be taken further. A ring of gold is a substance which enjoys a degree of autonomy and spontaneity *qua substance*, according to the received view. As Locke puts it:

> The particular parcel of matter which makes the ring I have on my finger is forwardly by most men supposed to have a real essence, whereby it is gold; and from whence those qualities flow which I find in it, viz. its peculiar colour, weight, hardness, fusibility, fixedness, and change of colour upon a slight touch of mercury & c. (*Essay* II.31.6)

Locke goes on to pour scorn on the idea that this real essence depends on the 'substantial form' of gold. That takes us further from understanding what gold is, since we have no idea of 'substantial form'. But Locke, unlike Leibniz, did not deny general essences. He did not deny that if it *were* possible to discover the 'necessary connexion' between the complex idea of gold and its properties then it would be possible to be as certain of scientific truths (like '*all gold is malleable*') as we can be of geometrical truths, e.g. about triangles (*Essay* IV.6.10).

Locke, we might say, was not denying the *truth* of the *inesse* principle in relation to real essences. It was part of his ideal of scientific knowledge even if one he thought could not be realized. He questioned some part of the Scholastic legacy but took other parts of it for granted, e.g. that substances like gold did have essences from which their properties could ideally, if not actually, be inferred. Leibniz also accepted some part of the Scholatic legacy but found that the requirements for being a substance could not be met by material substances as such. He was in any case, as I suggested earlier (Section 8.7), motivated by a nominalist tendency to deny that there were *general* natures in the universe and to say that the only essences there could be are *individual* essences.

Leibniz's statement of the principle of spontaneity in *Discourse* §33 makes use of this Scholastic language and provides some confirmation that it is indeed a nominalist counterpart to Scholastic assumptions about real essences:

> ... the true principle is this: We have said that everything which happens to the soul and to each substance follows from its concept; hence the idea itself, or the essence of the soul, carries with it that all its appearances or perceptions must arise spontaneously out of its own nature ....

Spontaneity and autonomy seem thus to have been immediate consequences of the thought that individual substances have unique essences or natures. That they have such unique essences or natures seems in turn to have been a requirement of their being 'complete' beings in the sense previously explained (see Section 8.5). In this way the theory of the individual substance is the counterpart in reality (*a parte rei*) of a general theory of truth, namely, the generalized *inesse* principle. The *inesse* principle only admits of generalization in virtue of a Scholastic theory of essences.[6] It is the application to *individual* substances of a principle formerly applied to *sorts* of substance ('secondary substances', as they were known) which permits the deduction of spontaneity and autonomy.

If that is true then the *Discourse* should be regarded as a *fundamentally* Neo-Scholastic work. Indeed Leibniz presents it in just that light: 'I know that I am putting forward a great paradox in claiming to rehabilitate ancient philosophy to some extent, and *to restore the rights of citizenship to substantial forms*, which have practically been banished' (§ 11, italics added). It seemed to Leibniz that such a revival did not in any way detract from Modern philosophy, since it was compatible with holding that all particular phenomena are to be explained mechanically (§ 10).

11.3 Spontaneity and Autonomy in the *New System*

In the *New System* the impossibility of interaction between substances is based, at least partially, on the consideration that substances must have 'real unity' (§ 14). But it is not clear there how spontaneity is to be inferred from unity. The thought is probably that articulated in the *Monadology*, where the early sections are dominated by the requirement that *monads* or simple substances must be indivisible. From this Leibniz infers the indestructibility of monads and indeed that they are wholly autonomous with respect to the rest of the creation:

> There is also no means of explaining how a monad can be altered or changed within itself by any other created thing, since it is impossible to displace anything in it or to conceive of the possibility of any internal motion being started, directed, increased, or diminished within it, as can occur in compounds, where change among the parts takes place. (§ 7)

But if there is no way in which a simple substance, as opposed to a complex one, can be modified from without, the changes which take place in it must all 'come from an *internal principle*'[7] (*Monadology*, § 11). Spontaneity and autonomy seem thus to follow in large measure from unity, understood as a requirement of atomic simplicity and indivisibility. This requirement, as we saw in the previous chapter, is played down in the *Discourse*—probably because of Leibniz's wish to include animals, plants, and other organic unities, as genuine substances. But in the later writings the emphasis on absolute indivisibility plays a pivotal role in Leibniz's thought, and complex substances are reduced to courtesy substances, as nothing more than well-founded phenomena.

The *New System*, as we have seen, represents Leibniz's theory of the mind-body relation as resulting from a quandary into which he had been thrown *after* arriving at a theory of the nature of substances in which the unity-as-indivisibility requirement was paramount. Malebranche's work confirmed him in the belief that 'in the strict metaphysical sense there is no real influence exerted by one created substance on another' (*New System* § 13). He was thus confirmed in what I have called the requirement of *autonomy* of created substances with respect to one another. He takes up and presents the case for *spontaneity* in the following terms:

> Being thus constrained to grant that it is impossible for the soul or for any other true substance to receive anything from without, except by Divine omnipotence, I was insensibly led to adopt a view which surprised me, but which seems inevitable... that God first created the soul, and every other real unity, in such a way that everything in it must spring from within itself, by a perfect spontaneity with regard to itself, and yet in a perfect *conformity* with things outside. (*New System* § 14)

Since, however, *autonomy* is in a certain sense secured by Malebranche's occasionalism and *spontaneity* does not follow from the requirement of *unity-as-indivisibility*, the theory of spontaneity is a hypothesis. It is to be preferred to the hypothesis of occasional causes, according to Leibniz, on the ground that it is out of place to invoke, as Malebranche did, a special divine intervention ('miracle') to explain the regular course of nature. The phenomena of harmony agree with both hypotheses, but the hypothesis of a *pre-established* harmony between *spontaneous* substances is more suited to divine wisdom, which is to do everything in the most orderly and economical way. The *New System* thus presents *spontaneity*, not as something explicable wholly *a priori* but as a possible way of explaining the phenomena.

11.4 Leibniz's Defence of the Pre-established Harmony

One of the most trenchant criticisms of Leibniz's *New System* was made by his friend Simon Foucher, who thought the system of pre-established harmony had a distinctly *ad hoc* character. '*In truth, sir, can we not see that these views are formed with a set purpose, and that these systems, coming after the event, have only been manufactured to save certain principles?*' (G i 426, quoted from Leibniz's reply, PW 128, G iv 496). Leibniz was unable to see any force to this objection. 'All hypotheses are formed *with a set purpose*', he retorted, 'and all systems come *after the event* to save phenomena or appearances' (PW 128, G iv 496). Leibniz professed to be unable to see what were the principles in favour of which he was supposed to be 'prejudiced'.

Leibniz's failure to grasp Foucher's point seems to be due to his own exaggeration of his agreement with the 'Cartesians' (Occasionalists). As Foucher understood it, Leibniz was agreeing with the 'Cartesians' that, since mind and body had nothing in common, they could not interact. Foucher's criticism is directed not exclusively at Leibniz's 'system' but equally at those of the Cartesians. The prejudice he seems to have had in mind is that interaction was impossible. He concludes that part of his critique by alluding to a way of allowing interaction which had the authority of Augustine. What was needed, from Foucher's standpoint, was a better theory of interaction than the one offered by Descartes himself—not an acceptance that interaction was impossible.

Leibniz, after briefly searching his conscience for signs of prejudice, concludes that Foucher could not have meant to imply that he was simply bolstering prejudices. He then makes an important methodological remark:

> If this means that I am led to my hypothesis by *a priori* reasons also, or by fixed principles, as is in fact the case, this is rather a commendation of the hypothesis than an objection to it. It commonly suffices for a hypothesis to be proved *a posteriori*, because it satisfies the phenomena; but when we have other reasons as well, and those *a priori*, it is so much the better. (PW 128, G iv 496)

The phenomena which Leibniz takes to need explanation are all the ordinary phenomena of what we call 'causes' and 'effects' but, more specifically, those relating to mind-body interaction. Amongst these phenomena is the fact that 'the soul has its seat in the body by an immediate presence, which could not be closer than it is' (PW 123, G iv 485). There is a particularly close correspondence between what goes on in an individual's mind and what is happening in his body. Interaction or '*transeunt* activity', in the jargon of Leibniz's day, was to him a *phenomenon* (see PW 128, G iv 496) to be explained. On an *a posteriori* basis there might be nothing to choose between various metaphysical theories. Hence the importance, for Leibniz (and others), of taking higher ground and advancing *a priori* reasons for preferring a particular theory. There was nothing scientifically odd about this procedure. The Copernican theory was preferred to the Ptolemaic one, at least for some time, on *a priori* grounds, e.g. simplicity.[8] For Leibniz 'the way of influence' (what would nowadays be called 'interactionism') was a *superficial* theory which maintained that substances do indeed interact. In the same way he regarded the Ptolemaic theory, according to which the sun does indeed rise in the morning, as a superficial theory which 'saved the phenomena' but as objectionable on *a priori* grounds.

Leibniz held that his 'system' of pre-established harmony was more than a mere hypothesis, since it had the support of *a priori* considerations which at the same time eliminated the two main alternative theories. In the first place there was Scholastic interactionism, which embodied the highly obscure and problematic notion of an 'influx'. Leibniz's objection to interactionism seems not to have rested primarily on these kinds of difficulties—which he was a past master at clarifying, had there been any point in doing so. Any kind of influx is excluded by the nature of true substances, in particular by the requirement of complete unity (indivisibility) and the implied requirement of complete autonomy relative to other finite substances. Perhaps, if he had lived to continue the debate, Foucher might have identified the unity requirement as a 'prejudice'. But, sceptic though he was about many matters, Foucher seems to have agreed with Leibniz that the unity of the soul afforded proof of its autonomy and so of its natural immortality. It is more likely that he would have wanted to represent the belief that the soul and the body have nothing in common as a prejudice. But Leibniz was far from denying that the soul and the body have anything in common—indeed his theory calls for many analogies between them.[9]

Leibniz's objection to the Malebranchian account of the mind-body relation is grounded in his acceptance of a principle (explored in the next chapter) that God has created a world which is as rich in its effects as it is simple in the basic laws from which they result. God can do miracles but even they, according to Leibniz (*Discourse* § 7), conform to the general order—with this difference, that human beings could not understand the laws of this general order sufficiently to be able to explain how miracles happen. But, as for the ordinary course of nature, of which the interaction of minds and bodies is a part, this is by no means beyond the reach of human understanding. Leibniz's principle of sufficient reason, which played an increasingly dominant role in his metaphysical reasoning, came to be more than the principle that everything is intelligible *to God*. He also used a version of it, with increasing confidence, as a principle relevant to scientific debates—as the principle that everything *in the natural order* is intelligible *to us*. On this basis he objected to philosophers like Malebranche who sought to explain phenomena by an immediate appeal to the intervention of God. A good philosopher will no more resort to a *deus ex machina* than a good playwright will use such an artifice to escape from the natural development of his plot.

11.5 Saving the Appearances of Interaction

In the *Discourse*, Leibniz was prepared to suppose that any bodies which make an *unum per se*, as a human being does, are substances. He therefore included organic unities generally, such as animals (and, slightly later, plants) as substances. He also allowed, at this stage, that there were incorporeal substances or spirits (§ 23). All substances had to have something like 'souls' or 'substantial forms' which constituted their principle of unity and identity. At the same time spirits were held to be a higher species of soul (§ 34). There is a tension in this account which corresponds to Leibniz's attempt to grapple with both what I have called an 'Aristotelian' and a 'Platonic' problem about unity at the same time. There is a tendency to represent souls generally in the 'Aristotelian' way, as 'forms of bodies', as what makes bodies true unities and therefore substances. There is a competing tendency, in the case of a special class of soul, namely spirits, to regard them in a 'Platonic' way as separate substances.

Corresponding to Leibniz's 'Aristotelian' moments there is a genuine *unity* of soul and body which makes a person, animal or whatever into a substance. Corresponding to his 'Platonic' moments soul and body are separate and their so-called 'unity' consists in the close harmony between what happens in each. Leibniz seems to have believed, at the time of writing the *Discourse*, that he had managed to have it both ways, that he had explained 'how our body belongs to us, but without its being attached to our essence' (§ 33). But we human beings *are* bodies, though not *mere* bodies, according to one point of view. According to that point of view, our bodies *are* attached to our essence. On the other hand, if *we* are essentially something immaterial, i.e. *spirits*, then that our bodies belong to us consists in nothing more than the special causal relationship which exists between each of us and our particular bodies. On this account, however, our bodies belong to us as our *shadows* do, not as substances which can have effects on us. The only true substances are souls or things like souls and it is only to substances that causal powers can be attributed in accordance with the principle *actiones sunt suppositorum*.

We have already seen, in the previous chapter, how Leibniz subordinated the 'Aristotelian' problem to the 'Platonic' one and was led to the conclusion that the only true substances were monads or indivisible immaterial things possessed of something analogous to perception and appetition or striving. From a staunch insistence that 'we must maintain that bodies are substances and not merely true phenomena like the rainbow' (BW 154, G ii 72) Leibniz was led to reduce matter generally to the level of true or 'well-founded' phenomena. By this reduction, however, it was not his intention to put our bodies on the level of shadows. For, unlike shadows, bodies are in some sense constituted by an infinite number of living things. My relation to my body is that of a dominant monad to a mass of lower-order monads which are both able to resist and to respond to my will. The mind-body problem, on Leibniz's later theory, is simply part of the general problem of how substances can communicate with one another.

The later theory supposes that a monad is always attached to some matter and so it is not, strictly speaking, a dualist theory.[10] There is only one kind of created substance, according to the later theory. God is the only immaterial substance. Our materiality is the badge of our finiteness and general imperfection. Matter undergoes constant change. The unity of an organism, like the unity of the universe as a whole, is for Leibniz a sort of political unity.[11] Just as the universe as a whole, and more especially that part of it constituted by beings like ourselves, forms a 'republic' under the Sovereign Being, so my body is like a republic of monads to a lesser degree answerable to me. Indeed the same would be true of the tiniest creature observable under a microscope. Of course human beings have special qualities, like consciousness, memory and reason, which other created beings lack. But these special qualities are not relevant to the general problem of the relations between substances.

11.5.1 Causality and 'Expression'

Leibniz held that what we ordinarily take to be 'causes' are in metaphysical rigour 'merely concomitant requisites'. (PW 90, C 521) There is, in the language of Malebranche and Hume, no necessary connection between what is true of a substance which is said to 'cause' what happens to another and what happens in that other substance. We could not actually derive what happens in the second substance from what is true of the first.

Nonetheless there is a place for talk about causality, in that phenomena occur according to regular sequences and we can learn from experience that certain events only occur in the presence of certain others or are invariably followed by others. Although there is no 'influx' from one kind of event to another, we commonly call 'causes' those which are always present when the effect occurs and never present when it does not. The process of reaching conclusions of such an inductive sort is one which, in common with Hume, Leibniz took to be an animal one. Unlike Hume, however, Leibniz accorded to our exercise of reason a critical role of eliminating certain observed sequences in forming our beliefs about the true order of nature (PPL 550, G vi 506).

The order of phenomena is thus, for Leibniz, a well-founded

one—one therefore which must find its counterpart in the 'perceptions' of monads. The theory offered by Leibniz to explain what happens at the basic level of monads (which underwrites causal relations at the phenomenal level) is his theory of expression.

According to this theory, every substance is an expression of the whole universe. In the *Discourse* Leibniz puts this by saying that 'when one considers properly the connexion between things, one can say that there are in the soul of Alexander . . . traces of everything that happens in the universe' (§ 8). This *a priori* claim is one which Leibniz believed to agree with 'our experience of nature'. A vessel full of liquid may, he suggests, be considered as a microcosm of the whole universe. As motion set up in the middle is propagated to the edges, so its 'effects' become less and less perceptible as it recedes from its point of origin (PW 90, C 521). But, however imperceptible, such causal chains have their effects throughout the whole universe. The soul of Alexander bears traces of the whole universe, but of some parts *more distinctly* than others. This is how each substance expresses the whole universe from a unique perspective. So far as most of the universe is concerned it is expressed by any given substance in a very confused way. For it is only in respect of certain actions that an individual is close to the centre of the vessel, to use Leibniz's metaphor.

According to Leibniz it is in the nature of individual created substances to have 'perceptions', i.e. to express the universe in various ways. It is in the nature of created substances to be passive as well as active. Corresponding to the passivity of such substances will be relatively confused expressions and corresponding to their activity will be relatively distinct ones. The special relation between myself and that congregation of monads which gives substance to my body is to be explained by this difference: 'that whose expression is the more distinct is judged to act, and that whose expression is the more confused is judged to be passive . . .' (PW 79, G vii 312). In virtue of my more distinct perceptions it is *I*, and not my body, who is properly said to do something when carrying out my will. When I am merely receiving sensory impressions, however, my perceptions are relatively confused.

11.6 Spontaneity as an Explanatory Hypothesis

It is a consequence of Leibniz's theory of spontaneity that all our ideas are innate and this is stressed in the *Discourse* (see § 26–9). But he is not thereby required to deny that our ideas sometimes correspond to an objective world outside us or even that, in the ordinary sense, we can speak as if *some* of our ideas were 'derived' from the senses. That view, though he thought it a superficial one, he was prepared to grant to Locke at the outset of the *New Essays* (NEHU 74) for the sake of developing discussion on other points. Such a correspondence is, strictly speaking, underwritten by a pre-established harmony. Moreover the relation implied by saying that one thing 'expresses' another does not, for Leibniz, have to be that of similarity. An algebraic equation can 'express' a circle, though it in no way resembles one (see PPL 207, G vii 263). Thus Leibniz can allow that ideas of secondary qualities do express or correspond in a precise way to properties of objects (NEHU 131).

Leibniz's theory of spontaneity was thus intended to be consistent with belief in a material world and to allow, if only by courtesy of strict metaphysics, that it contains what can loosely be called 'substances' which 'interact' with one another. His metaphysics was not intended in any way to subvert the language of practical life nor, for that matter, to pre-empt empirical investigations into the nature of matter. On the contrary, he himself looked for confirmation for his metaphysical theory in the results of such investigations. An important example of this is his belief that there is an inherent *force* in all created things. It may even be true to say that Leibniz's metaphysics was motivated in part by his belief that the 'dead matter' of Cartesian mechanics and other scientific theories of his day was not defensible in empirical terms. That, at any rate, is the motivation claimed by Leibniz in the *New System*:

> ...when I tried to get to the bottom of the actual principles of mechanics in order to give an explanation of the laws of nature which are known through experience, I became aware that the consideration of an *extended mass* is not of itself enough, and that use must also be made of the notion of

force, which is fully intelligible, although it falls within the sphere of metaphysics. (§ 2)

The spirit of Modern philosophy was above all hostile to explanations which were more obscure than what was to be explained. Without some way of making the concept of 'force' intelligible Leibniz could not have justified proposing its introduction in physics. At this point metaphysics could, he believed, come to the rescue of mechanics. For the metaphysical theory of spontaneously acting substances corresponds to and can underwrite the apparent scientific requirement that a constant quantity of force is preserved in the universe. God is not constantly required to 'top up' depleted force since He has built into the universe at its most fundamental level the capacity for conserving the force with which it was originally endowed. The 'dead matter' theories required God's constant intervention and to those for whom, like Malebranche, that was in any case a fact of mechanics it was a natural enough extension to solve the mind-body problem by invoking divine interventions of a like kind. Leibniz believed his theory of a pre-established order with spontaneously acting substances constituted an advance on both fronts. By postulating a perfect spontaneity in the basic constituents of the universe and a pre-established harmony between them Leibniz believed he was able to explain phenomena in physics and metaphysics which otherwise seemed to him to defy explanation.

11.6.1 Monads and Human Souls

From a twentieth century standpoint one of the most problematic assumptions made by Leibniz is that the basic constituents of the universe—the monads—are to be understood in terms of an analogy with human souls. There was nothing original in this assumption, which had been accepted by those who believed in substantial forms. Indeed Leibniz clearly linked his acceptance of this analogy with his attempt to rehabilitate substantial forms. Their nature, he claims in the *New System*, consists of force and 'from this there follows something analogous to sense and to appetite'. Hence, he goes on, 'it was necessary to form a conception of them resembling the notion we have of *souls*' (§ 3). All substances have something like perception insofar as they have the capacity to 'express' or 'represent' the universe and not, of course, in virtue of having conscious experiences. All substances have something like appetite insofar as they contain an 'internal principle which produces change from one perception to another' (*Monadology*, S 15) and not, of course, in virtue of having desires.

The analogy between substances generally and human souls needs careful qualification. But Leibniz attached an importance to it, defending it by saying that 'the nature of things is uniform, and our nature cannot differ infinitely from the other simple substances of which the whole universe consists' (PPL 537, G ii 270). This claim embodies a major principle which Leibniz deployed extensively from 1687 onwards—his principle of 'continuity'. This principle is sometimes expressed by saying that there are no 'gaps' in the created order. There is a huge difference between a human soul and the simple substances which give being, for example, to a lump of rock. But, according to Leibniz, the difference is not infinite. On the contrary the apparent 'gap' is bridged by a whole series of substances each of which differs from its neighbour only in the minutest detail.

The consequences for Leibniz's metaphysics of his analogy between the basic constituents of the universe and human souls are far-reaching. Leibniz made no bones about the fact that his 'system' provided a way of giving a good sense, amongst other views, to 'the vitalism of the Cabalists and hermetic philosophers who put a kind of feeling into everything' (PPL 496, G iv 524). Mechanistic explanations, Leibniz always insisted, are what should be sought for particular phenomena. But ultimately the universe is animated by spontaneously-acting beings. Whereas 'in the case of bodies everything happens mechanically, that is, through the intelligible qualities of bodies, namely magnitude, shape and motion; in the case of souls, everything is to be explained in vital terms, that is, through the intelligible qualities of the soul, namely perception and appetites' (PW 173, C 12).

A major doubt raised by Modern philosophy was whether there is room for purposive beings in a mechanistic universe. Leibniz's project of resolving this doubt brings together two dimensions of his metaphysics. One of these is his 'ontology', his theory of the kinds of basic entities which make up the universe. It is this dimension with which we have been mainly concerned in this part.

In later years Leibniz became increasingly interested in a somewhat different dimension of metaphysics, that which was concerned with the principles assumed in the other sciences. The role of metaphysics as 'the first of the sciences' was to provide a basis for the principles of the other sciences. In this conception of metaphysics Leibniz took himself to be following Aristotle, whom Leibniz credits with the view that 'metaphysics asks for nothing from the other sciences, and provides them with the principles they need' (NEHU 449f.). Metaphysics should seek to demonstrate the principles of the other sciences, i.e. to derive them from higher principles. These higher principles, as we shall see in Part Four, are purposive in character. They turn on Leibniz's belief that the world has a perfect Creator and therefore that it is formed in accordance with principles of perfection.

Notes

1 See his letter to Foucher of 16 April 1695. Leibniz's letter does not mention dying or posterity. Instead he inquires after Foucher's health, adding: 'for some time mine has not been of the soundest. That's what makes me think of publishing some of my thoughts, among others my system of the communication of substances' (G i 420).

2 Leibniz, significantly, did not adopt the autobiographical mode in the draft of the *New System*. His reason for adopting it in the published version may have been to present himself as a seeker after truth rather than as someone with 'a passion for preconceived opinions' (§ 1). Descartes implies a similar humility in his *Discourse* but it seems clear that both the *Discourse* and the *Meditations* offer an order of discovery which the reader is invited to retrace.

3 Translated from a plan for a work on science in Eduard Bodemann (ed.) *Die Leibniz Handschriften in der Königlichen Öffentlichen Bibliothek zu Hannover*, Hanover, 1895, xxxvii, iv, 9–10.

4 In introducing his 'agreeable opinion' to Foucher (quoted in Section 8.4 above), Leibniz wrote that it was 'very different from that of the author of the *Recherche*' (G i 382). The doubt, expressed in Leibniz's own time and even now, as to whether it really is that different from Malebranche seems to have been encouraged by playing down the doctrine of spontaneity. Leibniz himself seems to have done this, calling his theory 'the system of pre-established harmony', perhaps to avoid the charge of 'innovation'.

But, as we saw in Chapter 9, there is reason for doubting whether Leibniz succeeded in preserving contingency and spontaneity, and that could be taken as a doubt as to whether he effectively distances himself from Malebranche's view that God alone is a true cause.

5 The 'strong defence' of spontaneity is conspicuous in the notes Leibniz wrote in May 1686 (BW 118, G ii 47) in response to a letter from Arnauld and also, though less conspicuously, in his reply dated 14 July 1686 (BW 133–5, G ii 57f.). Leibniz appears, at this time, to have confused what is contained *in* something's nature with what arises *from* its nature. The former is a way of talking consequential upon the *inesse* principle, the latter is what is implied by talking of *spontaneity*. The separation is made in Leibniz's summary in his letter to Arnauld of 23 March 1690.

6 It is not true, therefore, that it is a 'logical' principle or (as has sometimes been supposed) that Leibniz's metaphysics is derived from his logic. The theory of essences or natures is metaphysical, whether general or individual. It is true that Leibniz arrived at his doctrine of the individual nature partly by 'logical' considerations such as those which allowed statements about individuals to be treated as universals (LP 66, C 377). But the unoriginality of the framework within which such developments were made should not distract attention from the fact that the language of 'essences' and 'natures' was laden with metaphysical commitments.

7 This probably connects in Leibniz's thought with substances being made in the image of God and God acting 'by the spontaneity of his excellent nature'. This phrase occurs in a paper on jurisprudence of around 1706, quoted from *The Political Writings of Leibniz* trans and ed. Patrick Riley, Cambridge, Cambridge University Press, 1972, p.71.

8 For Leibniz the fact that 'the simplest system is always preferred in astronomy' is based on what 'reason desires' (*Discourse* § 6).

9 Force in bodies, for instance, corresponds to 'appetite' in monads. Leibniz seems generally to have been committed to a thorough-going analogy between everything in the natural order (see below Section 11.6.1).

10 '... I see no reason, either religious or philosophical, which compels me to abandon the doctrine of the parallelism of soul and body to admit a perfect separation. For why cannot the soul always retain a subtle body organized after its own manner...?' (PPL 556, G vi 533).

11 There is some basis for comparison, Leibniz believed, between the way in which God is *dominant* in the universe and the soul or self is dominant in a human body (PW 136, G vii 302).

PART FOUR

The Place of Metaphysics

12   Metaphysics and the Natural Sciences

> By this we see, a little better than by what is commonly said about it, how
> the true physics should in fact be derived from the source of the divine
> perfections. It is God who is the ultimate reason of things, and the
> knowledge of God is no less the beginning of science than his essence and
> will are the beginning of beings. The most reasonable philosophers agree
> with this, but few of them can use it to discover any truths of importance.
> Perhaps these little samples will arouse some of them to go much further.
> (PPL 353, G iii 52)

These remarks were made by Leibniz in a paper he wrote in 1687
where he made a critique of Cartesian mechanics. That earlier
critique began what later became known as the *vis viva*
controversy. A version of it is included in *Discourse* § 17. But the
Discourse is rather vague about just what could be inferred for
physics from the assumption that the world was created by a
perfect being:[1]

> ...one can say that in whatever way God had created the world, it would
> always have been regular and in a certain order. But God has chosen the
> one which is the most perfect, that is to say the one which is at the same
> time the simplest in hypotheses and the richest in phenomena... (§ 6)

It may seem as if Leibniz is engaged, here and elsewhere, in the
pretentious exercise of deriving the nature of the world from the
nature of the divine wisdom. But Leibniz is careful to stress that
God does things because they are good—they are *not* good just
because God does them (*Discourse* § 2). There are, that is to say,
objective standards of goodness, as also of beauty, wisdom, and
so on, to which God conforms in a perfectly exemplary
way—standards which are independent of God's will. Leibniz
believed we could know what these standards are and *thereby*
know what kind of world an infinitely wise and powerful being
would create. Although, therefore, Leibniz's philosophy of

science cannot be separated from his theology, his theory of divine wisdom is derived from what he was prepared to count as 'wise' or 'rational'. God's construction of the world thus corresponds to Leibniz's standards for good scientific theorizing.

12.1 The Principle of Economy

Among these standards is that a theory should have as few hypotheses or assumptions as possible and as many consequences derivable from them as possible. That is why the most perfect world would be one which is 'simplest in hypotheses and richest in phenomena'. As Leibniz himself explains:

> ... in the matter of wisdom, decrees or hypotheses represent expenses in proportion as they are more independent of one another: for reason desires that multiplicity of hypotheses or principles should be avoided, in almost the same way as the simplest system is always preferred in astronomy. (*Discourse*, § 5)

That there is a God at all is something Leibniz characteristically infers from the common assumption that the universe is thoroughly intelligible and rational, together with the assumption that the world does not contain within itself the explanation for its existence (see Section 8.8 above). The first of these assumptions is as fundamental to Leibniz's philosophy as the principle of contradiction. In a vague form it pervades the whole of Leibniz's philosophy. It is only in his mature writings, however, that Leibniz began to spell out the implications of stating it more precisely. This process was begun in the *Discourse* and considerably developed in succeeding years.

The principle of sufficient reason can be articulated in many ways and is variously articulated by Leibniz at different times and with different issues at stake. In the *Discourse* it makes its appearance in the form of a denial that anything could happen in the universe which is 'absolutely irregular' (§ 6). Everything, he claims, can be subsumed under a rule or law. This is true even of miracles (§ 7) though they are distinguished from the ordinary course of events by the fact that human beings are not able to state the general laws which would explain their occurrence. Human beings could, however, hope to provide explanations for 'natural operations' and indeed the principle of sufficient reason was later used by Leibniz as a device for excluding the importation of 'occult' or otherwise mysterious properties into scientific explanations (PW 172f., C 11f.).

The orderliness of the universe is connected by Leibniz with its being *'regular'*, i.e. governed by rules. That in turn is connected with there being *explanations* or *reasons* for everything. The *Discourse* stresses regularity rather than explicability or rationality. But the way was open for Leibniz to explore further what is involved in the thought that there is a proper explanation for everything, i.e. that there is what we should count as a proper scientific explanation. The implications of this thought are hinted at in the *Discourse* by Leibniz's remark that the universe is the one which is 'the simplest in hypotheses and the richest in phenomena'. A *perfect* universe is one which would exemplify the scientific principle of economy in hypotheses to the highest degree.

There would, of course, be no virtue in a theory using only a few hypotheses if nothing could be explained by means of it. The principle of economy in hypotheses is that of preferring, as between theories which are *equally 'rich'* in consequences, the one which has fewest assumptions. Many different sorts of justification have been given for this principle. But Leibniz's justification is an extreme form of scientific realism. The world is so constituted that to construct theories which multiply hypotheses unnecessarily is to lose one's way in the search after truth.

12.2 Perfection and the Unity of Science

The late seventeenth century saw a remarkable burgeoning of the experimental sciences. There was what we would nowadays call a knowledge 'explosion'. Leibniz was clearly excited by this and eager to keep in touch with all the significant developments in the special sciences. Advances in microscope technology, for instance, had effectively brought into existence the discipline of micro-biology. Leibniz believed that this new branch of science provided confirmation of some results he had reached by metaphysical reasoning—that in every particle of matter there is contained a whole world of tiny creatures and that organic death is really a kind of transformation (*New System* § 7). But there were also many developments in the mathematical sciences like optics and mechanics. Leibniz was impressed by the principles apparently involved in theories of light. The fact that light seemed always to travel by the 'easiest' path seemed to him a wonderful illustration both of the economy of nature and of its purposiveness (*Discourse* § 22).

That there are purposes in nature was an assumption excluded from mechanics, where explanations were given solely in terms of 'efficient causes'. But Leibniz came to believe that Descartes' laws of motion could not be squared with the experimental results (*Discourse* § 17). This failure, he claimed, was linked to the fact that Descartes' account violated a fundamental principle which governed all changes in nature. The principle itself might be expressed in an old maxim, that nature does not proceed by 'leaps'. Leibniz called it his *principle of continuity*. Its implication for physics, he claimed, was that all changes take place gradually—indeed infinitely gradually.

Leibniz considered the principle of continuity to be a quite general principle which applied in physics no less than in geometry, and in zoology no less than metaphysics. Hence he was willing to infer from it that 'all the orders of natural beings form but a single chain in which different kinds like so many links clasp one another so firmly that it is impossible for the senses and imagination to fix the exact point where one begins or ends' (S 187). There are no sharp distinctions between species, the 'gradations' being known distinctly only by God. All form part of a 'great chain of being',[2] a chain with links between man and animals and animals and plants.

This speculation by Leibniz was a seminal one which, through Lamarck, contributed to the main line of development of the life sciences in the eighteenth century. Yet to us, it seems a *mere* speculation. For why should the principle of continuity admit of the generalization which licenses the inference that there are no 'leaps' between species? Leibniz's answer is to be found in the kind of unity he believed the sciences to have. It is inconsistent with the unity of science that physics and the life sciences should be seen as wholly autonomous branches of inquiry founded on principles which bore no relation to one another.[3] There had to be a convergence between the higher principles of the special sciences if the principle of economy was true. This convergence, Leibniz believed, could be brought out by metaphysics, by showing how the sciences were derivable from the divine perfections. His discovery of the principle of continuity encouraged Leibniz to develop this aspect of his metaphysics much further than he had done in the *Discourse*.

12.3 Perfection and Plenitude

Leibniz inherited the assumption, made use of in the Ontological Argument (see Section 5.4), that God possesses all the perfections and that therefore He is the most real being (*ens realissimum*). He sought to clarify this assumption in the *Discourse*, defining a 'perfection' by excluding from the 'perfections' only 'the forms or natures which are not susceptible of an ultimate degree' (§ 1). Among the perfections he could, accordingly, include knowledge, power and wisdom. To say that God's knowledge is infinitely more *perfect* than that of any human being is to say that it is infinitely more *real*. But not only is any given perfection possessed more fully by God but all perfections are. There is an infinite variety of such perfections which are in some way part of God's nature. Any world created by God must in both these respects be as full and as varied as possible. This line of thought may well have informed Leibniz's claim that God's choice of worlds must be of that which is 'richest in phenomena' (*Discourse* § 6).

12.4 The Identity of Indiscernibles

The *principle of economy* (of divine decrees and hypotheses) and the *principle of plenitude* (of substances and phenomena) really constitute a twin principle. There is no virtue in simplicity without variety or in profusion without order. Hence the world does not contain every substance that is possible in itself but only the number of substances that conforms to the requirements of order. The order of the universe needs to maximize the variety of the universe without duplication. The metaphor used by Leibniz to capture this is that the universe is a city of which there is an infinite variety of variously related views obtainable from different positions. Each substance is like a perspective point on this city. There are no two substances which are exactly alike since each has a unique perspective (*Discourse* § 9).

In the *Discourse* and in the writings of 1686–87 Leibniz sought to derive many of his metaphysical beliefs from his theory of the individual substance together with a general appeal to the fact that everything is connected with everything else. In particular he presented the identity of indiscernibles as a requirement of the *inesse* principle. Otherwise there could be several individual substances which shared the same full concept and there would be no principle of individuation for them. In the *Discourse*, as we have seen, Leibniz had an open mind as to what exactly could be taken as a 'true substance' in full metaphysical rigour. The identity of indiscernibles was intended to have the consequence, therefore, that there were no two organisms which differed only numerically. Leibniz did not, however, restrict the identity of indiscernibles in accordance with his later, more stringent, view of what could count as a simple substance. He took it to apply no less to complex entities like organisms and sought, accordingly, an alternative basis for it.

This search seems to have played a part in the displacement of the *inesse* principle from the pride of place it enjoyed in the *Discourse*.[4] At one stage Leibniz seems to have believed that he could derive the principle of sufficient reason from the *inesse* principle and so insist that 'it must be possible to give a reason' why different individuals are taken as *different* (PW 88, C 519). From this he concluded that 'two perfectly similar eggs, or two perfectly similar leaves or blades of grass, will never be found.' But this conclusion only follows if eggs, leaves, and so on are substances. If they are not substances, strictly speaking, and yet the identity of indiscernibles applies to them, the principle of sufficient reason must be more than a corollary of the *inesse* principle.

The principle of sufficient reason is the chief of a whole band of principles which Leibniz came to employ in later years, which included the principle of perfection and the twin principles of economy and plenitude. From these principles Leibniz inferred that the identity of indiscernibles applied quite generally. In his correspondence with Samuel Clarke (1715–16) Leibniz appealed to these principles to criticize the 'superficial' philosophy which supposed there were atoms or empty spaces. Leibniz had long believed that the universe was a *plenum* in which everything was interconnected with everything else. He eventually took the view that absolute space and time (as maintained by Newton and, following him, Clarke) was an abstraction. One of his arguments for this was that different parts of space and time considered in themselves, would be indiscernible. Indeed he claimed that 'these great principles of a Sufficient Reason and of the Identity of Indiscernibles change the state of metaphysics...' (G vii 373).

12.5 The Role of Metaphysics

The universe, Leibniz claimed, is governed by certain fundamental principles of order. These principles of order do not allow the different sciences to be *sui generis*, each with its own basic principles not reducible to or comparable with those of any other. Just as everything in the universe is perfectly connected, so everything in science is perfectly connected (S 185). On this basis Leibniz believed that there would always be a fundamental correspondence between the more profound aspects of every science. Metaphysics might, he believed, attempt to identify what these fundamental correspondences were.

By this means Leibniz claimed that mechanistic and purposive explanations of the world could ultimately be reconciled. A complete explanation of force could not be given in purely mechanistic terms, i.e. in terms of size, figure and motion. Its explanation had to be sought in metaphysics, in the conceptions of substance and soul which metaphysics provides (*New System* § 3). The role of metaphysics was thus to unify and complement the special sciences by explaining what they could not explain on their own terms. Metaphysics provided a broad explanatory framework which might indeed direct scientific investigation in certain ways (*Discourse* § 22) and even help to resolve questions (e.g. about atoms) which would otherwise be a matter for speculation. But metaphysics could not contradict unambiguous results of the special sciences. If Leibniz's conception of metaphysics was, in the well-known phrase, as 'the queen of the sciences', she was for Leibniz a constitutional monarch. Although Leibniz believed that metaphysics might *explain* the principles and fundamental concepts of the special sciences, he did not suppose that metaphysics might undertake to discover them.

The charge commonly levelled against 'Rationalist' metaphysics has been that it abrogated from the autonomy of the special sciences. But this charge cannot justly be made against Leibniz. He did, to be sure, believe that metaphysical claims could be more certain than theories embraced by some natural scientists. But these metaphysical claims were not self-evident. On the contrary, Leibniz characteristically argued for them on the basis of their fruitfulness in the sciences. His confidence in the law of continuity was based on its pertinence to the problems of mechanics. His application of this law in polemical discussions against 'action at a distance' and generally against any kinds of 'gaps' in nature involves a generalization from the cases where he believed its scientific credentials had been established. It is in virtue of the scientific credibility of this and other principles in the natural sciences that Leibniz came to the view that 'the true physics should in fact be derived from the divine perfections' (PPL 353, G iii 52). Leibniz was not proposing to make the natural sciences subservient to dogmas about 'the divine perfections'. On the contrary, as I have tried to bring out in this chapter, the natural sciences themselves supplied Leibniz with the relevant content for talk about 'perfection' in the construction of the universe. As the natural sciences increased in autonomy, so the conception of metaphysics as an autonomous discipline dear to Rationalism became increasingly difficult to defend. Metaphysics was well-begun in Leibniz's own life-time on the state of crisis about its own identity and validity which has largely dogged it since.

Notes

1 In spite of having the title *Traité sur les Perfections de Dieu*. The *Discourse* has a theological context. The scientific criticism of Descartes' laws of motion is illustrative.

2 This aspect of Leibniz's philosophy is discussed in A.O. Lovejoy's *The Great Chain of Being*, Cambridge, Mass., Harvard University Press, 1939, Chapter V.

3 Hence his claim, in the *New Essays* (quoted and discussed in Chapter 7, Note 12 above) that 'the foundations are always the same'.

4 That the principle of sufficient reason is richer than and so not a mere corollary of the *inesse* principle has been argued above, Chapter 8. See also O. Hanfling's 'Leibniz's Principle of Reason', *Studia Leibnitiana*, *9* (1980), pp. 67–73.

13   Science and Religion

Whoever considers these matters honestly will hold to the middle way in philosophy and do justice to theology as well as to physics... Nature has, as it were, an empire within an empire, a double kingdom, so to speak, of reason and necessity, or of forms and particles of matter, for just as all things are full of souls, they are also full of organic bodies. These kingdoms are governed, each by its own law, with no confusion between them, and the cause of perception and appetite is no more to be sought in the modes of extension than is the cause of nutrition and of the other organic functions to be sought in the forms or souls... By thus combining both types of interpretation, we shall serve, in the consideration of the individual phenomena of nature, both our welfare in life and our perfection of mind, and wisdom no less than piety. (PPL 409f., G iv 392)

With these words Leibniz concluded his 'Critical Remarks on the General Part of the Descartes' *Principles*', the most extended of his attempts in the 1690s to produce a definitive judgement on Descartes' philosophy. The religious orthodoxy of Descartes' philosophy had been questioned and indeed was denied by those wedded to Scholastic theology. Leibniz believed he was able to find a middle way between Scholastic and Modern philosophy and to reconcile science with piety. His doctrine of the two 'kingdoms'—what he later referred to respectively as the 'Kingdom of Nature' and the 'Kingdom of Grace'—sums up in a graphic way his proposals for an amicable division of the territory disputed between orthodox theology and science as conceived by philosophers in the Modern tradition.

It is commonplace that the intellectual authority of the Church had been challenged by Galileo and others—in particular the right of the Church to pronounce on the natural world had been questioned. Descartes' theory of matter was seen by many as a further incursion against this right. For, in the theory of transubstantiation (see Section 3.3 above), it was held that the consecrated bread underwent a physical transformation into the body of Christ. That theory had seemed intelligible to Scholastic philosophers but it made no sense in Cartesian terms. It was not necessary for Descartes to deny the theory outright. His philosophy was quickly put under suspicion of unorthodoxy and indeed, in some religious orders, the teaching of Cartesianism was banned outright.

Leibniz himself showed little inclination to impugn Descartes' religious orthodoxy beyond pointing out that there were unresolved difficulties in the way of 'doing justice to theology' in Cartesian terms. But this was one respect in which he regarded his metaphysics as a step forward. Writing to his Catholic employer in 1679 he claimed: 'There is another important thing in my philosophy which will give it access to the Jesuits and other theologians. This is my restoration of substantial forms, which the atomists and Cartesians claim to have exterminated' (PPL 261, A II 488). More generally, in the *Discourse*, Leibniz devoted a whole section to expatiating on the 'utility' of the principles he had expounded 'in matters of piety and religion' (§ 32). Again, in the *New System*, Leibniz did not hesitate to point out the 'advantages' of the hypothesis he was offering in showing, for instance, 'the immortality of our soul . . . in a marvellously clear light' (§ 16). These 'advantages' are not incidental to Leibniz's metaphysics. On the contrary it was one of his major objectives to secure them.

13.1 Leibniz's Alleged 'Bias' towards Theology

This fact has been a major stumbling-block to sympathetic treatment of Leibniz's philosophy and has been a major source of misinterpretation of it. Leibniz's attempt to secure these 'advantages' for faith and morals has been seen as unworthy of a true philosopher and even as a kind of intellectual dishonesty. This is one major source of the kind of view of Leibniz put forward by Russell:

> ... there are two systems of philosophy which may be regarded as representing Leibniz: one, which he proclaimed, was optimistic, orthodox, fantastic, and shallow; the other, which has been slowly unearthed from his

manuscripts by fairly recent editors, was profound, coherent, largely Spinozistic, and amazingly logical. (*History of Western Philosophy*, p.563)

Russell's accusation that Leibniz 'was wholly destitute of those higher philosophical virtues that are so notable in Spinoza' is based on his view that Leibniz was deliberately pandering to religious orthodoxy to further his career. But this greatly exaggerates Leibniz's orthodoxy and ignores the fact that Leibniz's refusal to turn Catholic was a frequent obstacle to his finding a better position than the one he held in Hanover. It is true that he was under pressure from friends at court to publish the *Theodicy*. But there is no reason whatever to suppose that his way of reconciling faith and reason was itself determined in any way by his need for patronage. Russell's accusation tells us more about his own conception of philosophical virtue than it does about Leibniz. His doctrine of the two philosophies of Leibniz turns out, on examination, to be a distinction between those parts of Leibniz's philosophy which fit in to some extent with what Russell took to be a proper way of doing philosophy and those parts which manifestly do not.

Central to Russell's accusation is the mistaken belief that, at least in his private writings, Leibniz was a 'rationalist' philosopher who sought to base his metaphysics on firm logical or epistemological foundations. This mistake, by no means peculiar to Russell, is partly motivated by a conception of how philosophy ought to be practised. Philosophy, according to this conception, is the ultimate arbiter of human knowledge, providing the basis on which any claims to knowledge are ultimately to be validated. It is held to be unworthy of a philosopher to take starting-points which are not themselves validated in this way. Accordingly it must always be improper for a philosopher to give a privileged status to beliefs which are held independently, such as Christian beliefs. That is a compromise of the judicial role of philosophy—in short, a form of 'bias'.

This conception of philosophy can recognize as legitimate, if erroneous, the competing programmes of Rationalism and Empiricism. Indeed it may be the prevalence of this conception which has made for the emphasis on this Gog and Magog of Modern philosophy in philosophical curricula. The expectation that Leibniz should be a Rationalist may, in some measure, have been reinforced by the requirement that philosophy should be the ultimate arbiter of claims to knowledge. However that may be, Leibniz made no pretence of living up to this expectation. On the contrary, he repeatedly claimed it as an advantage of his system that it could throw light on beliefs he regarded as admissible without the warrant of philosophy. Reason might subvert what is taken on faith or illuminate it, just as it may contradict or explain what we take ourselves to perceive through our senses. But the demand that what is accepted on authority be consistent with philosophy (on which Leibniz certainly wanted to insist) is importantly different from the demand that its acceptance is made conditional upon its having the support of philosophy. 'Doing justice to theology' or, for that matter, natural science would not be possible unless they enjoyed a degree of autonomy both from each other and from metaphysics. Metaphysics, as a unifying and explanatory science, needs, on Leibniz's understanding of it, to answer both to the results of natural science and to the requirements of piety. It may, therefore, not only be *hypothetical* in its content (as is, for instance, Leibniz's theory that all organic death involves not more than a transformation) but also *ideological*.

13.2 The Ideological Content of Leibniz's Metaphysics

The 'ideological' content of a metaphysical theory is that part of it which has some practical import and for that reason enjoys a protected status in the theory. Beliefs of an ideological kind survive the discovery that the reasons given for them are inadequate. Where they are found to be inconsistent with the theory being put forward it is the theory which is amended. Ideological beliefs enjoy a protected status and therefore a relative degree of stability as compared with other parts of a theory.

Evidence of such beliefs in Leibniz's metaphysics is brought to light by looking at his writings diachronically. There are, as we have seen, no major differences in the conclusions Leibniz drew in his *New System* compared with the relevant parts of the *Discourse*. But there are significant differences in the arguments offered and in the status claimed for the conclusions. The claim of spontaneity and autonomy in created substances and the corresponding denial of interaction between them, the principle of the identity of indiscernibles, and several other elements of Leibniz's metaphysics might appear, to judge from the *Discourse* alone, to be consequences drawn from what Leibniz at one time called his 'great principle'—that the predicate of any true proposition is to be found in the complete concept of its subject. But these conclusions are preserved in Leibniz's later philosophy on quite different bases. That he inferred them from his generalized *inesse* principle appears therefore to have been quite incidental to Leibniz's willingness to believe them. Their 'utility' in 'matters of piety and religion', on the other hand, is not.

Most of Leibniz's definitional requirements of substance (see Section 8.2 above) are ones on which he could invoke some support from past philosophers. The requirement that an individual substance must have some kind of unity, agency and autonomy, for instance, was commonplace enough. But Leibniz came to insist on true unity and that every created substance 'has a perfect spontaneity (which becomes freedom in the case of intelligent substances), that everything which happens to it is a consequence of its idea or being, and that nothing determines it, apart from God alone' (*Discourse* § 32). He recommends these results partly on the ground that they 'serve . . . to strengthen' religion: 'nothing gives us a better understanding of immortality than this independence and extent of the soul'. And such an understanding serves in turn to promote the sense of belonging to that community of minds which constitutes the 'Kingdom of Grace'.

The ultimate triumph of what Leibniz understands by the 'Kingdom of Grace' constitutes, in eschatological terms, a vindication of the *homme honnête* discussed earlier, in Chapter 7. Freedom and individuality are, or so we are to believe, ultimately reconcilable with absolute obedience to a higher rational order. Freedom does not require the possibility of arbitrary exercises of will. Nor does it require that future events are not foreseeable or ordained by God. Equally our absolute dependence on God does not mean that we are not true individual substances, with a unique identity and a capacity for 'spontaneous' action. But this ultimate triumph requires that humans are not just parts of a world describable in mechanist terms. This is underwritten by the unity of substances, for anything which is part of the world conceived in mechanistic terms is further divisible and so not a true unity. But Leibniz's theory of the individual substance does not just serve to 'strengthen' religion in general but a highly intellectual form of it.

In conventional terms Leibniz was not a pious man. He did not attend Church and gained the reputation of being an unbeliever. Leibniz's god was indeed the god of a philosopher. It is not surprising that Leibniz's doctrine that spirits are made in the image of God can be turned on its head. God becomes the absolutely rational philosopher-king who perfectly conforms to the eternal laws of justice and goodness. He is an *homme honnête* writ large and perfected, Whose actions are totally free of any wilfulness and Whose creation of the world exhibits perfect wisdom and goodness.

In allowing that there is an ideological content to Leibniz's theology and metaphysics one need not be committed to a reductionist theory about these subjects. It is simply that someone who believes that man is made in the image of God may well be drawn into defending a particular view of God in order to defend a particular view of man. Nor do I intend to detract from Leibniz's metaphysics by saying that some of its starting-points lie outside philosophy. My point is that noting these starting-points helps us to see why Leibniz was specially concerned with certain problems in particular and why he sought the solutions for them that he did.

13.3 Nature as 'an Empire within an Empire'

Leibniz's theory of pre-established harmony, although offered as a solution to the mind-body problem and more generally as a solution to the problem as to how substances can communicate with one another, serves him also as a theory of the relation between the two 'Kingdoms':

> The soul follows its own laws, and the body its own likewise, and they agree
> with each other by virtue of the harmony pre-established between all
> substances, since they are all representations of one and the same
> universe...
> Souls act according to the laws of final causes through their appetitions,
> ends, and means. Bodies according to the laws of efficient causes or the
> laws of motion. And the two kingdoms, that of efficient and that of final
> causes, are in harmony with one another. (*Monadology*, § 79f.)

The autonomy of the Kingdom of Nature corresponds with the
autonomy of natural science discussed in the previous chapter.
Accordingly, the principle of sufficient reason takes both a
purposive form (as the principle of perfection) and *mechanistic*
form, as the principle that 'in the case of bodies everything
occurs mechanically, that is, through the intelligible qualities of
bodies, namely, magnitude, shape and motion' (PW 173, C 12).
Yet the physical world cannot be sufficiently explained in
mechanistic terms, according to Leibniz. Physics must make use
of concepts like force which, he claims, can only be understood
in metaphysical terms. Thus nature is 'an empire within an
empire' (PPL 409, G iv 392) and ultimately the autonomy of
natural science is limited by the need to explain its concepts and
principles in terms drawn from metaphysics. To the extent that
natural science is autonomous, in Leibniz's view, the range of
matters concerning which it can claim to offer explanations is
limited.

Although Leibniz thus accommodated physics and theology
to one another, he did so on terms which limited the scope of
natural science. Yet these terms, as it seemed to him, accorded
entirely with the spirit of Modern science. Explanations had to
be in terms of 'intelligible notions'. If the understanding of the
world which could be achieved in terms of magnitude, shape
and motion was limited, that limitation was to be seen as having
its basis in human nature:

> Imagine that some angel wished to explain to us how bodies are made
> heavy; he could achieve nothing by speaking, however beautifully, about a
> substantial form, or sympathy, or other beings of this kind. Rather he
> would only satisfy our curious understanding when he gave us an
> explanation, sufficiently understood, which, when we have comprehended
> it, will enable us to demonstrate with geometric certainty the gravity must
> necessarily arise from it. This angel must therefore necessarily present only

such things as we can perceive distinctly. (PPL 289, from the unpublished manuscripts in Hanover, XXXVII, iv, 5)

Corresponding to the two kingdoms is a distinction between 'two kinds of distinct attributes, one of which must be sought in mathematics, the other in metaphysics'. Leibniz lists them as follows:

Mathematical science provides magnitude, figure, situation, and their variations, but metaphysics provides existence, duration, action and passion, force of acting, and end of action, or the perception of the agent. (PPL 289, unpublished manuscripts XXXVII, iv, 6)

Such lists of intelligible notions give teeth to the general requirement of the principle of sufficient reason. Within the mathematical sciences only explanations in terms of the 'primary' qualities are to be admitted; within metaphysics, only such explanations as involve notions we distinctly perceive in ourselves. The former kinds of explanation will be mechanistic: but the purposive explanations of metaphysics are more far-reaching, as are those explanations of why everything is as it is which lie outside human comprehension.

13.4 The 'Correction' of Metaphysics

Leibniz's attempt to 'do justice to theology as well as to physics' involved him in according a mediating role to metaphysics. But whereas there was at least some consensus amongst Modern philosophers as to what the fundamental explanatory categories of physics should be, there was no consensus in the case of metaphysics. At any rate, though there was perhaps some agreement as to what the fundamental explanatory categories of metaphysics were, there was no agreement as to how to understand them. As Leibniz claimed, in his 'Reflections on the Advancement of Real Metaphysics...':[1]

Substance, accident, cause, action, relation or proportion, and quantity and other terms are always being talked about, while their true notions have not yet been clarified: for these are fertile in beautiful truths while the ones we have are sterile. (*Correspondance de Bossuet*, Vol. 6, p. 523f.)

Leibniz proposed no easy route to the discovery of 'the true and fruitful concepts, not only of substance, but of cause ... (etc.)' (PPL 432, G iv 468). They were not to be justified by a kind of intuition such as would provide a starting-point for a Rationalist epistemology. They had to be justified by their fruitfulness in explaining the difficulties. 'The true sign of a clear and distinct notion is one's having the means for giving *a priori* proofs of many truths about it' (NEHU 219). A clear and distinct notion of substance is one which, *inter alia*, would enable one to explain how substances can communicate with one another. 'I hope', Leibniz once wrote, 'that this great problem will be resolved in such a clear manner, that that of itself will serve as a proof to judge that we have found the key to some of these things ...' (*Correspondance de Bossuet*, Vol. 6, pp. 527f.).

Metaphysics, so understood, is an interpretative science which seeks to explain whether, and in what sense, certain things are true which are commonly believed to be so. It takes such common beliefs as its 'data' and tries to find out how much reason there is for them. In this way it also sorts out conflicts between them, trying to find a 'good sense' for beliefs that are dismissed simply out of a 'sectarian spirit which imposes limits on itself by spurning others' (PPL 496, G iv 524).

Leibniz claimed that it was possible to preserve many of the insights of the philosophical 'sects' in a unified perspective:

> ...the vitalism of the Cabalists and the hermetic philosophers who put a kind of feeling into everything; the forms and entelechies of Aristotle and the Scholastics; and even the mechanical explanation of all particular phenomena by Democritus and the moderns; etc.—all of these are found united as if in a single perspective centre from which the object, which is obscured when considered from any other approach, reveals its regularity and the correspondence of its parts. (PPL 496, G iv 524)

Leibniz believed that one major fault in the metaphysics of his time was its failure to take a sufficiently catholic view of the 'phenomena' and therefore the 'difficulties' with which metaphysics should be concerned. It was this failure which led to the division of metaphysics into different sects, each over emphasizing the value of what it had to contribute. But there are two sides to this coin. For the selective view of the problems complained of in the Cartesians, for instance, is due to their willingness to put traditional beliefs on one side and to try to find a new and sounder basis for determining our beliefs about the world. In their defence it may be said that to take a catholic view of the metaphysical agenda is already to confer a privileged status on what are no more than received opinions. To justify a metaphysics on the basis that it can resolve traditional difficulties is in some measure to go in a circle. For these are difficulties only if there is something to be said for the beliefs on account of which they arise in the first place. A metaphysics which finds a way to accommodate these beliefs will have a theoretical counterpart to them. The circularity comes in when that accommodation is cited as a confirmation of the theory.

If, to take a conspicuous example, we accept the Platonic requirement that a substance be a real being, a true unity, then there is a difficulty for the common belief that there are material substances. One way of resolving this difficulty, proposed by Leibniz in the *Discourse*, was to say that material substances derive their unity from something non-material (a substantial form) and that their essence could not consist of extension alone. But it was open, as Arnauld pointed out, for a Cartesian to deny the assumption on which the difficulty arose: '...this fact, that the body has no true unity when its essence is extension, cannot be put forward to prove that extension is not of the essence of the body; for, perhaps, the essence of the body has no true unity' (BW 176f., G ii 87).

The difficulty that arises for Leibniz's metaphysics is that the 'true and fruitful' or 'distinct' notion of substance which he sought to justify by the light it shed on problems is itself caught up in this circularity.[2] He himself had joined in the complaint that only a Cartesian clearly and distinctly perceived as true what Descartes proposed as clear and distinct ideas. But with his own criteria of clarity and distinctness he seems to be hoist by his own petard. Or at any rate he seems to be to the extent that the confirmation of his metaphysics requires a peculiarly Leibnizian perception of the problems.

Notes

1 Leibniz's own French version of his *De primae philosophiae emendatione* paper was sent to Bossuet and is included by Ch. Urban and E. Levesque in their edition of *Correspondance de Bossuet*, Paris, 1909–23).
2 Circularity may be unavoidable in a problem-solving philosophy and it may be that the only kind of defence is that which may be offered for Leibniz's own philosophy, namely, that it is rich and (fairly) coherent in its theory and both sensitive and catholic in its treatment of problems. See Chapter 14 below.

14 The Virtues and Limits of a Problem-Solving Philosophy

We considered earlier (11.2) the criticism made by Foucher of the *New System*, that, like other systems of its kind, it had 'only been manufactured to save certain principles' (G i 426). Foucher, though unable or unwilling to speculate on how interaction between substances might be possible, was sceptical about the assumptions on which the mind-body problem was set up by Leibniz, Malebranche, and others. Leibniz, for his part, had credited Malebranche and other advocates of 'the system of occasional causes' with having 'gone a great way with regard to this problem by showing what cannot possibly take place' (*New System* § 13). His objection to their account was only that they had failed to resolve the difficulty, not that they had failed to diagnose it. Foucher's objection is a more radical one, that Leibniz and the occasionalists begged certain questions in their very diagnosis of the problem. The project of saving 'certain principles' in each case constrained what could be accepted as a solution.

These constraints, in Leibniz's case, relate particularly to the requirements he makes on what can strictly be counted as a substance, such as unity, autonomy and agency. It is because of such requirements that it seems to Leibniz that 'we must say that God first created the soul, and every other real unity, in such a way that everything in it must spring from within itself, by a perfect *spontaneity* with regard to itself, and yet in a perfect *conformity* with things outside' (*New System*, § 14). These requirements in turn seem to derive from Leibniz's moral and religious sensibilities.[1] On his own testimony this is true of the requirement that every substance is independent of every other created thing. He claimed to have found in the writings of St Theresa 'the fine thought that the Soul should conceive things as if there were only God and itself in the world. This yields a reflection which is even notable in philosophy and I employed it usefully in one of my hypotheses' (G Grua, ed., *G W Leibniz: Textes inedits*, Paris, 1948, p. 103). The unity of substances guarantees this independence and thus their 'natural immortality'. The hypothesis of spontaneity and harmony serves in turn to save the phenomena of interaction.

Leibniz's project of 'doing justice to theology' thus involves him in the attempt to produce an overall picture of the world within which certain beliefs, like belief in immortality, can remain credible. Whether or not it succeeds depends on whether the theory also does justice to the problems of physics and Modern philosophy which it addresses. Those who believe that philosophy should be 'objective' and not be the servant of any ideology will deny the legitimacy of the project. But that view of philosophy is not the only one. Indeed, it might be argued, the sheer scale and richness of Leibniz's metaphysics make it a model of what philosophical theorizing might be, if philosophy is not an autonomous subject borrowing nothing from outside itself. The hypothetical and ideological content of Leibniz's metaphysics no longer corresponds to any consensus about science or religion. But to note that may be to note a virtue in it as well as a limitation. For to the extent that metaphysics needs to be justified by reference to its capacity to solve the problems of its time, it cannot be impervious to changes which affect its starting-points. To the extent that the problems change a metaphysics which is addressed to them is bound to be ephemeral.

In reality, of course, the problems do not change equally quickly and some of Leibniz's problems (e.g. his freewill and mind-body problems) can, with suitable adjustments, be entered into as twentieth century problems. But much is lost if the twentieth century student of Leibniz refuses to look at Leibniz's problems on his own terms. The success of a metaphysics such as Leibniz's has to be judged by whether it achieves its objectives. His standing within the canon of great philosophers of the past depends partially on that assessment and on whether his way of doing philosophy affords a model of enduring interest. It should not be made to depend on whether he provides answers to the problems which preoccupy a subsequent generation of philosophers.

One of Leibniz's main objectives, I have been urging, was to restore the intellectual order which had been undermined both by the Reformation and by the rise of Modern philosophy. Any general assessment of the success of Leibniz's metaphysics should therefore give particular weight to how coherent it is.

14.1 The Coherence of Leibniz's Metaphysics

Leibniz claimed that he was able to 'hold to the middle way in philosophy and do justice to theology as well as to physics' (PPL 409, G iv 392). But there are tensions created by the fact that this 'middle way' had to be sought in a single unitary theory. In particular his theory of the 'double kingdom', of two sets of laws in perfect harmony with one another, commits him to a sharp dichotomy between the human and moral world, on the one hand, and the rest of nature, on the other. Yet there are elements in his theory which commit him to denying any such dichotomy.

There is, for instance, a tension between what the world must be like to be scientifically perfect, namely, as rich as possible in its variety of species, and what the world must be like to be morally perfect, namely, designed so that the virtuous are rewarded and the wicked punished. God's purposes for nature require that there is a continuity between all species and that human beings are at one end of a finely-graduated natural order.

Corresponding to this thought, Leibniz shows a willingness to extend to other forms of life features reserved by other philosophers for human beings. Against the Cartesians, Leibniz protested that 'to ascribe a substantial form and perception, or a soul, to man alone is as ridiculous as to believe that everything has been made for man alone and that the earth is the centre of the universe' (PPL 289, unpublished Hanover manuscripts, XXXVII, iv 6). But elsewhere Leibniz expresses just such a ('ridiculous') thought: 'it may truly be said that all the rest is made for them [minds] alone' (PW 118, G iv 481). On some occasions he emphasizes the continuity, on others the discontinuity between human beings and the rest of the natural order. According to his law of continuity (see 12.2 above) there ought to be a series of infinitely small graduations between human beings and the next species closest to our own. But elsewhere he stresses that '*minds* or rational souls ... are of a superior order and have incomparably more perfection than those forms embedded in matter...' (G iv 479). In the *Discourse* he allows that *every* substance is 'like a mirror of God' which 'bears in some way the stamp of the infinite wisdom and omnipotence of God, and imitates him as far as it is able' (§ 9). Elsewhere only rational souls are 'made in the image of God' (*New System* § 5).

Leibniz made some attempts to iron out these inconsistencies, settling, in his later writings, for instance, on the view that only rational souls are made in the image of God, substances in general being only mirrors of the universe. But the tension is a deep-seated one. It is crucial for Leibniz to insist on the *continuities* between human beings and other living things in order to use our own case as a true analogue for understanding other living things. Having concluded that the nature of substances consists of force, Leibniz concluded that 'from this there follows something analogous to perception and to appetite; and that therefore it was necessary to form a conception of them resembling our ordinary notion of *souls*' (*New System* § 3). The more the discontinuities between human beings and (other) animals are stressed the more strain is put on this crucial analogy. If there are gross discontinuities between humans and animals then it is natural to suppose that there are other discontinuities further down the line and that there is no reason to suppose that all substances have even the 'little perceptions' Leibniz insists on frequently (e.g. *Monadology* § 21) in his later writings. The more Leibniz emphasizes what is exceptional about the human case the more he subverts its status as a paradigm of what it is to be a substance. The more that status is in doubt the less credibility can be attached to the claim that there are substances diffused throughout nature with 'a true unity which corresponds to what is called the *I* in us' (*New System* § 11).

Leibniz's 'double kingdom' theory was intended to be an advance on the severe Cartesian dichotomy between the mental and the physical. For, although the two kingdoms have their own laws, one is ultimately included in the other. The two kingdoms are thus supposed to be intelligibly related to one another in a way Descartes had failed to explain in the case of mind and matter (see, e.g., PW 121, G iv 483). But, as we saw earlier (Chapter 10), Leibniz seems to have been torn between 'Aristotelian' moments in which he regarded the soul as the form of the body, constituting it as a substance, and 'Platonic' moments in which he regarded the soul as a separate substance in its own right. In his 'Platonic' moments he is much closer to Descartes, denying any real union of the soul and the body over and above the harmony pre-established between them (e.g. *New System* § 14). In his 'Aristotelian' moments he is willing to allow that there is '*some real metaphysical union* between the soul and the organic body' (PPL 598, G ii 370), although he concedes that he cannot explain it. On the whole his later writings, apart from the correspondence with the Jesuit Des Bosses, seem to give more weight to a Platonic conception of the soul. That conception, however, only partially fits with regarding the mind-body problem as a special case of the problem as to how substances can communicate with one another. For, on Leibniz's own theory, bodies destitute of souls are not substances properly speaking at all.

There is a way out of this problem which might help Leibniz's cause. That is to say that human beings have animal souls, as well as minds, and that it is in virtue of their animal souls that they are living organisms. Their minds 'have special laws which set them above the revolutions of matter' (*New System* § 5), but as living organisms they are subject to just the decay and transformation which (on Leibniz's speculation) is the lot of other living things. On this interpretation minds and living bodies are substances in their own right.

There are times at which Leibniz writes as if humans are a kind of animal with something super-added:

> Men act like brutes so far as the sequences of their perceptions arise through the principle of memory only, like those empirical physicians who have mere practice without theory. We are all merely empiricists as regards three-fourths of our actions. For example, when we expect it to be day tomorrow, we are behaving as empiricists, because until now it has always happened thus. The astronomer alone knows this by reason.
>
> But it is the knowledge of necessary and eternal truths which distinguishes us from mere animals, and gives us *reason* and the sciences,

raising us to knowledge of ourselves and of God. It is this in us which we
call the rational soul or *mind* (*Monadology* § 28f.)

But this way of thinking of animals does not fit the 'double
kingdom' theory. For, insofar as we do act like 'brutes', we do
so in a way which needs to be explained in purposive terms. By
parity of reasoning it should be supposed that the explanation
of animal behaviour should also be given in purposive terms.
Teleological explanations are, however, those which belong to
the 'Kingdom of Grace' rather than the 'Kingdom of Nature'.
The 'double kingdom' theory allows that 'God governs minds
as a prince governs his subjects' but requires that 'he disposes of
other substances as an engineer handles his machines' (*New
System* § 5). Although ultimately it is necessary to bring in final
causes to explain nature, the explanations to be looked for in the
natural sciences are in terms of efficient causes. The 'organism
of living things is nothing other than a divine mechanism' (PW
178, C 16)—divine, and thus ultimately to be understood in
purposive terms, but nonetheless a mechanism so far as
practical scientific investigation is concerned.

These tensions are echoed in Leibniz's theory of the material
world. Leibniz seems to have been torn between a desire to
accommodate material substances as a genuine part of the
natural order and a willingness to see them reduced to mere
phenomena. Under pressure from Arnauld he articulated the
choice: 'if there are no corporeal substances such as I claim, it
follows that bodies are only true phenomena like the rainbow'
(BW 162, G ii 77). In some sense, as we have seen (Chapter 10),
he believed, in the end, that he could have it both ways: that
there could be 'compound substances' even although matter is
'a phenomenon like a rainbow' (*Prinicples of Nature and of
Grace* § 1). This later view suggests that the Kingdom of Nature
is a world of appearances only, deriving its reality as a reflexion
of what is happening at the more fundamental, monadic, level.
This view accords with Leibniz's tendency to a Platonic
scepticism and even to a form of idealism. But a philosopher
who insisted that matter does not consist of extension alone
could hardly be content to go down that road. Corporeal
bodies, in Leibniz's dynamics, are by no means comparable to
rainbows. It presupposed, on the contrary, 'a bodily substance

which involves the power to act and to resist, and which exists everywhere as corporeal mass, the diffusion of which is contained in extension' (PPL 445, GM vi 248). That view requires that material bodies really do possess various kinds of force, even if metaphysics needs to be called in to make the notion of 'force' intelligible.

The 'double kingdom' theory is thus fraught with difficulties which Leibniz left at various stages of resolution. His metaphysics, in consequence, is neither wholly complete nor wholly coherent. Nor is this a remarkable result. Few philosophers have sought to advance on anything like as broad an intellectual front as Leibniz. Only by attempting to do so could he have hoped to achieve such large aims as reconciling Scholastic and Modern philosophy or the purposive view of the world required by belief in a Providence with the mechanistic character of modern natural science. It was widely believed, at least in Germany, that he had met with some measure of success. But even on his own terms that success was by no means complete.

14.2 Leibniz's Work as a Model of Philosophy

The study of past philosophers might be defended by reference to general considerations about the value of scholarship. But, in our tradition of philosophy, this study is generally confined to those who are included in the canon of 'great' philosophers or who are claimed to be worth such inclusion. It is widely, if not universally, agreed that an understanding of these great philosophers of the past is a prerequisite in anyone who aspires to doing philosophy at a professional level. Part of the reason for this is that the classics of the subject provide models of how philosophy might be done and have been held to be models of how philosophy ought to be done. Their critical reception has contributed and continues to contribute to the practice of what we call 'doing philosophy'. They may be held up as examples of how *not* to do philosophy in one generation and as a source of inspiration to the next. In the process they also admit of being stereotyped and in turn of fresh interpretation.

Leibniz's posthumous career has not been exceptional in

these respects, except perhaps in the variety of ways of doing philosophy which his writings have been taken to exemplify. The tradition of eighteenth century German philosophy of which he was represented as the founder was from the start dogmatic (as opposed to 'sceptical' or problem-related), anti-empirical and idealistic. That tradition, which began the stereotyping of Leibniz, was informed by a relatively small number of Leibniz texts. In the meantime, expiricist philosophers in the British Isles held up Leibniz, if they discussed him at all, as exemplary of a way of doing philosophy which is not viable.

The split between the German tradition and that of the British was not overcome in the nineteenth century by the considerable influence exercised by German philosophy, especially that of Kant and Hegel. The British took sides and 'rationalism' became a common label for Kant's style of philosophy. Though it might be said that there was an empiricist 'school', the legend of a competing rationalist 'school' seems to have its origins in the nineteenth century. The published exchanges between Whewell and John Stuart Mill, for instance, are evidence that something like competing schools existed in the nineteenth century. But it seems only in the twentieth century that the trio of Descartes, Spinoza and Leibniz have been celebrated as the founding fathers of Rationalism.[2]

The influence of the work of Couturat and Russell at the turn of century may well have decisively influenced this trend so far as Leibniz is concerned. Previously unpublished manuscripts came to light which showed how Leibniz thought of unfolding his metaphysics as a deductive system.[3] Though other interpretations continued to be published, it became established practice to expound Leibniz's thought by showing how his system could be derived from a small number of premises.

This interpretation would only help us to understand Leibniz if his procedure were similar to that of Descartes. But, as I have tried to bring out, Leibniz did not proceed by trying to find intuitive certainties on which to build. The deductive mode of exposition was indeed the established way of putting forward an explanatory theory in the seventeenth century. But it was also the format of non-rationalist works, most famously Newton's *Principia*.

The interpretation of Leibniz's work as a model of rationalist philosophy has been due, I claimed in the Introductory Essay, as much to expections of what philosophy should be like as it is to the textual evidence which lends support to it. Such impositions are endemic in what has been practised as 'history of philosophy'. For, of course, the models of past philosophy are complex, problematic writings which can only be represented in a short compass by selecting what is thought most important. Not surprisingly, Leibniz has been hailed as an idealist by idealists, an eclectic by eclectics and as a rationalist by those who believe that philosophy should be concerned above all with the foundations of human knowledge. Those who are intellectually at a sufficient distance from idealism, eclecticism or foundationism will have little difficulty in finding serious discouragement for these interpretations in Leibniz's writings. But just that intellectual distance is compromised by anyone, including the present author, who attempts to see the work of a past philosopher as a model of how philosophy might be done.

In attempting to present Leibniz's work as a 'problem-solving' philosophy I have undoubtedly been reacting both against the dominant interpretation of Leibniz as a rationalist and against the long established, if no longer dominant, conception of philosophy as concerned with underwriting other forms of inquiry. Each of these reactions finds a separate expression in recent literature.[4] In bringing them together I hope to have enhanced the interest of Leibniz for philosophers who regard themselves as post-foundationist.

Leibniz himself, it should be said, did not think of his departure from foundationist philosophy in the radical terms of philosophers such as the later Wittgenstein. His avowed concern, rather, was with how philosophy might progress in the meantime even though the kinds of foundation sought by Descartes could not be laid. He claimed not to be pre-empting the possibility of a later stage of philosophy which would be fully demonstrative. In practice, however, it was sufficient for Leibniz that human knowledge could be more perfect than it is and that, such as it is, it could be represented as a partial approximation to divine knowledge. That human knowledge could never attain to the rationalist ideal exemplified in God's knowledge of the world is a corollary of Leibniz's understanding of matter and therefore of material beings as essentially imperfect. It is difficult to see how Leibniz could have explained this imperfection, and the associated need to rely on our senses for most of what we know about the world, as a merely temporary phase of human intellectual history.

A problem-solving philosophy is subject to quite different constraints from a foundationist ('rationalist' or 'empiricist') philosophy. It can be piecemeal to the extent that some problems can be dealt with in isolation from others. I have concentrated, in Leibniz's case, on problems which are interconnected and which call for a more systematic solution. Others, like the problems of evil (addressed in the *Theodicy*), I have left aside, in spite of the importance Leibniz attached to them. Such problems only exist as problems because certain things are believed which are not obviously consistent with one another and which nonetheless are seen as being in some sense right. The task of the problem-solving philosopher is to find a way of explaining how and in what sense each of the apparently conflicting beliefs in question can be defended. Such a task is constrained by a presumption in favour of these beliefs and by the need to find a solution. In accepting such constraints Leibniz practised philosophy more as the Scholastics had done (see Chapter 2 above) than after the fashion of Descartes. A foundationist philosopher may restrict himself to just those problems which arise within his own programme. Thus Descartes needed to give some answer to the mind-body problem but thought himself excused from addressing other major problems, such as the problem of freewill.

Leibniz can hardly be said to have offered a theory of problem-solving philosophy. His criteria for distinguishing between what is presumptively true and what is presumptively false ('paradoxical'), for instance, are not made clear. His suggestion that truth in metaphysics can be measured by 'fruitfulness' leaves much unexplained. Nonetheless Leibniz practised problem-solving philosophy on a scale which raised it to the dignity of a system or theory. As such Leibniz's work continues to provide a model of what philosophy might be.

Notes

1 For enlargement on this claim, see Sections 7.4 and 13.2 above.

2 See my 'Leibniz's Break with Cartesian "Rationalism"', in A. Holland (ed.), *Philosophy; its History and its Historiography*, Dordrecht, D. Reidel, forthcoming.

3 For instance, his 'Primary Truths' paper, first published by Couturat in C 518–523, translated in PW 87–92.

4 For instance, George MacDonald Ross's recent book on *Leibniz* for the Oxford past Master's series offers a similar non-rationalist interpretation of Leibniz's writings, though Ross lays greater stress on the Socratic aspects of those writings than I have done. A recent attack on 'foundationism', Richard Rorty's *Philosophy and the Mirror of Nature*, is concerned with what philosophy might be if not an autonomous discipline providing the foundations for other disciplines. Rorty has little to say about Leibniz, in whom he might have found an unexpected ally on some matters. Interestingly, however, Leibniz's writings point to an alternative conception of what philosophy might be, if not the foundation of other disciplines, from that presented by Rorty.

Bibliography of Works Referred to in Text

A Leibniz's Works

(i) Original Language Editions
Deutsche Akademie der Wissenshaften (ed.) *Sämtliche Schriften und Briefe*, Darmstadt and Leipzig, 1923- . Definitive, but far from complete edition. [Referred to above as 'A', followed by series, volume and page number]
Buchenau, A. and Cassirer, E. (eds.) *G.W. Leibniz: Philosophische Werke*, 4 vols, Leipzig, 1906–25.
Couturat, Louis (ed.) *Opuscules et Fragments inédits de Leibniz*, Paris, 1903. [Abbreviated above as 'C']
Erdmann, J.E. (ed.) *G.G. Leibnitii opera philosophiae quae exstant*, 2 vols, Berlin, 1840.
Foucher de Careil (ed.) *Nouvelles Lettres et Opuscules inédits de Leibniz*, Paris, Didot Frères, 1857. [Abbreviated above as 'F de C']
Gerhardt, C.I. (ed.) *Mathematische Schriften*, 7 vols, Berlin and Halle, 1849–60. [Abbreviated above as 'GM']
Gerhardt, C.I. (ed.) *Philosophischen Schriften*, 7 vols, Berlin, 1875–90. [Abbreviated above as 'G']
Grua, G. (ed.) *Textes inédits*, Paris, Presses Universitaires de France, 1948.
O. Klopp (ed.) *Die Werke von Leibniz*, Hanover, Klindworth Verlag, 1864–84.

(ii) English Language Editions
Loemker, L.E. (trans and ed.) *Gottfried Wilhelm Leibniz: Philosophical Papers and Letters*, 2nd ed;, Dordrecht, D. Reidel, 1969. [Abbreviated above as 'PPL']
Lucas, P.G. and Grint, L. (trans) *Leibniz: Discourse on Metaphysics*, Manchester, Manchester University Press, 1953.

Montgomery, G.R. (trans) *Leibniz: Basic Writings: Discourse on Metaphysics: Correspondence with Arnauld etc.*, La Salle, Ill., Open Court, 1902. [Abbreviated above as 'BW']
Parkinson, G.H.R. (trans and ed.) *Leibniz: Logical Papers*, Oxford, Clarendon Press, 1966. [Abbreviated above as 'LP']
Parkinson, G.H.R. (ed.), Parkinson and Mary Morris (trans) *Leibniz: Philosophical Writings*, London, J.M. Dent and Sons; Totowa, N.J., Rowman and Littlefield, 1973. [Abbreviated above as 'PW']
Remnant, P., and Bennett, J., (eds. & trans) *G.W. Leibniz: New Essays on Human Understanding*, Cambridge, Cambridge University Press, 1981. [Abbreviated above as 'NEHU']
Riley, Patrick (trans and ed.) *The Political Writings of Leibniz*, Cambridge, Cambridge University Press, 1972.
Russell, C.W. (ed. and trans) *System of Theology*, London, Burns and Lambert, 1850.
Wiener, P.P., (ed.) *Leibniz: Selections*, New York, Charles Scribner's Sons, 1951. [Abbreviated above as 'S']

B Works Read by Leibniz (Listed Chronologically by date of Publication)

Molina, Luis de, *Liberi Arbitrii cum Gratiae Donis, Divina Praescientia, Providentia, Praedestinatione et Reprobatione Concordia*, 1588.
Suarez, Francisco, *Disputationes Metaphysicae*, 1597.
Fromond, Libertus, *Libyrinthus de Compositione Continui*, 1631.
Descartes, *Meditations on the First Philosophy*, 1641.
Descartes, René, *Principles of Philosophy*, Latin edition 1644, trans R.P. Miller and V.R. Miller, Dordrecht, D. Reidel, 1983.
Spinoza, Benedict, *The Principles of Descartes' Philosophy*, 1663, trans H.H. Briton, Chicago, Ill., 1905.
Spinoza, *Tractatus Theologico-Politicus*, Amsterdam, 1670, trans A.G. Wernham in *The Political Works of Spinoza*, Oxford, 1958.

Malebranche, Nicolas, *De la recherche de la vérité*, 1674/5, trans *The Search after Truth*, by T.M. Lennon and P.J. Olscamp, Columbus, Ohio State University Press, 1980.

Malebranche, Nicolas, *Traité de la Nature et de la Grace*, Paris, 1680.

Foucher, Simon, *Critique de la Recherche de la Vérité*, 1675, ed. and intro. R.A. Watson, Johnson Reprint Company, 1969.

Spinoza, *De Deo* (posth. 1678) (*Ethics*, Part I).

Foucher (Simon), *Dissertation sur la Recherche de la Vérité, contenant l'Apologie des Academiciens*, Paris, 1687.

Huet, Pierre-Daniel, *Censura Philosophiae Cartesianae*, 1689.

Locke, John, *Essay Concerning Human Understanding*, 1690.

Bayle, Pierre, *Historical and Critical Dictionary*, 1697, 2nd ed. 1702, *Selections* trans R.H. Popkin, Indianapolis, Ind., Bobbs Merrill, 1965.

Berkeley, George, *Principles of Human Knowledge*, 1710.

C Modern Commentaries and Historiographical Literature

Adams, R.A., 'Leibniz's Theories of Contingency, *Essays on the Philosophy of Leibniz*, ed. Mark Kulstad, Houston, Texas (*Rice University Studies*, Vol. 63, No. 4) 1977, pp. 1–41.

Barber, W.H., *Leibniz in France from Arnauld to Voltaire*, Oxford, Oxford University Press, 1955.

Broad, C.D. (ed. C.Lewy) *Leibniz: An Introduction* (lectures given in 1948–50) Cambridge, Cambridge University Press, 1975.

Brown, Stuart, 'Leibniz's Break with Cartesian "Rationalism"', in A. Holland (ed.), *Philosophy: its History and its Historiography*, Dordrecht, Reidel, forthcoming.

Costabel, Pierre, *Leibniz and dynamics*, trans R.E.W. Maddison, London, Metheun, 1973.

Couturat, Louis, R. Allison Ryan (trans), 'On Leibniz's Metaphysics' in Harry G. Frankfurt (ed.) *Leibniz: a collection of critical essays*, New York, Doubleday, 1972.

Craig, E.J., 'Philosophy and philosophies', *Philosophy*, Vol. 58, No. 224, April 1983, pp. 189–201.

Davillé, Le. 'Le Séjour de Leibniz à Paris', *Archiv für Geschichte der Philosophie*, *32*, 1920, 14ff.; *33*, 1921, 67ff., 165ff.

Furth, Montgomery, 'Monadology', *Philosophical Review*, Vol. 76, 1976. Reprinted in H.G.Frankfurt (ed.), *Leibniz: A Collection of Critical Essays*, Paris, University of Notre Dame Press, 1976.

Hanfling, O., 'Leibniz's Principle of Reason', *Studia Leibnitiana*, *9*, 1980, pp. 67–73.

Hazard, Paul, *The European Mind*, 1680–1715, trans J.L. May, Harmondsworth, Penguin Books, 1964.

Kuhn, Thomas S., *The Structure of Scientific Revolutions*, Chicago, University of Chicago Press, 1962, 2nd Ed. 1970.

Loemker, L.E., 'A Note on the Origin and Problem of Leibniz's Discourse of 1686', *Journal of the History of Ideas*, 1947, pp. 449–66.

Lovejoy, A.O., *The Great Chain of Being*, Cambridge, Mass., Harvard UP, 1939.

Meyer, R.W., *Leibniz and the Seventeenth Century Revolution*, trans J.P. Stern, Cambridge, Bowes and Bowes, 1952.

Papineau, David, 'The *Vis Viva* Controversy', *Studies in History and Philosophy of Science*, *8*, 1977, pp. 111–42. Reprinted in R.S. Woolhouse (ed.) *Leibniz: Metaphysics and Philosophy of Science*, Oxford, Oxford University Press, 1981, pp. 139–56.

Parkinson, G.H.R., *Logic and Reality in Leibniz's Metaphysics*, Oxford, Clarendon Press, 1965.

Parkinson, G.H.R., *Leibniz on Human Freedom*, Wiesbaden, Steiner, 1970.

Parkinson, G.H.R., 'Leibniz's Paris Writings in Relation to Spinoza', in *Leibniz à Paris (1672–1676)*, Wiesbaden, Steiner, 1978, Vol. II.

Popkin, R.H. *A History of Scepticism from Erasmus to Spinoza*, Berkeley, Calif., University of California, 1979.

Popkin, R.H., 'Leibniz and the French Sceptics', *Revue Internationale de Philosophie*, *76–77*, 1966, pp. 228–48.

Rabbe, F., *Étude philosophique, L'abbé Simon Foucher chanoine de la Sainte Chappelle de Dijon*, Paris, Didier, 1867.

Rescher, Nicholas, *The philosophy of Leibniz*, Engelwood Cliffs, N.J., Prentice Hall, 1967.

Rescher, Nicholas, 'Leibniz and the Concept of a System', *Studia Leibnitiana 13*, 1981, pp. 114–22.

Robinet, A., *Malebranche et Leibniz*, Paris, Vrin, 1955.

Rorty, Richard, *Philosophy and the Mirror of Nature*, Oxford, Blackwell, 1980.

Ross, George MacDonald, *Leibniz*, (Past Masters Series) Oxford University Press, 1984.

Russell, Bertrand, *A Critical Exposition of the Philosophy of Leibniz*, London, George Allen and Unwin, 1900.

Russell, Bertrand, *History of Western Philosophy*, 1946, new ed., London, George Allen and Unwin, 1961.

Stein, L., *Leibniz und Spinoza*, Berlin, 1890.

Watson, Richard A., *The Downfall of Cartesianism*, 1673–1712, The Hague, Nijhoff, 1966.

Indexes

Compiled by R. N. D. Martin

1. Leibniz' Writings

a) Named works, General and Specific References

Confession of Nature against Atheists: 118, 151

Critical Remarks on the General Part of Descartes' Principles of Philosophy: 37, 43, 37, 69, 186

'Dialogue on the Connection between Words and Things': 60

'Discourse touching the Method of Certitude ...': 48

Discourse on Metaphysics: 8, 10, 25, 42, 47, 79, 84f., 91, 95f., 129, 142, 146f., 149f., 153, 155, 158f., 182, 185, 189, 195
§1: 181
§2: 123, 177
§5–7: 91, 198, 113, 165, 173, 177–8, 181
§8: 89, 91, 98, 100–1, 106, 109–11, 115, 117, 153, 168
§9: 29, 36, 65, 70, 89, 98, 101–2. 110f., 113–14, 117, 149, 159, 182, 200
§10–11: 138, 141, 161
§12: 42, 149, 152
§13: 110, 118, 122–3, 197
§14: 113, 117, 157, 197
§16, 187
§17: 177, 180
§22: 180, 184
§23: 165
§24: 66
§26–9: 90, 98, 169

§32: 105, 113, 187, 190
§33: 158, 160, 166
§34: 100, 114, 118, 138, 152, 165
§35: 152

Disputation on the Principle of Individuation: 17, 30

Dissertation on the Art of Combinations: 64

Mars Christianissimus: 67

'Meditations on Knowledge, Truth and Ideas': 76, 91

Monadology: 6, 161
§7: 161
§11: 161
§15: 171
§21: 200
§28f.: 201–2
§79: 192

New Essays on Human Understanding (NEHU): 3, 7, 185
NEHU 65: 28
NEHU 71: 92
NEHU 74: 169
NEHU 105: 141
NEHU 107f.: 64
NEHU 131: 169
NEHU 218: 78
NEHU 219: 78, 194
NEHU 317: 28, 138
NEHU 362: 75
NEHU 367: 153
NEHU 372: 81
NEHU 375: 69
NEHU 392: 49
NEHU 407f.: 64

3. Select Index of Topics